COMMON CORE STANDARDS
IN DIVERSE CLASSROOMS

COMMON CORE STANDARDS
IN DIVERSE CLASSROOMS

Essential Practices for Developing Academic Language
and Disciplinary Literacy

JEFF ZWIERS
SUSAN O'HARA
ROBERT PRITCHARD

STENHOUSE PUBLISHERS
PORTLAND, MAINE

Stenhouse Publishers

www.stenhouse.com

Library of Congress Cataloging-in-Publication Data

Zwiers, Jeff.

  Common core standards in diverse classrooms : essential practices for developing academic language and disciplinary literacy / Jeff Zwiers, Susan O'Hara, and Robert Pritchard.

      pages cm

  Includes bibliographical references and index.

  ISBN 978-1-57110-997-2 (pbk. : alk. paper) -- ISBN 978-1-62531-009-5 (ebook) 1. English language--Study and teaching--Foreign speakers. 2. Academic language--Study and teaching--United States. 3. Language arts--Standards--United States. I. O'Hara, Susan. II. Pritchard, Robert Henry, 1947- III. Title.

  PE1128.A2Z84 2014

  428.0071--dc23

                                                          2013040074

Cover and interior design by Blue Design, Portland, Maine (www.bluedes.com)

Manufactured in the United States of America

PRINTED ON 30% PCW
RECYCLED PAPER

20 19 18 17 16 15 14 9 8 7 6 5 4 3

CONTENTS

Acknowledgments

We are deeply thankful for the collaborations and conversations with outstanding teachers and educators such as Betty Achinstein, Diane August, Timothy Boals, Martha Castellon, Mariana Castro, Gary Cook, Emily Davis, Gil Diaz, Angie Estonina, Austyn Fudge, Margo Gottlieb, Michelle Griffith, Kenji Hakuta, Steve Hammack, Bonnie Hansen, Chris Hiltbrand, Patrick Hurley, Allison Hyde, Ann Jaquith, Fermin Jaramillo, Denise Kilpatrick, Nicole Knight, Linda Montes, Debi Pitta, Octavio Rodriguez, Kristin Stout, and Yee Wan. We would also like to thank the federal Office of English Language Acquisition (OELA), which, through a National Professional Development Grant, supported portions of this work.

Introduction

Language yearns to be used in meaningful ways.

Many lessons still focus on filling students' minds with as many "parts" and "pieces" as possible. Yet what is needed for the Common Core State Standards (CCSS; the Standards), and especially in diverse classrooms, is an increased focus on helping students put the pieces together. Students must learn to *use* pieces such as facts, rules, and word meanings to understand and communicate whole ideas in meaningful ways across disciplines. Students do not need to use perfect English, but dealing in whole ideas will require significant changes in how we teach content, language, and literacy in every lesson.

The Common Core State Standards require an unprecedented emphasis on developing the sophisticated language and literacy of each discipline. However, many students lack sufficient baselines of academic language and literacy to engage successfully in CCSS lessons at grade level. Granted, some of these differences stem from nonschool factors such as home language variations, rarely being read to, and lack of literacy resources. Then again, in our observations of many lessons across different grade levels and subject areas, we saw a range of school factors that we can improve, two of which were as follows: (1) Many popular lesson activities such as sentence starters, think-pair-shares, and vocabulary exercises were not powerful enough to build students' abilities to understand and communicate complex whole ideas. (2) In diverse classrooms with large numbers of English learners and others who struggle with school's language and literacy demands (called "academic English learners" [AELs] in this book), the teaching was even more focused on disconnected pieces than in nondiverse classrooms with high percentages of proficient English speakers.

We therefore wrote this book to provide educators with a practical resource for teaching Common Core State Standards to students who need accelerated growth in their academic language and literacy. The practices focus squarely on increasing the quality of students' understanding, thinking, and communicating. This book is for teachers of students who need extra support and practice in (1) comprehending and learning from complex texts; (2) communicating complex ideas orally, visually, and in writing; and/or (3) engaging in authentic conversations about content.

In our research we identified a handful of essential practices to address these needs. These practices focus on teaching students the language and literacy skills that support Common Core literacy, math, and English Language Arts (ELA) standards. The three practices with the highest impact are using complex texts, fortifying complex output, and fostering academic interaction (Chapters 4, 6, and 8). These are supported by the three crosscutting practices of clarifying, modeling, and guiding (Chapter 3), and the foundational practice of designing instruction (Chapter 2). This book describes these seven practices in detail with many classroom examples and full lesson examples (Chapters 5, 7, and 9). We top it all off with practical ways to foster professional development and systemwide capacity (Chapter 10).

Objectives of This Book

This book seeks to do the following:

- Clarify how to support the learning of the complex language that students need for reaching the Common Core and other new standards.

- Provide clear and practical ways to realize the instructional shifts needed with implementation of new standards in diverse classrooms. These include shifting from access to ownership; from piece skills to whole-message skills; from focusing on content to focusing on language-literacy-thinking-content; from individual to collaborative skills; from playing school to learning in school; from checklists of strategies to frames of practice; from tests to assessment and beyond; and from silos to capacity.

- Provide practical frameworks for understanding the practices that have the highest impact on students' development of complex language and literacy needed for Common Core and related standards.

- Provide practical descriptions and concrete examples of how to use texts to develop students' complex language; improve students' complex speaking, writing, and communication of ideas; and develop students' abilities to engage in interactions that produce learning.

- Provide ways to maximize students' independence in using texts to learn, communicating with high-quality oral and written output, and interacting to effectively build ideas with others.

- Provide ways to work at the coach, professional development, school, and district levels to support the work and build capacity to implement the work across an educational system.

The Common Core State Standards provide us with plenty to do, but they are not the entire picture. Many of the same language demands are also found in standards outlined in the Next Generation Science Standards, the World-Class Instructional Design and Assessment (WIDA) English Language Development (ELD) Standards, English Language Development standards (of various states), the English Language Proficiency Development Framework (CCSSO 2012), state history and social science standards, and 21st-Century Skills, which have also informed this work. What these documents and standards have in common is the urgent need to develop grade-level language and literacy skills. As we succeed in addressing this need across the horizontal and vertical axes of schooling, all learners will not only meet but exceed the many "standards" that come their way in the future.

CHAPTER 1

Framing the Teaching of Academic Language and Disciplinary Literacy

Often the frame is as important as the picture within it.

anguage is the main axle of learning in any discipline—especially now. Everywhere you look in the Common Core State Standards (CCSS; the Standards), you see a wide range of complex language and literacy demands. For example, the CCSS emphasize the teaching of argument-based reasoning, reading and writing complex texts, and engaging in authentic academic discussions across disciplines. Such skills demand much more sophisticated abilities to use language than learning that is based on memorization, recitation, and choosing right answers from a list. Moreover, these language and literacy demands tend to be much greater for the many students who are still learning how to use language in ways that are valued in the texts and tasks of school.

The new standards intensify the need for every teacher to develop the language, thinking, and literacy skills of grade-level texts and tasks in each discipline. We must teach students how to put ideas together and communicate them in purposeful ways. Putting pieces together to form real ideas requires students to develop their abilities to use complex forms of academic language, often called "complex language" in this book. For example, reciting the definition of *reciprocal* is not complex, whereas justifying why a person would use the reciprocal of a fraction to solve a problem is complex.

For students to meet and exceed the Common Core State Standards, it is no longer enough to provide them with basic "access" to content through highly "sheltered" instruction. Students need accelerated growth in using complex language in grade-level tasks in mainstream classrooms. Adding a few strategies such as visual aids, sentence starters, and pair-shares to each lesson isn't enough. Lessons must be designed to help students use language—even if it is not perfect—to put the "pieces" together and build whole ideas in a discipline. Lessons must also give students the exposure, tools, scaffolding, and practice that they need. In a nutshell, we can no longer shelter our diverse students from complex language, literacy, or disciplinary thinking at grade level.

The students who most need accelerated growth in language and literacy to meet grade-level demands are academic English learners. Academic English learners are numerous and diverse in our schools. The term *academic English learners* (AELs) often evokes images of students who have immigrated within the last several years, but these students are only a subgroup of AELs. Many academic English learners have been in U.S. schools for multiple years and speak social versions of English quite well. These students are sometimes called "long-term English learners." Many academic English learners have grown up in English-speaking homes using variations or dialects of English that differ significantly from the English used and expected in school. Finally, many academic English learners have grown up speaking English at home and have simply struggled with the ways in which school asks them to read, write, speak, listen to, or converse in academic English. (For international and bilingual settings, *English* in this paragraph can be replaced by any language used to learn in a school, such as Spanish, Turkish, or Japanese.)

Most AELs need increased exposure to interactions and literacy experiences that provide a "critical mass" of complex academic language use and background knowledge needed to thrive more independently at grade-level tasks in the average U.S. school. This critical mass helps many "mainstream" students (non-AELs) to more smoothly adapt to and acquire school ways of using language. Academic English learners, on the other hand, can have triple the work: (1) many lack background and cultural knowledge that helps to learn new content (i.e., large numbers of mainstream students actually learn much of their content outside of school); (2) they are still learning social and cultural English; and (3) they are learning complex uses of academic English. And yet, while it is tempting to blame the backgrounds of the students for their struggles, we must look instead at the ways in which we can and must shift our practices of instruction and assessment to meet the needs of these students.

The Just-Right Mix of Content and Language

Before we begin to look at how to do extra things during a lesson to develop language, it is important to think about how much language development work should be in a lesson. A good rule of thumb is to use just enough language teaching to support the depth and clarity of the communication happening in the activity or task—without reducing the engagement levels. In most cases, upping the amount (and quality) of language development in a lesson or activity will actually increase the engagement because it reinforces the clarity of complex concepts. But overstuffing a lesson with vocabulary activities, sentence frames for every answer, and other language activities (even those in this book), will tend to reduce the amount of engaging, enduring, and meaningful learning. Language learning, in itself, isn't all that interesting to most students. But as students use more complex forms of language to accomplish interesting tasks, they learn more content and their language skills improve.

This book describes practices and activities that help teachers move from too little emphasis on developing language up a few notches so that students, especially academic English learners, can maximize their learning of content, language, and literacy in every lesson. This book endeavors to get educators to think about the types of teaching that develop engaging and enduring learning of both content and language.

We are not saying that math, science, and history teachers must now pile onto the many rules of English grammar to what they already teach. What we are arguing is the importance of answering two questions: How can I use content teaching to build students' language of my discipline? How much can I realistically do to improve students' language and literacy? Many teachers are already developing language in powerful ways simply through well-designed content activities. Indeed, the most engaging and effective content-teaching strategies can also be effective language-teaching activities, especially when supported by some of the practices described in this book.

Consider your own abilities to use complex academic language; most of them developed from engaging in motivating activities that involved reading challenging texts, communicating ideas, and interacting with others to accomplish challenging tasks.

Complex Academic Language

You can't get very far in school and life without using complex language, though many try. Content-area concepts, thinking skills, and literacy all depend on students' abilities to use complex language. What we call "complex language" in this book is a subset of features and skills within the much broader category of academic language. The broad term *academic language* tends to include any language used to describe abstract ideas and cognitive processes in school (Schleppegrell 2004; Swartz 2001; Zwiers 2008). Vocabulary, in particular, is often equated with academic language. Yet the bulk of what we call complex language involves putting clauses, sentences, paragraphs, and other elements together to construct, negotiate, and communicate clear and whole academic messages. While many activities in this book do include vocabulary-related elements, one of our main goals in these chapters is teaching students how to understand and create complex messages in a discipline. We believe that too much school time has been spent on non-complex language, on the pieces; it is time to intensify our focus on equipping students to read, think, talk, and write in ways that will prepare them for the future.

Figure 1.1 shows the three main dimensions of academic language and associated skills. In the Sentence and Message dimensions, students are doing something useful with the words: they are building complex messages. The activities and lessons in this book emphasize developing the Message dimension. Even though the Word/Phrase dimension is important, we believe that (1) it tends to be the easiest to assess and teach; (2) many other resources are available on teaching words (i.e., books on academic vocabulary); (3) many teachers have asked for ways to help students communicate longer and more complex messages; (4) the Common Core and other standards emphasize communication of meaningful ideas and reasoning; and (5) we have observed the need for more emphasis on teaching AELs how to learn and communicate beyond word and sentence levels.

FIGURE 1.1

Dimensions, features, and skills of complex academic language use (adapted from WIDA 2012)

DIMENSIONS	FEATURES	SKILLS
Message	• Clarity and coherence • Register for participants and purposes • Density of ideas and their relationships • Message organization and structure (visuals, paragraphs) • Organization of sentences	• Create a logical flow of and connections between ideas, knowing how ideas develop and need to develop. • Match language with the purpose of the message (clear, complete, focused, logical, appropriate to the discipline). • Create, clarify, fortify, and negotiate ideas.
Sentence	• Sentence structure (compound/complex) and length • Transitions and connectives • Complex verb tenses and passive voice • Pronouns and references	• Craft sentences to be clear. • Use of a variety of sentence types to clarify a message and condense information. • Combine ideas, phrases, and clauses.
Word/Phrase	• Cross-disciplinary terms • Figurative expressions and multiple meanings • Content vocabulary • Affixes, roots, and transformations	• Choose and use the best words and phrases to communicate. • Figure out the meaning of new words and terms. • Use and clarify new words to build ideas or create products.

In looking at the three dimensions in Figure 1.1, it can help to imagine a word as color, which communicates some meaning. Put words together into a sentence and you get more meaning, but it is still limited, like the figures and elements of a painting. Put the figures together and you compose a message, like the painting in the Message dimension in Figure 1.1. We need to move beyond the teaching of just the vocabulary (colors) in the first dimension and the grammar rules (forming of figures) in the second dimension to teaching students how to construct a wide variety of complex, original, and whole messages (paintings) (Carr, Sexton, and Lagunoff 2006; Zwiers 2008). Most of these messages require critical thinking skills and abilities to use language within particular functions and settings (Echevarria, Vogt, and Short 2008; Schleppegrell 2005).

Consider differences between the two excerpts from a lesson on the same topic in Figure 1.2.

FIGURE 1.2
Sample of academic and complex language use (intermediate)

Academic Language Use	Complex Language Use
T: OK, class, tell your partners what you think the meaning of the word *conquer* is. Use complete sentences and start with the frame on the board, which is, I think conquer means to. . . . Now repeat with me. I think conquer means to. . . . A: I think *conquer* means to take over someone else's land. It means to make war on others and control them. B: I think *conquer* means that the stronger guys win. They take the government and take all the money. A: Yeah, *conquer* is taking over the government and making up taxes.	T: OK, class, discuss in your pairs two different motivations for conquering and use examples to support your ideas. Try to come up with a main motivation. C: Conquerors wanted to conquer because of religion. He thought others needed their God. Like it says here that they had a "view to convert them to the holy faith." D: However, I think conquerors wanted money. They conquer to get rich. Think of all the gold, I think it was a trillion dollars of it, that Spain got. C: Like José said yesterday, maybe religion was an excuse, like, to conquer, and they really wanted gold and silver and to be rich.

Lesson time is very limited. The more time we spend on one thing (e.g., vocabulary), the less time we have to spend on others (e.g., communicating complex ideas). Mohan (2006), for example, strongly argues for more complex language in science: "Simplified understandings of explicit language instruction, in leading to simplified science talk, result in simplified science" (52). These are further elaborated upon in the shifts described in the next section.

Key CCSS Shifts for Teaching Academic English Learners

Even though the Common Core documents do not tell teachers how to teach, there are many new resources that describe how teaching should change as a result of the Standards. Most of the "shifts," as these changes are commonly called, apply to the teaching of all students. Yet we also believe that there are additional, "deeper" instructional shifts that are necessary for the effective teaching of academic English learners. To provide a comprehensive view of the many shifts, we first summarize the commonly cited shifts and briefly describe their implications for the teaching of academic English learners. Second, we describe the additional paradigm and instructional shifts that we have identified as essential to consider in the instruction and assessment of academic English learners.

Figure 1.3 shows four commonly discussed shifts in practice that have accompanied many presentations about the Common Core. In the second column we mention several important implications and nuances of these shifts for teaching academic English learners.

FIGURE 1.3

Common Common Core instructional "shifts" and their implications for AELs

COMMON SHIFTS	IMPLICATIONS FOR TEACHING ACADEMIC ENGLISH LEARNERS
Building knowledge through content-rich nonfiction	This shift tends to focus on elementary school and ELD/ESL settings that have overemphasized fiction texts. Most AELs often need to gain higher amounts of academic knowledge across disciplines for current and future learning experiences, much of which comes only from nonfiction, in school. Thus, extra doses of nonfiction, combined with extra teaching of their language and structures, benefit AELs.
Reading and writing grounded in evidence	AELs need extra instruction on the school expectations for what constitutes strong and weak evidence for an idea, claim, opinion, etc. Finding and using evidence involves value systems that can differ across cultures. AELs need focused instruction and modeling on how to value certain pieces of evidence over others.
Regular practice with complex texts and academic language	For AELs, the "regular practice" should involve extra attention to how authors use language in texts to convey micro- and macro-ideas. This means close and "wide-angle" reading strategies. Using complex texts for AELs means more support than for non-AELs. That is, just analyzing a key sentence will not be enough for students to understand and acquire the language of the text (see Chapter 4).
Rigorous pursuit of conceptual understanding, procedural skill, and application	While this is a math shift, it applies across disciplines. The heightened emphasis on conceptual understanding and application presents challenges for AELs, especially related to assessment. We must figure out how to assess complex conceptual understanding despite students' lack of advanced academic English. We need to do both: build students' complex language as we assess higher-order thinking and conceptual understandings.

As we analyzed the Common Core State Standards and considered the variety of academic English learner needs, and as we have worked with numerous teachers and coaches on implementation of the CCSS, we discovered additional "shifts" in instruction and assessment needed to help diverse students succeed. These AEL shifts, as we call them, also serve as objectives for this book. As you read each chapter, you will see how the essential instructional practices work together to support various shifts. We believe that these AEL shifts, combined with the common shifts in Figure 1.3, provide a solid outline of the major changes needed to help students in most diverse classrooms.

AEL SHIFT 1: FROM ACCESS TO OWNERSHIP

Plenty of resources and professional development programs focus on providing English learners with better "access" to the content. Much of what is called "sheltered," "intervention," or "English language learner" (ELL) instruction is focused on providing academic English learners with increased access to a lesson's content. *Sheltered instruction* is teaching that usually includes extra uses of visual aids, modified teacher talk, gestures, and background-building activities for texts. Yet in many cases the instruction just achieves *access*; it fails to foster students' *ownership* of the language and thinking such that they can communicate complete grade-level ideas. In addition, sheltered instruction can often "water down" complex language in order to provide easy access to content, lacking an emphasis on building students' abilities to use and learn language from complex texts. This shift focuses on providing students the power to possess and use language in ways that are valued by experts in the discipline. It also emphasizes ways to serve academic English learners in mainstream classes that are not tracked, so that they do not fall behind their grade-level peers and so that they can benefit from working with peers at higher and lower levels of language proficiency. This book emphasizes moving beyond basic access to focusing on building the disciplinary communication and knowledge-working skills that students will need for future grade levels, college, and career success.

AEL SHIFT 2: FROM "PIECE" SKILLS TO "WHOLE MESSAGE" SKILLS

One of the most negative effects of multiple-choice, test-based instruction is the intense focus on "pieces" of content knowledge and language. Students have been asked to memorize vocabulary meanings, grammar rules, sentence stems, and a range of facts extracted from long lists of standards. This focus is quantitative in nature. It views learning as accumulating discrete facts, word meanings, grammar rules, etc. "The more, the better," so they say. The tests in recent years have promoted this view as well. Parts and pieces are easier to test. "The more items correct, the more the student has learned," so they think. In this book, however, we emphasize helping students to put the pieces together: to use increasingly advanced levels of academic discourse skills to communicate complex authentic messages in real ways. We must be like basketball coaches who, rather than having players spend all of their workout time on free throws and dribbling drills, have players engage in scrimmages, practice games, and real games.

Students have spent too much time memorizing and playing games with words when they should be using words to craft meaningful ideas of value to the world. They have spent too much time thinking of language and learning as choosing the right answer rather than choosing how to best communicate to an audience based on the task and purpose. Many students are yearning for chances to be creative and to stop regurgitating pieces of other people's ideas. Fortunately, the new standards and assessments emphasize putting ideas together, using critical thinking skills, collaborating, and doing tasks that better prepare students for the future. Yet, even with the new assessments, we must resist the strong and ingrained temptations to look at the sample test questions, break them down, and thus continue to focus on pieces at the expense of teaching students how to communicate complete messages. We must reimagine what learning looks like. Rather than points for facts and word meanings, we need to have a vision of students using the facts and meanings to think and communicate meaningful ideas. Such skills are vital for each student's future, yet they are not nearly as easy to count up and grade as their abilities to choose answers on bubbly tests.

Another way of viewing this shift is moving from direct to indirect teaching. Now, this might raise a few eyebrows since "direct" and "explicit" approaches have gained momentum in recent years. Direct approaches have also been associated with yearly test score gains. Such approaches tend to be "clean," that is, they focus on one concept or skill, they tell students what it will be in the beginning of class, and they use assessment and lesson activities focused on that concept or skill. Yet much of language learning is actually indirect. It comes from using language (reading, writing, listening, speaking, interacting) to accomplish a wide variety of engaging and discipline-valued tasks.

We must shift from emphasizing the "clean" pacing guides to embrace the "messiness" of complex language building. That is, the development of language is a dynamic social process that is far from linear and instead "spirals" up and out over time in different ways for different students at different rates. We cannot, for example, check off in October a student's learning of a standard such as "Explain how an author uses reasons and evidence to support particular points in a text" (CCSS.ELA-Literacy.RI.4.8). We have to monitor growth in this skill during the entire year (and over the years) with a wide range of texts. The best ways to ensure that this muddy process of language and literacy growth is happening is to maximize the amount of complex text that students are reading, the authentic and purposeful communication of ideas in writing and oral interactions, and the valuing of students' ideas throughout each lesson. The more immersed students are in using complex language to think and communicate, the more the language sticks and grows in their minds.

The practices in this book address this shift. For example, fortifying complex output (the focus of Chapter 6) emphasizes building students' abilities to speak and write complex ideas by linking and organizing multiple sentences for real audiences. Likewise, the high-impact practice of fostering complex interactions (described in Chapter 8) emphasizes developing students' abilities to engage in face-to-face interactions in order to co-construct ideas about the discipline, rather than memorizing other people's ideas or repeating sentence starters back and forth.

AEL SHIFT 3: FROM FOCUSING ON CONTENT TO FOCUSING ON LANGUAGE-LITERACY-CONTENT

We have a somewhat extreme point of view: complex language and literacy skills that can be learned in each content area are as important as the content itself. And the best way to build complex language and literacy is through highly engaging content learning. Students need to know a discipline's facts, concepts, and skills. Students need to learn these things in order to know and learn more things. Academic English learners, moreover, often need to learn more school-valued content knowledge than their more proficient-in-academic-English peers. Yet this doesn't mean that we should focus more on content by reducing language and literacy demands. We have been doing this. Rather, and this is somewhat counterintuitive, we must realize the large roles that complex language and literacy skills play in content learning. We must develop our pedagogical language knowledge (PLK) (Bunch 2013; Galguera 2011; Zwiers 2008), similar to Shulman's (1986) notion of pedagogical content knowledge (PCK). In other words, teachers need to know the language that is running the learning show in each lesson. The more proficient we are at developing complex language and literacy skills, the better our students learn the content in enduring ways. And vice versa.

AEL SHIFT 4: FROM INDIVIDUAL TO COLLABORATIVE

Particularly in schools with large numbers of academic English learners, lessons have focused on building up the skills and knowledge of each individual student. Students have been asked to focus much of their learning time on independent practice in preparation for the tests. The CCSS, on the other hand, value the skills of communication and collaboration, which are both the goals and the means for achieving other learning objectives. The better students get at negotiating and explaining content ideas, the better they learn them. The better students get at communication, the better prepared they are for communicating in college, careers, and life.

Thus, we must shift from just filling students' heads with knowledge to having students collaboratively build and communicate ideas. Students cannot build disciplinary ideas without complex language skills. This means reducing the time spent having students fill in blanks and, instead, having students negotiate and clarify with one another the meanings of the words that would go in the blanks—and then *using* the words to construct clear and authentic messages. We must apprentice students into being able to do many of the things that historians, mathematicians, authors, and scientists do as they collaborate in real-world settings. For example, even in second grade, students can argue whether they would recommend to others to live in the country or the city. In fifth grade, students can learn how to give presentations on the importance of exercising and eating in healthy ways. The more that students communicate to accomplish engaging and realistic tasks, the better their learning of content sticks in their minds.

AEL SHIFT 5: FROM PLAYING SCHOOL TO LEARNING

Large numbers of students begin to become disinterested in school learning after fourth grade. Many begin to build their skills at "playing school." This can be particularly true of academic English learners, who are more likely to lose interest in school because (1) they can't keep up with the language and literacy demands of texts and tasks each day; and (2) lessons do not connect to students' languages and cultures. As a result, students learn to keep quiet, turn in work (even if copied), minimally answer questions, talk as little as possible in class and group discussions, and stay beneath the radar as they navigate through school. Too many students play this game for too many years. They learn very little, even though they pass classes and even though they do moderately well on state tests.

We must continue to strive to reduce this school game playing and build a culture in the classroom that focuses on learning. Other shifts, in fact, can help build this culture. For example, as students begin to own language and use it to communicate authentic and whole messages, as teachers allow and value collaboration, and as schools treat students as thinkers with ideas worth sharing, a learning culture can form. Indeed, one of the purposes of using the practices in this book is to foster such a culture.

AEL SHIFT 6: FROM CHECKLISTS OF STRATEGIES TO FRAMES OF PRACTICE

Often, teacher books, webinars, and slide presentations offer a smorgasbord of teaching suggestions such as *Put language objectives on the board, Use visuals and gestures, Use paragraph frames for writing, Provide sentence stems for think-pair-shares, Preteach vocabulary for difficult texts, Use jigsaws,* etc. While many of these practices are effective, there has been little agreement on which to choose and when for which students, or how they best fit together in strategic ways. We advocate moving away from simply choosing from long lists of instructional practices to seeing the practices in strategic frames that show how they reinforce one another. The frame in Figure 1.4, for example, shows how essential practices can support one another in lessons. Throughout the chapters in this book, and especially in 5, 7, and 9, we describe how the practices work together to develop language and literacy.

AEL SHIFT 7: FROM TESTS TO ASSESSMENT AND BEYOND

This shift is somewhat controversial, but we include it anyway to spark some extra reflection. Under the No Child Left Behind (NCLB) Act, many of the classroom practices for academic English learners focused on improving test scores. This meant loads of activities and time spent on learning how to—individually and silently—read many short unrelated texts, choose or guess the right answer, read the test questions beforehand and look for answers, memorize grammar rules, write with writing "formulas," and navigate the various parts of tests in a short amount of time. The focus was quantitative: getting as many facts and rules learned as possible, and then using them to score high on tests. The new Standards, however, are more qualitative. They emphasize the quality of conceptual understandings, arguments, ideas, and communication.

Some of the most important language and skills, such as conversing with others to solve a problem or create new ideas, are too difficult, expensive, and subjective to assess every year in standardized ways. And yet, such skills are vital, especially for academic English learners. This is the somewhat controversial part: we must shift to teaching what students will need the most for their futures. We can use the assessments to guide us in some areas, but we will need to teach well beyond them when necessary. For example, we work with teachers who assess paired conversations in the last month of each semester. Students don't know the exact day they will need to have an intelligent conversation (much like in real life), so they prepare and practice throughout the semester. Teachers realize that this doesn't explicitly prepare students for yearly high-stakes tests, but they believe that this preparation counts more than most of the things that are easily counted.

AEL SHIFT 8: FROM SILOS TO CAPACITY

All of the previous shifts, of course, require yet another meta-shift: changing the educational system from isolated pockets of practice to an integrated capacity-building model. This model includes coaching, collaboration, observations, data analysis, conversations, leadership practices, culture, and policies that support complex language and literacy for academic English learners. This shift requires educators at all levels in a system to know what to communicate and how to communicate it. Chapter 10 outlines several ideas for addressing these levels. Chapter 10 also provides an observation tool based on these shifts (Figure 10.8).

✚ ✚ ✚

Each of these shifts, of course, is a continuum. Many teachers have already shifted or have been shifting in the ways previously described. We need to learn from them. Most of us, however, can bump up a notch or two on each of the shift continuums. The rest of this book provides a range of ideas for doing so. In the next section, we jump right in with an overview of research-based practices for developing complex language and literacy.

Essential Practices for Developing Complex Language and Literacy in Every Subject

Numerous checklists, protocols, rubrics, and approaches for teaching English language learners have been developed. The majority of protocols that we reviewed focused broadly on components of "sheltered" instruction, an approach largely based on the idea that academic English learners can learn content knowledge and skills when taught in English if the instruction makes the content comprehensible, explicit, and highly engaging. Yet as we mentioned in AEL Shift 1, students need to own the language and knowledge to be learned, not just access them. In other words, schools should not give students basic "access to fish," but instead teach students how to study, understand, catch, use, raise, and sell the "fish." This means extra emphasis on providing students with the language and communication skills to be able to learn more content more deeply, more collaboratively, and less dependently on the teacher over time.

The "essential practices," as we call them in our work, enable all teachers to focus on becoming more effective language teachers of the complex academic language and literacy skills of the Common Core State Standards, etc. These practices were identified and refined by research, expert consensus, and ongoing analysis of classroom instruction and assessment (O'Hara, Zwiers, and Pritchard 2013). Refer to Appendix A for a more detailed account of the research.

Our analysis of the Standards revealed a core set of skills that are common across grade levels and disciplines. These "common core across the Common Core" skills include making conjectures, presenting explanations, constructing arguments with sound reasoning and logical evidence, questioning assumptions, understanding multiple perspectives, making sense of complex texts, and negotiating meaning in academic discussions with others across subject areas (CCSS 2012). By analyzing the kinds of teaching moves that foster such skills and their language, we generated and refined the essential teaching practices in the next section.

FRAMES OF ESSENTIAL PRACTICES

Our research (see Appendix A) revealed not just a list, but ways in which the essential instructional practices support one another. We therefore organized the practices into three "frames," one of which is shown in Figure 1.4. Each frame consists of a high-impact essential practice at the top supported by three crosscutting practices and a foundational practice that are common across the three frames. We identified three of the essential practices as having the highest impact: using complex text, fortifying complex output, and fostering academic interactions. A frame has the high-impact practice (e.g., using complex text) at the top, which depends on three crosscutting practices: clarifying complex language, modeling complex language, and guiding learning of complex language. These are all supported by the foundational practice, designing activities and lessons.

Many teaching checklists contain discrete practices that do not relate to one another in significant ways. Unlike lists, the frames show the interconnectedness and interdependence of the practices. The frames help educators see how the essential practices support one another, and they help teachers focus on the essential practices with the highest impact at the top of each frame. Within each practice are more observable and detailed "strands." The frame example in Figure 1.4 is for using complex texts (see Chapter 4). The other two frames are headed up by the core practices of fortifying complex output (see Chapter 6) and fostering academic interactions (the subject of Chapter 8).

FIGURE 1.4

Essential practice frame for using complex texts

HIGH-IMPACT CORE PRACTICE	**Using Complex Texts** (CON) Use texts to build content understandings (LIT) Use texts to teach disciplinary literacy skills (BLT) Use texts to build language of disciplinary thinking		
CROSSCUTTING CORE PRACTICES	**Clarifying Complex Language** (CLR) Use clarification methods to make oral and written academic language understandable (DIF) Differentiate clarification methods (CHK) Check for language comprehension and adjust instruction	**Modeling Complex Language** (MLZ) Model complex language in students' "learning zones" (FOC) Use focused and thorough modeling or models of complex language (DEC) Deconstruct target language and develop metalinguistic knowledge and skills	**Guiding Learning of Complex Language** (PRO) Prompt for and provide target language (FAS) Formatively assess learning of target language (FBK) Provide useful and specific feedback
FOUNDATIONAL CORE PRACTICES	**Designing Activities and Lessons** (OBJ) Create language-supported content objectives (AUT) Structure tasks to be engaging and require authentic communication using target language (BLD) Build on student linguistic and cultural strengths and needs		

The first of three high-impact practices is using complex texts, which focuses on developing students' overall abilities to practice with and learn the language of complex texts (August, Artzi, and Mazrum 2010; Wong Fillmore and Fillmore 2011). The teacher (a) engages students in analysis of how a text's organization, syntax, and word choices combine to create meaning, and (b) fosters analytical discussions of authors' use of language to convey certain meanings for given purposes. This essential practice develops students' overall language while also strengthening their disciplinary thinking skills, comprehension habits, and content knowledge of specific texts (Urquhart and Weir 1998).

The second high-impact practice is fortifying complex output, which focuses on structuring, strengthening, and supporting the quantity and quality of students' production of original, extended academic messages that require complex language (Cazden 2001; Chafe 1982; Mercer 2000; Swain 1985). The teacher provides and scaffolds multiple opportunities for students to communicate ideas in activities such as oral presentations and answering teacher questions. Output also includes producing complex texts such as essays, articles, web pages, and multimedia presentations. The teacher provides opportunities and supports students in using academic language (vocabulary, syntax, discourse) to produce texts that communicate clear, meaningful, and original academic messages (Harklau 2002).

Perhaps the most challenging high-impact practice is fostering complex interactions, which focuses on structuring and strengthening student-to-student interactions that use academic language. *Interaction* consists of students responding to one another, building and challenging ideas, and negotiating meaning. The teacher provides and scaffolds multiple opportunities for students to interact with original, academic messages that require academic language (Cazden 2001; Lemke 1990; Long 1981; Mercer and Littleton 2007).

The first of three crosscutting practices, clarifying complex language, focuses on using a range of communication strategies to make written and spoken academic language input (oral, written) comprehensible to students (Dutro and Moran 2003; Krashen and Brown 2007). The language should be just beyond current levels of students' competence (not too difficult or too easy) in order to push them to new levels. The teacher should use varied communication strategies (gestures, drama, visuals, repetition, rate of speech, intonation), differentiate for varying levels of language proficiency, and check for comprehension throughout the lesson.

Another crosscutting practice is modeling complex language. It focuses on how effectively a teacher models (or provides a model for) the use of the target language needed to clearly speak, listen, read, and/or write in order to support content learning and its assessment (Anstrom et al. 2010; Gibbons 2002; Zwiers 2008). At high levels of enactment, the teacher might model target academic language to make a scientific argument, hypothesize about the outcome of an experiment, cite evidence to support a thesis, and so on. The teacher also *deconstructs* what is being modeled, which means to break down and explain the linguistic components or processes for students (Scarcella 2003; Schleppegrell 2004) and engage in discussions about language and its purposes.

The most complicated crosscutting practice is guiding learning of complex language, which focuses on how well the teacher adapts and supports language tasks to meet students' current levels and needs. This includes asking questions that prompt students to use academic language while providing the language for student use; formatively assessing students' learning and use of target academic language; and providing helpful and specific feedback on the effectiveness of students' use of language to communicate academic messages.

The foundational practice of designing activities and lessons focuses on how clearly a teacher crafts language objectives and instructional activities into lessons. A teacher should identify the essential academic language demands (at the word, sentence, and message levels) that students need in order to complete the lesson's texts and tasks and show mastery of the skill or concept to be learned (Bailey 2007; O'Hara, Zwiers, and Pritchard 2013). The teacher then designs engaging tasks that require authentic and meaningful use of the target language. Such tasks should require original oral or written language to be used to bridge information gaps and to negotiate meaning (Gibbons 2002; Van den Branden 2000; Zwiers 2008). The teacher supports the tasks with materials such as visual aids, real objects, word walls, and posters. The teacher also considers ways to build on students' linguistic and cultural backgrounds to inform instruction.

Please note that these are not *all* the practices that teachers must use during a lesson. The ones in these chapters support students' development of academic thinking, literacy, and communication skills. Teachers must combine these with additional instructional practices and lesson activities that focus on content-area learning, classroom management, motivation, and so on. Yes, rocket scientists have it easy.

THE INTERWOVEN NATURE OF STUDENT LEARNING

Figure 1.5 provides a rough picture of how three key dimensions of learning support one another. In the bottom box, Essential Skills correspond directly to the essential practices highlighted in this book. These are skills that we can "give" to students to work on each year of school and beyond. We develop these skills through our teacher practices, which support one another in each lesson. For example, the practice of using complex texts provides textual language and content for students to use as they produce output and as they interact. Fostering academic interactions during and after reading allows students to understand complex texts and authentically practice language and content skills. Fortifying academic output helps students to practice putting complex ideas into oral and written language, which prepares them for engaging in interactions.

The essential skills help students to develop two other core dimensions of learning in the top two boxes, complex language and disciplinary literacy along with content understandings and thinking skills. These top two dimensions provide purposes and ideas for the activities in which the essential skills are developed. For example, in a language arts lesson, your content objective is interpreting symbolism in a novel; students need to read the challenging text and use complex language in their written essays in which they need to support ideas about a symbol; they need to develop output skills for their writing and interaction skills as they talk with partners about the text; their interactions help them to clarify and add to their understanding of symbols in the story.

FIGURE 1.5
Interdependent components of student learning

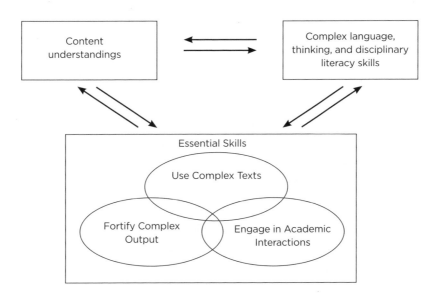

An important aspect of this diagram is the equal status of the top two boxes. While many educators throughout the years have put content on the top of most models for learning, we believe that it is time to place more value on language, literacy, and thinking. In fact, when we think of our own learning experiences, we realize that we remember a small percentage of the content of the many lessons we had in school. We haven't needed many of school's facts and concepts, or we relearned them. Yet the language, literacy, and thinking skills that we developed were actually more useful in the long run. In a sense, the content we learned in school, coupled with many out-of-school language uses, were supporting our linguistic and cognitive development, not vice versa.

UNDERLYING PRINCIPLES

Language and literacy development for the Common Core State Standards is much more intricate (i.e., messy) than the many checklists of research-based practices make it out to be. Each day, week, and year, the expert teaching of academic English learners involves a strategic cycle of creating, adapting, observing, analyzing, and reflecting. It's rocket science on multiple levels. So, just as rocket science is based on underlying physical laws and principles, the essential practices and lessons in this book are based on several pedagogical principles:

a. All students, including English learners at all levels of proficiency, need to develop their complex language and literacy skills. We cannot wait until "they are more proficient," and we cannot stop developing language when we think they are "proficient."

b. Most abilities to use complex language develop indirectly and naturally as a result of using language to communicate academic messages and "get things done." This means that we must design engaging and authentic tasks that allow and encourage students to push themselves to use more complex language to communicate. We will seldom know the exact language that they learn or when they learn it.

c. Spending extra time and effort teaching the complex language of literacy and thinking is vital for students' successful learning of challenging academic standards such as Common Core, Next Generation Science, WIDA ELD, and others. We must become more knowledgeable and skillful language teachers who address the most pressing receptive, productive, and interactive language demands in every lesson.

d. Like the double-stitched heavy thread in a pair of jeans, these practices need to be woven into lessons. Even though weaving in the practices seems to make teaching even more complicated, it strengthens it. Without a solid emphasis on the learning of complex language and literacy, lesson-based learning will unravel and not last, like a pair of jeans with weak stitching.

e. We must achieve an effective mix between more implicit (principle b) and more explicit (principle c) development of complex language. All lessons should be engaging, and within them we must find the right balance between not doing anything extra for language and overdoing the language part such that the engagement and ideas are bogged down by too many language-focused activities.

f. We must increase the use of instructional activities that value the voices and ideas of all students, especially learners at beginning and intermediate levels of proficiency who are often reticent to participate.

g. We must fortify our coaching, systems, and policies in order to cultivate and sustain the growth of the practices that promote growth in complex language and literacy.

The rest of this book describes each of the essential practices and ways they are used in real classrooms. We start at the bottom of the essential practice frames and work our way up. Chapter 2 outlines three strands of foundational practice, including how to put everything together into a well-designed lesson. Chapter 3 describes the crosscutting practices of clarifying, modeling, and guiding language learning. Chapters 4 through 9 describe the high-impact practices and annotated sample lessons in four different classroom settings: second-grade math, fifth-grade language arts, eighth-grade science, and tenth-grade history. Chapter 10 zooms out to look at how to coach, collaborate, and build sustained system capacity for the growth of students' complex language and literacy.

Summary

One of the exciting features of the Common Core State Standards is their emphasis on building students' abilities to communicate. Every day, every student should be learning more of each discipline's complex academic language, deeper levels of content understanding, and ways to improve communication with others. The teaching of academic English learners, in particular, needs to pay extra attention to complex language. Complex language roughly consists of the sentence construction and message organization strategies that are used to clarify and communicate ideas in a discipline. Complex language is vital for effective content learning, and vice versa.

CHAPTER 2

Designing Activities and Lessons

The bigger the building, the stronger its foundation needs to be.

The building of complex language and literacy is exciting and highly challenging. It needs a solid "foundation" that is based on knowing how the learning of content, thinking, literacy, and language reinforce one another within a lesson. At the bottom of each of the three essential practice frames, you see that designing activities and lessons forms the foundation for the other practices. While not everything can be planned, many lessons can be *better* planned. An ounce of planning is worth a pound of confusion avoidance and pedagogical triage when it comes to the complexity of language development in each lesson.

REFLECTION TOOL FOR DESIGNING ACTIVITIES AND LESSONS

In every chapter from here on there are tools for reflecting on improvement of the strands within each practice. Each reflection tool briefly describes the different strands, which are more tangible and observable, that make up the practice. Each tool can be modified to look more like a rubric and to have more space for note taking.

Throughout this book, the rows in each reflection tool should be seen as "interlaced" components, that strengthen learning as they work together. Even though they are separate in Figure 2.1, they often overlap. These strands should be woven together before, during, and after instruction. You will also notice three-letter codes after each strand. The codes can be used to bulk up lesson plans and to take notes during classroom observations.

FIGURE 2.1

Teacher reflection tool for designing activities and lessons

Strands of Designing Activities and Lessons	Limited Evidence	Acceptable Evidence	Strong Evidence
Identify complex language demands to create language objectives that support content objectives (OBJ)			
Structure tasks to be engaging and require authentic and original communication using complex language (AUT)			
Build on students' background knowledge, language, and cultural strengths (BLD)			

STRAND 1 OF DESIGNING: Identify Complex Language Demands to Create Language Objectives (OBJ)

One of the first things we need to do before we design the lesson is to take a close look at what and how we are teaching in order to identify the language that supports and communicates learning. If we don't develop a clear idea of the language that we need to emphasize during a lesson, then the language learning tends to get watered down by the many things happening in the lesson.

In too many settings, academic language development has been reduced to teaching vocabulary meanings. For example, a teacher might create a short list of difficult words and think of them as the language demands of the lesson. Yet for the Common Core and other important standards across disciplines, we must look for complex language in the message and syntax dimensions of academic language (refer to Figure 1.1). Other educators have identified language demands mostly by unpacking standards (Clancy and Hruska 2005). Yet it is also vital to analyze the texts and tasks used in a lesson. Therefore, we developed a set of steps that help a teacher identify the most pressing complex language demands and then use them to create language objectives.

STEPS FOR CREATING LANGUAGE OBJECTIVES

In the first column of Figure 2.2 are several steps for creating language objectives based on the identification of language demands in a lesson or unit. In the second column are examples from a seventh-grade teacher that correspond to each step. Figure 2.3 is a visual organizer that you can use to keep track of the information that you gather during the steps in Figure 2.2.

FIGURE 2.2

Steps and examples for identifying language demands to create language objectives

STEPS	EXAMPLE
Step 1. Reflect on the complex language needs of the students in the class. What language knowledge and skills do they most need to develop? Analyze their written work and listen to their conversations. Have short interactions with them to gauge their language abilities.	My seventh-grade history students struggle to support their ideas with good examples. They also lack clarity when evaluating the relevance or strength of an argument. Some students do not connect their ideas well.
Step 2. Analyze the "content" objective for message organization (i.e., discourse) demands; then sentence-level demands; and then word and phrase demands.	For example, here is a Common Core Anchor Standard: "Integrate and evaluate information presented in diverse media and formats, including visually, quantitatively, and orally" (CCSS.ELA-Literacy.CCRA.SL.2).
Step 3. Analyze texts that will be used. Texts include written texts, oral messages, videos, and visuals. Identify the most challenging language for message organization (i.e., discourse) demands; then sentence-level demands; and then word and phrase demands.	The textbook weaves narratives and expository sections together. Students are challenged to integrate them with boxed text, primary source pieces, and visuals. They need to closely read the texts for contradictory and nuanced language.
Step 4. Analyze tasks that will be used, including assessment tasks. Tasks include activities and products. Identify the most challenging language for message organization (i.e., discourse) demands; then sentence-level demands; and then word and phrase demands.	They need the language of negotiating conflicting ideas in pairs and small groups. They need to summarize long paragraphs and recognize bias in them. They need to connect their sentences as they describe their evaluations of the information presented about the Black Plague.
Step 5. Choose the most pressing demands. Look back at the lesson objective and decide which language is most useful for learning and showing learning of the objective.	Most pressing would be skills of describing the criteria used to evaluate texts and images presented about the Black Plague.
Step 6. Use the language identified in Step 5 to create a clear language objective. The objective will usually have a function (communication or thinking skill); and may or may not have specific terms or syntax strategies in it.	Objective: Students will be better able to use and explain criteria for evaluating textbook and primary source information, using strong topic sentences supported by details and examples from the text.

FIGURE 2.3

Visual organizer for identifying language demands and creating language objectives

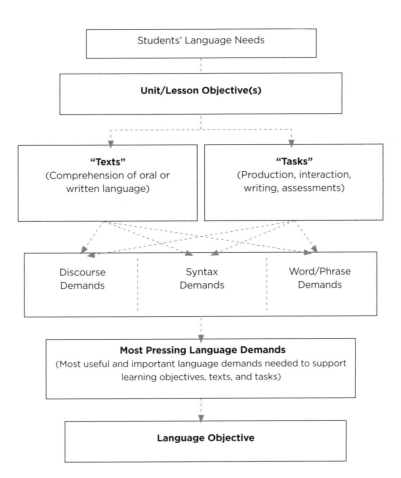

In most cases, a content objective consists of something that students need to do or know. This is often a skill, display of knowledge, or communication function—all of which need language. Thus, the language objective should directly support the content objective. Sometimes in ELA or English lessons, the content and language objectives are the same. Figure 2.4 provides examples of content objectives in math, science, English, and history in the first column, with language objectives that support them in the second column. The content objective might be based on standards from Common Core State Standards, Next Generation Science Standards, WIDA English Language Development Standards, History-Social Science Standards, etc. Focal skills and functions are underlined in the chart.

FIGURE 2.4

Content objectives and language objectives that support them

CONTENT OBJECTIVE	LANGUAGE OBJECTIVE THAT SUPPORTS IT
Students will be able to *determine* a theme or central idea of a short story and how it is conveyed through particular details. (CCSS.ELA-Literacy.RL.6.2)	Students will be able to use topic sentences with linked supporting sentences in oral and written forms to explain how the details from a text support interpretations of themes in a novel.
Students will be able to *explain* events in a scientific article on volcanoes, including what happened and why, based on specific information in the text. (CCSS.ELA-Literacy.RI.4.3)	Students will be able to organize ideas into paragraphs that describe causes and effects in sequential order, using cause–effect terms (*influenced, resulted from, led to*).
Students will be able to *analyze* the relationship between a primary and a secondary source on the topic of the "Reconstruction." (CCSS.ELA-Literacy.RH.6-8.9)	Students will be able to argue the corroboration and non-corroboration of letters (primary sources) and the textbook chapter (secondary source) using compare-and-contrast paragraphs.
Students will be able to *solve, in two different ways,* multistep word problems using the four operations. (CCSS.Math.Content.4.OA.A.3)	Students will be able to clearly explain the sequence of steps for solving a word problem, using transition words and the correct present-tense command verb form.
Students will be able to *critique* the scientific explanations proposed by peers on the topic of solar energy by *citing relevant evidence* and *supporting an argument* with data. (NGSS: 5-LS1-1)	Students, in a discussion, will be able to appropriately critique the ideas of others and organize and support their own ideas, using a topic-evidence-explanation structure for oral and written paragraphs.

Notice that the language objectives in Figure 2.4 tend to emphasize message–dimension language skills, not just grammar and vocabulary. This focus, as we mentioned in Chapter 1, is much "messier" than having language objectives that focus on word meanings and grammar rules. Yet if we don't teach these more complex ways of using language, many students will not be able to communicate well in academic and professional settings. You should also notice that many of the language objectives actually have the content objective embedded in them.

Most of the Common Core State Standards directly involve (1) understanding complex oral, visual, and written messages; (2) communicating complex ideas to others with oral, written, or multimedia output; and (3) interacting with others to construct meaning. Not coincidentally, these emphases correspond directly to the three high-impact practices in this book. For example, in the standard "Analyze the structure an author uses to organize a text, including how the major sections contribute to the whole and to an understanding of the topic" (CCSS.ELA-Literacy.RST.6-8.5), students must use organizational features of complex text to understand how it is put together. In the third-grade standard, "Use linking words and phrases (e.g., *also, another, and, more, but*) to connect ideas within categories of information" (CCSS.ELA-Literacy.W.3.2c), students must link their ideas to show their understanding of how knowledge is structured in a discipline. And in the math standard, "They justify their conclusions, communicate them to others, and respond to the arguments of others" (CCSS.Math.Practice.MP3), students must support their ideas as they evaluate and respond to the arguments of others. Thus, seeing the language that undergirds each standard can help us create effective language objectives.

We realize that most teachers don't have the time to write down detailed language objectives for every lesson. Some teachers have language objectives that span across weeks, units, or even longer. Other teachers have a small set of varying objectives that they mentally bring up as lesson tasks require. What is most important is not having the language objective nicely written up in the front of the room, but having a clear idea of the most important language skills needed for the lesson and strategically devoting some of the teaching to them.

STRAND 2 OF DESIGNING: Structure Engaging Tasks That Require Authentic and Original Communication (AUT)

This strand is actually less evident in lessons than you might think. Much of what students do in school is fake. Even though we are supposed to be preparing students for the real rigors of postsecondary education and careers, in many settings certain inauthentic patterns of instruction and assessment have become ingrained. Many students learn to go through the motions of schooling, even without realizing it. The problem is that the language-processing cells in our human minds are made for real communication. Students' minds can get dulled and lulled over time when solely focused on getting points on quizzes, answering questions for teacher praise, and writing essays for an audience of one for letter grades.

Students' minds are made to communicate with real people for real purposes. For example, people in many work settings usually read to be informed, write to convey ideas that are used to get something done, and interact with practical purposes in mind. There is usually a valuable product or solution to a problem at the end of all this communication. So, how can we do this in school? Granted, putting thirty young people in a room for six hours will never emulate most real-world settings, but we can improve the authenticity, rigor, and engagement in many lessons. We can start by asking ourselves the following questions as we design learning activities:

- Would I enjoy this activity?

- Does it allow students with different language proficiencies and background knowledge to participate?

- Does it have an interesting product or solution? Is it just busywork?

- Would experts in the discipline do something like this?

- Will it better prepare students for thinking or communication in college, careers, or real life?

- Does it involve integration of interacting with others about ideas from texts?

- Does it require students to create, clarify, fortify, or negotiate complex, original, and whole ideas?

- Is it cognitively challenging?

- Does it offer students choices?

- Does it connect to student interests?

- Does it allow students to raise and answer their own questions?

- Are there sufficient supports (content, cognitive, linguistic)?

- Is there sufficient use of materials such as objects, visuals, and auxiliary texts?

Granted, no task has all of these things. And we are not claiming that we can make *all* tasks truly authentic and engaging for *all* students *all* of the time. But we can make it one of our ongoing teacher habits to try different engagement techniques so that our lesson activities are more authentic more of the time. For example, one technique is to make sure that students are communicating information that others don't know. If listeners know it already, they don't need to listen, and the talker doesn't need to work to clarify the message either. Many common activities can be adjusted to have students talk and listen more authentically.

Engaging tasks involve shaping ideas with original and linked sentences for a given purpose. It is more work to formulate original messages, especially in oral communication with a live person listening. Unfortunately, many students have built up habits of getting by in school with the least effort expended. In the area of communication, they figure out how to use other people's words to convey messages. They copy and repeat from the texts, other students, sentence frames, and so on. They say just one-word answers, claim that they don't know, or agree with the previous answer. Many students are also afraid of making mistakes and speaking academically in front of peers.

We must push students, through the use of tasks that they care about, to challenge themselves to put their ideas together with more complex language. We realize that not all students care about all topics and tasks that we can offer in classroom lessons, but we can create activities that engage students in more real world–like communication than the simple tasks focused on definitions and right answers. In fact, we know several math and science teachers who, through their thoughtful design of engaging and language-rich activities, develop their students' language abilities much better than if they "directly" taught language through repetitive exercises.

Examples of engaging content activities that also serve as complex language development tasks are found in Chapters 4 through 9 of this book.

STRAND 3 OF DESIGNING: Build on Background Knowledge, Culture, and Language (BLD)

When designing lessons that effectively target complex language development, we need to use students' background knowledge, culture, language knowledge, and language abilities as resources (Fang and Schleppegrell 2010). This idea sounds great on paper, but how do we, in a real classroom each day, truly *use* students' backgrounds as *resources*?

BACKGROUND CONTENT KNOWLEDGE

Connecting to and building up background knowledge is both vital and difficult. First, we must know what students know and don't know related to the next lesson, unit, and remaining months of the year. We can give students preassessment questionnaires that relate to the unit. For example, "What do you know about earthquakes? How do you think mountains form? What is a volcano? What questions do you have about these things?" We then analyze the answers and get a sense of students' knowledge.

We can provide lesson activities that will help students develop, maintain, and utilize background knowledge necessary for success in classrooms. These approaches may include encouraging wide reading and the use of multiple texts as a way to become familiar with relevant concepts that will allow them to read, write, and talk with increasing confidence. We can also develop students' knowledge about a topic through classroom discussions, pictures, and videos. Because many academic English learners do not have extensive experience with the variety of genres and text structures used in mainstream texts, graphic organizers can provide opportunities to represent patterns of narrative and expository texts. More detailed examples of these and other approaches will be discussed in later chapters.

CULTURE

The cultural aspects of how families and communities communicate, as well as what they value and focus on in relationships, shape students' language and literacy in school. For these reasons, we must increase our knowledge of students' cultural backgrounds and communication approaches by asking how they, their families, and their communities communicate and educate. The stereotypes in many books about cultural and socio-economic differences are usually insufficient. We need to go to the sources: the students and their families. For example, a third grader in a nearby school never says more than one sentence when responding, and the family explained that in their country of origin students were only allowed to respond with the fact-based answers in one short sentence. In another school, a seventh grader feels that "talking school" and doing well on writing assignments doesn't make him look cool in front of his friends. For more comprehensive looks at cultural factors that influence language development, see work by Shirley Brice Heath (1983) and Lisa Delpit (2006).

KNOWLEDGE ABOUT LANGUAGE

The first component of language knowledge that we must build in students is their knowledge of the importance of improving one's language abilities. Students must come to realize that language is powerful for succeeding in life and that they must push themselves every day to be better users of language. This idea might clash with many students' notions that language is memorizing word meanings and grammar rules and that the goal in school is to say just enough to get by. Rather, we must be passionate about the power of language, emphasizing that the ideas valued in the future will require highly complex language skills, many of which are not tested in school.

The second aspect is the knowledge of language learning strategies. One of the best gifts we can give students is a set of language learning strategies that kick in even when they are not in school. We should model what we do to learn complex language. For example, we can show how we stop and think about a difficult sentence in a text and say something like, "I will remember that in science texts I need to identify the main subject and verb in long sentences." Students should learn additional strategies such as extensive reading, rereading, talking about texts and academic topics with adults and proficient speakers, writing summaries and critiques to remember what was read, asking why and how questions, listening to audiobooks, watching documentaries, and solving complex problems. The goal here is for students to realize that language learning is not just on the shoulders of the school.

The third aspect of knowledge about language is knowing what complex language is. Complex language, as shown in Figure 1.1, involves the messy discourse features such as message organization, density of ideas, register, and coherence of ideas. They should also know the skills such as matching language to its purpose, crafting a logical order of ideas, fortifying, and negotiating ideas with others. They should know that many academic messages are made up of an idea, its support, and explanation of its support (Toulmin 2003). This structure, in fact, is emphasized in the Common Core State Standards. Students also need to know that most long sentences have a main subject and verb, which are supported by other clauses and phrases. Finally, students need to know that the more complex an idea is, the more confusion there will be between two people who have very different word meanings and language backgrounds that they use to construct shared ideas.

LANGUAGE ABILITIES

For useful knowledge of students' language abilities, we need to dig. While scores on standardized tests of academic knowledge and language proficiency can provide us with some information, they rarely provide us with enough to plan instruction on a daily basis. We can start by using the observation tools, such as those found in the beginning of Chapters 4, 6, and 8, to assess students' complex language use. Additional assessment methods that may be useful include classroom observations over time, oral miscue analysis, story retellings, tape recordings of oral reading, student interactions, reading logs, writing folders, and student–teacher conferences.

We then use language ability information to help us design activities. One way to use language abilities as a resource is to engage in discussions about language use and differences. Students can share how they might communicate an idea and compare it with how the text or expert in a discipline says it. Another way is to do what one fourth-grade teacher did in her history lessons: she had students present information about their family history, quoting parents and grandparents and describing cultural values and practices. And an English teacher in a different school used students' abilities to argue as resources for persuasive discussions and writing assignments.

Putting It All Together into Strategically Designed Lessons

Even though some folks have reduced lesson plan design to filling in five- or seven-step templates, we strongly believe that an effective lesson is a strategic combination of art and science that serves a particular set of student needs and objectives at a point in time. Students are always changing and need well-designed lessons that match their learning needs. This is even truer for diverse classrooms.

To effectively design lessons, each teacher needs to be a researcher–artist–linguist–content expert–presenter–facilitator–evaluator. As researchers, we gather data on language abilities and use it to design activities. As artists, we brainstorm a wide variety of ways to communicate and solidify ideas and skills to be learned. As linguists, we analyze the language that we, texts, and students will use in the lesson. As content experts, we focus on the key concepts that students must learn. As presenters, we consider the best visual, verbal, kinesthetic, and interactive approaches for presenting new material. As facilitators, we figure out how to best foster students' growing independence in using knowledge and skills. And as evaluators, we create systems of assessment that best inform us and our students of their progress toward learning goals. Perhaps we should be paid seven times as much?

The purpose of this section is only to provide a brief introduction to possible ways in which we can strategically combine the various activities and practices that will be further explained in later chapters. It might help to bookmark this section to easily return to it.

To develop complex language in each lesson and throughout the year, it helps to use a macro- and micro-scaffolding approach (Schleppegrell and O'Hallaron 2011). Macro-scaffolding means gradually reducing support for complex language and literacy skills during the semester or year, designing lessons that build on previous lessons and units, and working toward larger language targets for students. For example, if students began to use more advanced language to compare and evaluate the contributions of characters to a novel's plot and theme, we would design similar yet more challenging models, supports, and tasks for the lessons in the successive units. Micro-scaffolding, on the other hand, means structuring activities within a lesson such that there is gradual building of students' independence by the time the lesson ends. A teacher might, for example, start the lesson by modeling how she analyzes a primary source for bias, have groups work together to find bias and fill in a visual organizer, and finally have students write an analysis on their own at the end of the period.

COMPLEX LANGUAGE AND LITERACY LESSON TOOLBOX

The set of tools in Figure 2.5 somewhat favors a certain order of activities, but is highly flexible. For example, when we begin to design three successive lessons (such as those in Chapters 5, 7, and 9), we tend to emphasize the use of complex texts in the first lesson and at the beginning of each lesson. Texts are effective ways to show students how the authors of the discipline use language. Text, be it written, visual, or oral, also provides content and language input for use in subsequent learning activities, which often emphasize output and interaction. Throughout the lesson the teacher needs to use additional practices such as clarifying, modeling, and guiding language learning by observing and providing feedback. We focus on output in the second lesson, to provide students with immediate practice in communicating ideas in the discipline. The third lesson challenges students to practice, face-to-face, their output skills in real time in order to create, clarify, fortify, and negotiate ideas.

In Figure 2.5, a sample lesson plan outline (fifth-grade ELA, with a focus on using complex texts) is included on the right to show how the tools can be strategically pulled from the "box" and placed into the lesson.

FIGURE 2.5

Academic language development practices toolbox and sample lesson

ALD TOOLBOX	SAMPLE LESSON OUTLINE

CCSS/Content Objectives and their language objectives
Connect to backgrounds and past learning
Wide-Angle Reading (emphasize disciplinary literacy and discourse) (TXT)
• Focus on purpose and background along with one column (type, structure, thinking, organizing, remembering, questions, key terms)
• Use pair-shares (OUT) and interactions (INT)
• Model how to read this type of text (author's choices, etc.)
Close Reading (emphasize content and syntax/vocabulary) (TXT)
• Model thinking and rereading during read-alouds (MOD)
• Text-based questions at word, sentence, paragraph, and whole-text dimensions . . . based on CCSS
• Clarify text language that we want students to use in conversations and in writing (CLR)
• Refer to wide-angle reading
Output Activity to use language and content of text
• Grids; continuums; opinion cards, writing organizers
• Provide language (syntax and discourse frames) from the text
• Students think in linked sentences before output
• Formatively assess
Whole-Class Conversation Practice in preparation for pair/group CCs
• Hand motions for conversation moves
• Student–student modeling ("If you were Kiara's partner, how would you respond? How might a person respond to deepen or extend the conversation?")
• All eyes on speaker; what to do when listening to speaker to build own ideas for own conversations
Conversation Models (MOD)
• Fishbowl conversation (two students or a student and teacher)
• Written conversation model on screen; highlight focal thinking skill(s), language, and CC skill(s)
• "What to say next" cards:
  • If short, ask to elaborate or for example
  • If short, ask for other example, or if partner doesn't have one, provide your own
  • If long, paraphrase, or ask to clarify or elaborate on one part
  • When partner finished with idea and examples from both of you, challenge with different idea and start over
  • Ask thinking questions: What does . . . mean? How does this help us to understand . . . ?
Constructive Conversations (INT)
• Card-based conversations (e.g., sort and prioritize) with guided practice
• Supported-then-Unsupported CC with different partners
• Clarify purpose, prompt, and language to be used.
• Review hand motion, visual, and stems of focal skill
• Formative assessment during: observe with CC card. Observe for sample language or ideas to share with whole class (back-and-forth, create–fortify–negotiate, nonverbal, multiple-linked-sentences, CC skills, disciplinary thinking
• Student self-assessment of CCs
	1. Objectives: Interpret the theme(s) of a short story using idea–support–explain message organization; evaluate, prioritize, and justify theme ideas.
	2. Connect: Why write and read stories? What usually happens in a story? Give examples of stories you have read.
	3. Wide-angle reading: Model with hand motions for purpose, share in pairs to fill in framework, then lead discussion. First read: What's this about?
	4. Close reading: (Refer to wide-angle reading visual at end)—What does *"His hope, an open ocean of colliding waves"* mean? Second read: themes and support.
	5. Output practice: Halfway through story: interview grid: *What is a possible theme and why?* (Build ideas in each interview; less looking at the text.) Use linked sentences and complex language.
	6. Whole-class conversation: Start with pair-share, with wait time to link sentences: *What might be the most important theme?* Share out and discuss: Be ready to answer; I ask them what to say next to fellow students (be like a teacher).
	7. Fishbowl model: Choose most important and apparent theme and argue why; review "what to say next" cards.
	8. Constructive conversations: Prepare by taking notes on theme idea, its support, and explanation. Have a CC. Then CC with second partner without using notes. I observe for back-and-forth; negotiate meaning; support ideas and their explanations. Students self-assess on these.
	9. Whole-class wrap-up conversation:
	Connect to content and language objectives.
	10. Final writing of theme paragraph:
	Model use of new language and ideas from conversations
	Think-pair-share on what they will write
	Remind to use new language

The toolbox helped teachers create the lessons in Chapters 5, 7, and 9. The annotated lessons in each chapter describe consecutive lessons across different disciplines in different grade levels. Each chapter emphasizes the high-impact practice of the chapter before it. For example, lessons in Chapter 5 focus on using complex text, lessons in Chapter 7 focus on fortifying complex output, and in Chapter 9 the lessons focus on fostering academic interactions. The lessons also build on the learning from previous lessons.

Summary

The teaching of complex language needs a solid foundation made up of three strands: identifying complex language demands to create language objectives; structuring tasks to be engaging and to require authentic and original communication; and building on students' backgrounds. This chapter provided tools and practical strategies for fortifying these strands across grade levels and disciplines. This chapter also highlighted the need for that fortifying to be as planned as possible in order to effectively teach language and literacy alongside content instruction. The next chapter moves us up the practice frames to describe the vital crosscutting practices for developing complex language and literacy.

CHAPTER 3

Clarifying, Modeling, and Guiding

From the raw materials to the manufacturing, to the supply chain to the retail outlets— students need to know how language works.

In Chapter 2 we looked at how to identify the complex language that we need to emphasize during a lesson. We considered different ways to strategically design lessons and activities. But we can't plan everything. We don't have the time to write everything into a lesson plan, nor do we know precisely how and what we will teach during the lesson. Students tend to throw a myriad of wrenches (and crowbars) into the lesson mix. We must therefore hone our "crosscutting" practices, which support the high-impact practices of Chapters 4, 6, and 8. This chapter describes the crosscutting practices, examples across disciplines and grade levels, and how to weave them together in lessons.

Clarifying Complex Language

In order for language to be learned, it must be understood. Clarifying involves the strategic use of various methods for helping students understand the complex language of texts and oral communication. We all can improve in the use of the three strands of clarifying. For example, even if a teacher draws a clear diagram of the complex concept of magnetism on the wall and then acts it out, some students still might not understand enough to remember it. The activity might be fun, and students might be able to draw or act it out, but they still might struggle to match the words to the concept—or to put the concept into words in their minds. The teacher will improve clarification by weaving the strands of this practice together.

TEACHER REFLECTION TOOL FOR CLARIFYING

There are three important strands of clarifying, shown in Figure 3.1. The first strand, the focus of many professional development sessions for teaching academic English learners, is perhaps the best known of the three. You can use this chapter and your own experiences to help you clarify the differences between the levels of evidence for each strand in your setting. This can also be a helpful activity for an inquiry team.

FIGURE 3.1

Teacher reflection tool for clarifying complex language

STRANDS OF CLARIFYING	LIMITED EVIDENCE	ACCEPTABLE EVIDENCE	STRONG EVIDENCE
Strategically use clarification methods to make complex language understandable to all students (CLR)			
Use a variety of clarification methods that are appropriately differentiated for the multiple levels of language proficiency represented in the class. (DIF)			
Use multiple approaches to check for complex language comprehension and appropriately adjust instruction. (CHK)			

METHODS FOR CLARIFYING COMPLEX LANGUAGE

Most of the clarification methods in Figure 3.2 are not new to most educators who are familiar with language teaching and English language learner (ELL) instructional approaches. What is new, however, is the shift in emphasis from using these strategies to build basic language to using them to build complex language. Drawing vocabulary meanings or acting out isolated sentences are quick and common methods, for example, but clarifying complex language for the "whole-message" dimension is not so common or quick. For example, it is more challenging to clarify how a speaker connects sentences and ideas in a speech than to clarify the challenging words and figurative expressions in the speech.

The methods in the first column of Figure 3.2 are commonly used to clarify language inside and outside of the classroom. While these methods are often used to help students understand content vocabulary, column 2 describes how to use them to develop more sophisticated uses of academic language. It is and will always be easier to limit our clarification energies to vocabulary. It is in our blood to act out and draw the meanings of words—and we must still do these things. Yet we must also push our talents and teacher creativity to adapt and design methods for teaching more complex uses of language.

FIGURE 3.2

Methods for clarifying complex language

CLARIFICATION METHOD	HOW METHOD CAN BE USED FOR MAKING COMPLEX LANGUAGE UNDERSTANDABLE
Movement and gestures	Students can be trained to look for language that requires (triggers) certain comprehension skills, such as comparing, persuading, or problem solving. For comparing, students learn to put one hand out, and then another when reading transitions such as *on the other hand, on the contrary, but, however,* and *yet.* For persuading, they might put both arms out and act like a scale, weighing certain ideas as they are described in the text.
Visuals and graphic organizers	The consistent use of graphic organizers, or icons that show thinking skills, can be effective. They should be connected to text types and text clues. For example, a science chapter can map onto a semantic map as students learn categories and subcategories of information. Icons can be used during reading to show parts of the text where readers must use thinking skills such as evaluation, inference, empathy, synthesis, comparison, etc. Listeners might jot down ethos–logos–pathos icons as they listen to a speech.
Hands-on activities	Students can use quotations from the text on cards to become experts on them; they can share their predictions or interpretations. They can also literally cut sentence cards up and put them back together to work on syntax skills.
Drama	Students act out scenarios while using target language. Students memorize certain dialogs from a text and practice how to say and also act out the parts. They can also do improvisation activities.
Repeated exposure (to complex text structures)	Students listen to audio-recorded texts multiple times; reread sections and short texts with different focuses; use language posters and associated visuals on the walls, and refer to them.
Intonation, stress, and pace	Teacher reads text aloud with proper intonation, stresses, and pauses to build students' fluency and exposure to complex syntax.
"Translating"	There may be times when you strategically use primary language or more common language to make the academic language of texts and oral classroom discourse more understandable to all students.

Then again, we must not overclarify. We must not create dependence on us to clarify every instance of complex language. Students must be taught to wrestle with the language of a text or message, hypothesize possible meanings, and then take steps to confirm or modify their understandings. We must, as quickly as possible, remove our supports and scaffolds so that by the end of a lesson, unit, or year, students are more independent users of the language they need to use in the discipline.

CLARIFYING FOR HIGH-IMPACT PRACTICES

Each of the high-impact practices depends on the clarification of language in different ways.

Clarifying for Using Complex Texts

There is a subtle yet significant difference between making the text's *content* comprehensible and making the text's *language* comprehensible. It is common for a teacher to clarify the content meaning of a text by modifying the text; choosing easier texts; and drawing, acting out, or paraphrasing difficult sentences and paragraphs. Yet these practices can enable students to avoid the mental work and vital practice of connecting the text's complex language to the meanings emerging from reading. We must train students to rely on the teacher less and less and to clarify on their own the language that they encounter.

Most of the time, you will be clarifying the language of some form of text, not only for students to comprehend the text, but also for their eventual use in output and interaction tasks. In fact, texts often provide the language that we would like students to use in their presentations, written products, and interactions. Thus, if students are to become independent meaning makers, we must use the text to teach them new ways to use disciplinary language to comprehend and create meanings. Both content and language need to expand and deepen in the Common Core paradigm. The Standards, for example, strongly advocate clarifying how and why the author connected ideas within and across paragraphs in a text.

Clarifying for Fortifying Complex Output

When we have a good idea of what we want students to say or write, we must clarify the terms, syntax, and whole-message strategies so that students are able to use them meaningfully. For example, if you want students to be able to describe what they think the theme of a novel is, you need to make sure that students understand (1) the disciplinary vocabulary of the description (*main character, plot, theme, motives, symbolism, represent*, etc.); (2) the syntax often used in supporting an idea (*Because . . . , Even though . . . The evidence shows that . . .*); and (3) the message-construction methods for connecting the sentences and organizing paragraphs (e.g., transitions, logical paragraph order). A teacher might use hand motions or highlight examples of transitions to emphasize certain aspects of language that students should use as they produce output.

Clarifying for Fostering Academic Interactions

A significant challenge arising from Common Core discussions is clarifying what a good conversation sounds like. We must come up with the language we want to hear between students before we clarify it. Once we know what we want students to say, we can then use methods to make it clear to them. For example, if you decide that you want to hear students use negotiation language when they argue for and against genetic testing in seventh-grade science, you write down sample conversations, show them to students, and act out the weighing of criteria and the language associated with it.

STRAND 1 OF CLARIFYING: Strategically Use Clarifying Methods (CLR)

It can be tempting to fill up a lesson with a handful of methods from a checklist of teaching practices. Yet, much like a symphony, these methods need to be strategically woven together at the right times during a lesson. This strand emphasizes thoughtful combining of clarification methods informed by ongoing formative assessment of students' needs. Refer to Chapter 1 for additional lesson planning suggestions.

So, how do we strategically combine clarification methods? How do we decide which to use, in which order, and how to tweak them for the best results? Here are a few suggestions.

1.   Formatively assess students' understanding and uses of the complex language they will need for the lesson. Analyze writing and oral production to identify the genres, text structures, syntax features, thinking skills, and terms that cause communication problems for students.

2.   Consider which strategies support one another and develop a logical sequence for their use. For example, a visual representation can often be supported by movement, as when a teacher combines arrows and shapes with hand motions to show how sentences in a paragraph can be linked.

3.   *Think* backward and *build* forward. Envision the most difficult skills and language that students will need and plan the clarification methods so that the early ones support the later ones. If students need to analyze primary sources to prepare a persuasive speech, the teacher might progress from clarifying text language with movement, to taking notes on a visual organizer like a continuum, to clarifying the language of persuasive speeches by listening to them multiple times and becoming experts on specific paragraphs.

CLASSROOM EXAMPLES OF STRATEGIC CLARIFYING

First-Grade Science: Using hands-on objects
Mr. Shane is teaching students to orally explain (CCSS.ELA-Literacy.CCRA.SL.4-5) the seasons resulting from the Earth's rotation around the Sun. Each group has a large yellow rubber balloon and a blue tennis ball with a stick through it as its axis. Mr. Shane clarifies language that they will need in their groups by moving the tennis

ball around and explaining as students emulate his motions: "The Earth is on a tilted axis. (Everyone tilt the axis of your Earth!) It rotates around the Sun. This rotation takes a whole year. How many days? Three hundred and sixty-five. Now we are in the Northern Hemisphere so we are closer to the Sun half of the year and far away the other half. What season is it when we are close, like this?"

Sixth-Grade Math: Using movements and visuals

To clarify the language of ratios (CCSS.Math.Content.6.RP.A.1), Ms. Vu begins by using several examples in the room: "What is the ratio of ears to noses in this room?" "What is the ratio of noses to fingers in this room?" "What is the ratio of fingers to eyes in this room?" She also models the explanation when asked why. "For every ten fingers in this room, there are two eyes. We could also say that for every five fingers in this room, there is one eye. The numbers might change, but the ratio stays the same. This is like two fractions. The fraction one-half is equivalent to two-fourths, even though the numbers are different." She writes on the board and shows how the colon symbolizes the ratio and the expression *to* of the ratio. Then students are asked to come up with ratios and say, "The ratio of _____ to _____ is [number] to [number]. This is because for every [number] _____, there are [number] _____." She then introduces the terms *odds* and *chances* and *probability* with coins, asking, "Out of these nine different pennies from different years, what are the odds that I pick the 1994 penny out of my pocket?"

Tenth-Grade History: Using drama and vocal emphasis

Ms. Lopez is teaching students to analyze imperialism in Latin America through the eyes of both the colonizers and the colonized (CCSS.ELA-Literacy.RH.9-10.6). She has students analyze primary sources and clarifies language they need to understand and use: "One thing that historians do is *compare perspectives* of people in the past. They then need to argue for the importance of understanding different people's *perspectives*, especially if they weren't famous. I might write or say '*According to* this Aztec poem, the author felt that the entire world was falling apart, but also that it might have been part of the *prophecy*.' Now I will move to the other side of the room to describe a *colonizer's perspective*. '*According to* this journal entry, they *were motivated by* their lust for gold and power.' Now I will look for more information about how the superstition of the Aztecs and the greed of the Spaniards *played a role* in the conquest and even *influenced* religion and culture." She also writes these terms on the board.

STRAND 2 OF CLARIFYING: Differentiate Methods for Levels of Language Proficiency

Given the immense diversity of student backgrounds, readiness levels, interests, learning styles, personalities, and language proficiency levels, differentiation is a must (Fairbairn and Jones-Vo 2010). Differentiation of clarification methods is based on your knowledge of students' language levels and learning needs. Start by asking yourself what you already know about your students' linguistic knowledge and language proficiency. Consider how you can learn more through classroom observation and assessment activities. Use this information to determine the range of language proficiency in your classroom and how you might respond to that range.

We must remember that differentiated language instruction is different from individualized instruction. As Irujo (2004, 72) argues, "Every student is not learning something different; they are all learning the same thing, but in different ways. And every student does not need to be taught individually; differentiating instruction is a matter of presenting the same task in different ways and at different levels, so that all students can approach it in their own ways." A teacher should know which students learn better through visual organizers; which students prefer movement; which students like to talk, read, and write; etc. The teacher then uses this information for differentiation. The teacher will strategically design and sequence the clarification activities depending on the content and task of the lesson and the language proficiency levels of his students.

Differentiated instruction means ensuring students have multiple options for understanding language, making sense of ideas, and expressing what they learn. More specifically, it means that we plan varied approaches to how they will learn it (process); how they will show what they have learned (product); and/or the setting or context in which the learning occurs (environment). Here are some ways in which we can differentiate according to product, process, and environment to clarify complex language for students.

- *Differentiate the product.* A teacher can have students write from different perspectives or to different audiences in a format of their own choosing. For example, a social studies teacher gives the same writer perspective (presidential candidate) and audience (the general public) to all students, but allows students to choose the topic (e.g., getting votes because of pro-union views) and the format (a campaign speech, a poster, a TV ad, an op-ed piece for the local newspaper).

- *Differentiate the process.* Perspective and background knowledge of a topic significantly influence a student's understanding and interpretation of language. Students can try "filtered reading," which involves reading a text multiple times with different focuses, or filters, each time. For example, for an article on acid rain, students may reread the selection three times with three filters: reading with a filter for persuasive language, reading with a filter for evaluating the quality of evidence and reasoning, and reading with a filter for learning the content. The students also borrow key language from the text for use in an output or interaction task.

- *Differentiate the environment.* Flexible grouping is the practice of grouping students according to their learning needs and the objectives of a particular lesson. These groups can be formed and re-formed depending on the particular activity and language-learning goals for the lesson. For example, one lesson might begin with the entire class watching a video, followed by differentiated discussion in small groups before returning to a whole-class setting to share the small-group ideas. In this type of approach, the needs of the students and the objectives of the lesson determine whether and how long flexible groups last.

At the same time, we must take care to not overdifferentiate. One of the emphases of the Common Core is that all students must develop grade-level thinking skills and disciplinary literacy. It is highly common and tempting to differentiate by requiring easier products (e.g., shorter essays), giving easier texts, and requiring easier skills (e.g., compare instead of evaluate). When academic English learners are overdifferentiated over long periods of time, the gaps between them and mainstream peers widen.

CLASSROOM EXAMPLES OF DIFFERENTIATING CLARIFICATION METHODS

Third-Grade ELA: *Focusing on differentiating the product*
Ms. Kaye is teaching students to describe characters in stories (CCSS.ELA-Literacy. RL.3.3). Students who need extra work on sentence linking are in several groups, and students who need extra work on paragraph organizing are in other groups. Students will switch, but they spend extra time where they need the most practice. The sentence-linking groups are asked to create sentences that begin with *Because, Given that,* and *Due to.* The teacher clarifies these terms with model sentences that use evidence from the text. For the paragraph organization groups she clarifies how to analyze the order of several paragraphs on cards. Students then organize different color-coded sets of paragraphs in logical order and explain why they chose that order.

Eighth-Grade History: *Focusing on differentiating the process*
As part of a Civil War unit, Mr. Lott gives students different quotations from Abraham Lincoln. He strategically gives quotations of different lengths to different groups and

asks all groups to analyze them. They need to discuss whether the quotation is evidence of possible racist views held by Lincoln and, if so, why. Mr. Lott spends extra time with some groups and gives them support cards that students use to ask and answer questions with complex language. Groups then share their ideas on a racism continuum up front.

Eleventh-Grade Physics: Focusing on differentiating the environment

The teacher, Mr. Steele, starts with a whole-class demonstration of a horizontally launched projectile and how to calculate where it will land. He clarifies the language that students will need to use to explain their results: "You can roll the ball on the table all you want. You should record the necessary data" —he writes numbers on a table on the board— "to determine the average speed, but it cannot roll off the table until I come to observe. I will grade you on your accuracy, that is, how close your calculations are to the observed phenomenon. In other words, the real measurement. Your calculations are all you have. You will want to control the variables, which means to make everything consistent, as much as possible. . . . " He has groups of four explain to each other what they plan to do. Then he strategically pairs students according to language proficiency and their abilities to work with others. The pairs then use the language from the board to gather data and make the calculations in preparation for the launch.

STRAND 3 OF CLARIFYING: Check for Comprehension of Complex Language

This strand includes using different methods to check for comprehension of complex language at strategic times during the lesson. This usually happens during or right after the use of clarification methods. Here are different ways to check for comprehension:

- Asking clarification questions. These can include What does it mean to . . . ? How does the author use language to . . . ? How would you say this in your own words? How would a historian say this? When asking questions, it is important to provide sufficient wait time and time to write their thoughts, so that students can process the language and formulate answers. Questions can be to the whole class, groups, pairs, and individuals. Listen closely to their answers.

- Having students write on paper or mini-whiteboards (or plastic over white paper) to show their responses. This offers a quick look at what the whole class is understanding.

- Having students use nonverbal signals such as hand signals, movement, gestures, and drawings to show understanding and lack of it. They can hold up cards (or sticky notes) or put different colors up on their desks (green for "got it," pink for "don't get it," etc.).

- Analyzing student assessments. While we are often looking for content learning in student assessments, we can get a good look at their complex language abilities by looking at their writing. Analyze how they structure paragraphs and essay-length written products. Notice any incorrect and awkward uses of academic language.

- Responding and adjusting in appropriate ways when we realize that clarification isn't happening. We need to quickly figure out what we can do that will clarify the idea and language. This can mean repeating what we said before, or more likely, using a different clarification method.

CLASSROOM EXAMPLES OF CHECKING FOR COMPREHENSION OF COMPLEX LANGUAGE

Second-Grade Math: Using nonverbal cues
Mr. Costa is teaching students how to explain their solution methods for solving word problems involving money (CCSS.Math.Content.2.MD.C.8). As students share their ideas for solving problems, he helps to clarify them to the class. All along he has students use one finger to agree with an idea, two fingers to expand on that idea, three fingers to disagree, and four to show confusion. He observes the cues from each student and re-explains ideas when there is confusion or when there is agreement with an incorrect idea.

Fourth-Grade Science: Using mini-whiteboard responses in response to clarifying questions
Ms. Johnson has students represent their conclusions on a whiteboard from a lab that taught them how to convert electrical energy into magnetism used for a small motor. They must use words and other means of representing scientific ideas (e.g., graphs, diagrams, visual models). Each pair presents and justifies the explanations in groups of four as a form of peer review in preparation for whole-class sharing.

Sixth-Grade ELA: Using observations of paired conversations
As Mr. Parisi reads an argument-based article on climate change aloud, he stops and uses verbal explanations to clarify the language of bias in the article. Then he prompts pairs to talk about the bias that they saw. He notices that most didn't see the bias. He quickly uses a visual organizer, like a balance scale, and puts the biased terms on each side, highlighting that one side is much "heavier." In the subsequent pair activity, the students show more understanding and use the terms from the text and mini-lesson in their answers.

Modeling Complex Language

Even though the practice of modeling is "obvious" and one of the first practices promoted (but not always taught) in teacher preparation and induction programs, becoming good at it is more difficult than it seems—especially the modeling of complex language use. Effective modeling involves much more than reading aloud, thinking aloud, word walls, or using new words correctly in sentences. Because so much complex language is happening and needs to happen in a lesson, strategic, planned, and intentional modeling is a must. Here we outline some key elements to consider when modeling complex language.

- *Before the actual modeling, tell students what you will be modeling and why.* For the "why," connect the modeling to the objectives of the lesson and how the skill can be used beyond school. For example, you might say, "Today I will be modeling for you how to sculpt the main idea of an article on genetic testing. This will help us with our objective for the day [CCSS.ELA-Lit.RI.5.2], which is 'Determine two or more main ideas of a text and explain how they are supported by key details. . . .' This skill will help you every time you read any article, website, or report in the workplace and life."

- *Model how to overcome obstacles and avoid errors.* One of the major goals of language is to communicate. And there can be many obstacles to clear communication between two or more people. It helps to model common issues and how to address them. For example, a sixth-grade teacher might notice that students have been able to find evidence for their persuasive writing but they don't vary their sentences enough. The teacher creates a non-model with short sentences to exaggerate the choppiness of such writing. Then she uses that same paragraph and models how to vary its sentences to make it sound more academic.

- *Engage in discussions about language.* Students need to understand how language works, and one way is to engage in discussions facilitated by the teacher. We can model how we think about the use of language in a text we are reading or that we are writing. For example, in tenth-grade English, Ms. Locke engages students in a discussion about the language used in Zora Neale Hurston's (1937/1998) *Their Eyes Were Watching God*. She leads a discussion about how culture, thought, and identities are portrayed by the language of the characters in the book. She reads the quote, "Love is lak de sea. It's uh movin' thing, but still and all, it takes its shape from de shore it meets, and it's different with every shore." Then she has students discuss in pairs and then the whole group how Hurston weaves dialect, figurative language, and standard prose to communicate themes and characterization in the novel.

MODELING FOR HIGH-IMPACT PRACTICES

Each of the high-impact practices depends on the modeling of language in different ways.

Modeling the Use of Complex Language in Texts

One of the greatest benefits of academic texts is the complex language that they offer. Texts provide a much higher level of complexity than that of spoken language—so much so, that we need to focus our modeling on a certain feature of the text or students will be overwhelmed. A teacher might, for instance, model how to chunk the long sentences in a science textbook chapter. The teacher thinks aloud as he reads a sentence, modeling for students how to prioritize the main information and use the subordinate clauses and phrases to support it.

Modeling the Production of Complex Output

The modeling of oral and written output is the most common form of modeling in school settings. Even so, the quantity and quality of modeling could improve in many classrooms. Many academic English learners need to see more than one model of an essay or project, as well as the thought processes used to construct them. Likewise, the modeling of oral communication could be improved in many lessons. A teacher might focus on modeling the communication of certain types of thinking skills (e.g., evaluation, argumentation, perspective-taking) and highlight the language used to describe them.

Modeling Academic Interactions

One of the most complex things that we see in a classroom is an interaction between two students that focuses on an academic topic. Yet good interactions are seldom modeled enough in K–12 settings. It is important to focus on the most relevant and needed skill or language and then remind students of it and remodel it throughout the lesson. A good place to start is modeling the prompts and responses of conversation skills (see Chapter 8) such as creating, clarifying, fortifying, and negotiating ideas.

TEACHER REFLECTION TOOL FOR MODELING

We must learn how to be strategic in our modeling for each text, activity, and group of students. Strategic modeling consists of several strands, shown in Figure 3.3. You can use this chapter and your own experiences to help you clarify the differences between the levels of evidence for each strand in your setting. This can also be a helpful activity for an inquiry team.

FIGURE 3.3

Teacher reflection tool for modeling complex language

STRANDS OF MODELING	LIMITED EVIDENCE	ACCEPTABLE EVIDENCE	STRONG EVIDENCE
Model in the learning zone: Adjust the modeling of language use from students' current levels and challenges to the next levels most needed for the lesson. (MLZ)			
Focused and thorough: Clearly and completely model and/or provide models of target complex language that supports content learning. (FOC)			
Deconstruct target language and develop metalinguistic awareness: Clearly and completely deconstruct the language being modeled; engage in discussions about complex language. (DEC)			

STRAND 1 OF MODELING: Model in the Learning Zone (MLZ)

Teacher modeling can be too advanced … or not advanced enough. In many classrooms we have seen modeling of language and literacy that students already know and can do well; in other classrooms we have seen modeling of language and literacy that is too far beyond students' current abilities. We must know where students are, and model what they need next, without overwhelming or confusing them. We call this the "learning zone," based primarily on Vygotsky's (1986) "zone of proximal development" (ZPD) and various branches of it, such as scaffolding (Wood, Bruner, and Ross 1976) and the gradual release of responsibility (Pearson and Gallagher 1983). Guiding complex language learning, the next practice in this chapter, encompasses similar ideas.

It is natural to think that the larger message dimension of complex language is too big (beyond students' learning zones) and therefore we should just model vocabulary and syntax dimensions most of the time. However, the message dimension needs the most modeling of all. Indeed, the other two dimensions are also modeled as we model how to construct whole messages. For example, as a history teacher models how to present a slide presentation of a historical argument about the effects of World War I, she models syntax and vocabulary at the same time. She also models the questions she has and the choices she makes about how to communicate to a given audience. She models how she prunes certain ideas so she doesn't water down or muddy up her message.

Modeling is meant to push students' knowledge and skills further than where they are now. We must model what they need next, without overwhelming them. For example, a seventh-grade teacher knows that her students know the meanings of the bold words in the history text (*feudalism, lords, serfs, vassals, fiefs,* etc.), but not how to use them in an argument. She uses the terms as she models, but she highlights how to construct the argument, modeling how to compare and contrast perspectives and how to evaluate feudalism's role in history. She models the thinking and its language, as well as communication strategies.

We can get an idea of the complex language that we need to model by observing students' language as they perform tasks in the classroom. Of course, this means assigning tasks that allow students to show their learning and thinking in some way. Language that we should model might also come from the language objective or other observations of student work. If students have been struggling to understand long sentences in a history textbook chapter, for example, we can model the thought processes of chunking sentences and keying in on certain terms that mark transitions and subordinate information.

Here are several complex language skills that usually need effective modeling.

- Use new vocabulary in authentic communication of ideas
- Use qualifiers and hedge terms to qualify messages (*likely, suggested that, could mean that, might*)
- Keep thoughts ordered, logical, and consistent
- Support ideas with evidence
- Use connectives such as *although, despite, so that, on the other hand* . . .
- Use subordinate clauses
- Distinguish and define abstract terms
- Use academic idioms, analogies, and metaphors
- React to inappropriate language

MODELING NON-MODELS

One way to model is to start with non-models. By looking at what not to do, and perhaps comparing it with what students often do, they can see what they need to do to improve. For example, a fourth-grade teacher might use a transcript of a paired conversation about why animals adapt, like the one here.

Student A: It says that animals change.

Student B: Yeah, like giraffes and their necks.

Student A: I saw one at the zoo. It was eating way high up on a tree.

Student B: I saw this gorilla; it went right up to the glass and scared a little kid.

The teacher asked students what Students A and B should have done in their conversation. The teacher listened and then synthesized and highlighted the main skills that students needed modeled for them, such as focusing on the prompt, coming up with additional examples and ideas from the text, clarifying ideas with elaboration and paraphrasing, etc. He then put up a good model on the same topic and had students look for skills and "moves" that helped the conversation.

Other non-models can be in the form of incomplete or unclear answers to questions, examples and modifications of past students' products, non-fluent reading aloud, and shallow think-alouds. Of course, we must be extra careful to ensure that students know that we are using *non*-models, and not models. And then we must clearly and completely model what we want students to do and know.

CLASSROOM EXAMPLES OF MODELING IN THE LEARNING ZONE

Third-Grade ELA: *Focusing on reading informational texts*
Ms. Gupta has observed that her students often struggle to see how paragraphs work together in nonfiction texts. She decides to model for students how to see and describe the logical cause–effect connections between particular paragraphs in a text (CCSS.ELA-Literacy.RI.3.8). She reads an article on pollution and models how she (1) emphasizes the topic sentence of a paragraph in her head and supports it with the other sentences; (2) summarizes the paragraph; (3) causally connects the paragraph to the previous paragraph; and (4) makes predictions about how it will connect to the next paragraph. She says, "Remember that paragraphs have ideas that are explained with their sentences. And authors connect the paragraphs to help readers understand. This paragraph was about how huge amounts of litter hurt marine life. The paragraph before explains how the litter gets into the ocean. And I think the next paragraph might explain what we can do."

Seventh-Grade Math: *Focusing on writing explanations*
Mr. Flores observed that his students were not clearly explaining their reasoning as they solved problems involving area, volume, and surface area of two- and three-dimensional objects (CCSS.Math.Content.7.G.B.6). He models how to think through and write up explanations: "It helps me to start with the term 'Given that.' So I write, 'Given that there is half of a sphere on top of a rectangular building, I needed to find the surface area of the exposed part using the formula $4\pi r^2$ and cut the answer in half. For the formula I needed the radius, which was half of the width of the building.' Notice how I am explaining why I need something and where I find it. I want to know these things, so put them into your explanations."

Ninth-Grade Science: Focusing on building ideas in interactions

Ms. Cheney has noticed that students are not building ideas in their conversations. She models this skill with another student on the current unit topic of the beginnings of the universe. She has a student help her model the conversation: "OK, David, why and how do we measure the age of the Earth?" "From rocks, I think. Scientists use radio dating to find out how old they are. But I'm not sure how that works." "They use radiometric dating that measures the radioactive decay in materials over time. It is like radiocarbon dating used on organic materials." "They found that the Earth is like 4.6 billion years old. It formed around the time of the Big Bang." "Interesting. But why do we want to know all this? It was a long time ago." "Maybe to understand how to create a new Earth, when the sun burns out." Ms. Cheney then addresses the class: "Did you notice how we built on the first idea and then moved on?"

STRAND 2 OF MODELING: Be Focused and Thorough (FOC)

In our classroom observations of modeling for growth in complex language, we have seen the need for more focus. Focused modeling means choosing a feature of complex language and being crystal-clear on what it is, why it is important, and how to use it. Before modeling, it helps to envision exactly what a good model is of what you want to see or hear from students. We should consider how proficient speakers, listeners, readers, writers, and conversers use a skill to accomplish purposes in the discipline. For example, if you are teaching students to logically link sentences in science, you can model by (1) explaining that you will be looking at ways to link sentences in scientific writing throughout the year; (2) showing why linking sentences is important in a text (e.g., to clarify cause-and-effect relationships between ideas); (3) looking at models of how authors link sentences in science articles; and (4) showing how you link sentences in a sample science article you are writing.

Modeling also needs to be thorough, which means that we don't just model a skill once and move on. Complex language skills are perhaps the most in need of modeling throughout a lesson and throughout the year for several reasons. First, the skills can't be memorized. Each sentence that students say or write to authentically communicate their ideas in a lesson is new; it is crafted and synthesized from many previous models of similar sentences. Second, complex language skills are much more abstract than content knowledge and skills. Because of this abstract and subjective nature, students' brains need large amounts of modeling of disciplinary language uses every day. Third, thorough modeling includes differentiated modeling, which helps the many students who tend not to effectively process modeling in whole-group settings.

CLASSROOM EXAMPLES OF FOCUSED AND THOROUGH MODELING

Second-Grade Social Science: Focusing on modeling of oral output

Ms. Chen is teaching students about the roles of people who influence the economy. She is also teaching students how to present information with supporting evidence (CCSS. ELA-Literacy.CCRA.SL.4). After reading about several different people who influence the economy, Ms. Chen models an oral presentation that students will practice and then give in front of the class: "I will now model for you how to connect sentences to give an oral presentation. Oral presentations are important in many classes and jobs in the future. They can show people what you know and teach them things. Ready? This person is a consumer. He is important to the economy because he buys products and services. For example, yesterday he bought milk. That money helped the grocery store and it helped the dairy farm that provided the milk to the store. OK. Now I want you to practice with your partners." Ms. Chen then goes around to groups and models her presentation several more times.

Sixth-Grade History: Focused on modeling the use of complex text

Mr. Bailey models for students how to be looking for text that prompts certain historical thinking skills. The modeling also highlights the idea that students can use this language in their own creation of messages. The modeling shows students how history knowledge is often organized and presented in the paragraphs of historical texts, and how to process the information so that it is understood and retained. Mr. B: "This chapter is exciting. Now I want to model how I read history textbook chapters. First, I prepare my brain for several types of historian thinking. What are they?" (Students share ideas). "Yes, cause and effect, maybe some bias, connections, and so on. Read along with me: *During the 900s, many Mayas moved away from their cities in the southern lowlands. Some archaeologists believe that overcrowding in the cities led to this migration, while others argue that war between the cities forced people to leave. Still others think that farming practices, diseases, and invaders played large roles in what came to be the collapse of the Classic period.* First of all, I saw the opening sentence and what did I think? That I need to remember this date and fact for a test? No. I wondered why! This got my 'cause-and-effect radar' going and I saw several terms such as *led to*, *forced people to*, and *played large roles*. I also saw some historian theory terms such as *believe that, argue that,* and *think that*. This interests me a lot because they still don't know. Maybe *I* can come up with a good answer. Now I might expect further explanation of these theories, and if I need to describe my own theory after doing more research, I can use the cause-and-effect terms and the theorizing terms from this text."

Eighth-Grade ELA: Focusing on academic interactions

As the class has been reading *The Giver* (Lowry 2002), Mr. Falk has noticed that students are not building up ideas as they talk; they have been just popcorning ideas back and forth. Mr. Falk is focusing on the skill of acknowledging new information expressed by others and justifying one's own views (CCSS.ELA-Literacy.SL.8.1d). He asks one student to come to the middle of the room in a fishbowl format, surrounded by students.

Teacher:	OK, class. Cindy and I are going to model how to build up ideas in a conversation. How can we build ideas? [Students call out.] Yes, by clarifying and supporting them with examples and evidence. OK, Cindy, let's talk about *The Giver*. How would I start the conversation? Should I ask you what you liked about it?
Cindy:	I think you should ask about the theme.
Teacher:	OK. What do you think the main theme was?
Cindy:	I thought an important one was that memory of the past is important, even if it is painful.
Teacher:	Well, I think the theme is being able to choose. They didn't have choices. OK. What did I just do?
Cindy:	You didn't build on my idea.
Teacher:	OK. How might I build on it?
Cindy:	You could ask for my evidence that supports it, like, from the book.
Teacher:	OK. What is your evidence?
Cindy:	Well, Jonas receives the memories, and a lot of them are violent and ugly. But others are beautiful and happy.
Teacher:	And there was that part where he liked the feeling of love. He said it was warm.
Cindy:	I agree. So everyone didn't remember any bad things, right? But they also didn't remember good things like love. They were like robots. We need to remember good and bad or we aren't human. And we need to choose.

Teacher: Great. Did you notice how we kept building on your idea? Now we might move on to build up one of my ideas. At the end we might even decide which theme is stronger.

The teacher modeled what good conversers do in a constructive conversation. The teacher even used a non-example of changing the topic and pointed this out to students. Later in the lesson, the teacher had two students model the conversation that the teacher had observed. Model conversations are never perfect, but over time they are effective at modeling interaction skills for students, especially for the students who volunteer to model.

STRAND 3 OF MODELING: Deconstruct Target Language and Develop Metalinguistic Awareness (DEC)

This strand of modeling helps students to understand how complex language works. One part of this strand is to deconstruct what is being modeled, which means to break down and explain for students what the language is doing. It does not mean testing students on word parts and grammar rules or diagramming sentences. Rather, it means showing students how authors and speakers make language choices to construct meaning in ways that meet the expectations of the message and situation. For example, we might highlight how a politician uses qualifying terms and figurative language in a speech to motivate and impress listeners without completely committing to certain causes or ideas.

We should also facilitate discussions and reflections on how language varies across content areas and contexts by discussing with students real-life applications and purposes of language (e.g., self-advocacy, social change, identity). For instance, a teacher might lead a discussion on how dialects influence users' access to power within the community. Metalinguistic knowledge allows students to take a wide-angle look at how authors, speakers, and they themselves use language for different purposes. In a nutshell, it provides more ownership of language.

CLASSROOM EXAMPLES OF DECONSTRUCTING COMPLEX LANGUAGE FOR METALINGUISTIC AWARENESS

Third-Grade Math: Focusing on deconstructing mathematical reasoning
Mr. Hall is teaching students how to determine the unknown whole number in a multiplication or division equation (CCSS.Math.Content.3.OA.A.4), as well as how to reason abstractly and quantitatively (CCSS.Math.Practice.MP2). He starts with this problem: "Sammy had a bag of forty-eight marbles. He decided to give them all to his six friends. If each friend got the same number of marbles, how many did each friend receive?"

First, he models his explanation of how to solve it: "I always remember that a problem gives me information and I need to do something with it to answer a question. I can solve this problem by picturing a bag of forty-eight marbles and . . . Hmmm. Should I add six friends to the forty-eight marbles? No. I can't add marbles and friends. They are very different units, right? That means I can't subtract either. I know each friend gets part of the forty-eight, so I will divide. I get eight marbles per friend. Does that make sense? Yes. I can multiply it by six and see if I get forty-eight. Yes. No applause, please. Now you do the same with the next two problems: one partner do number two and the other do number three."

Fifth-Grade History: Focusing on metalinguistic awareness of argumentation in writing
Ms. Irving has students set personal goals for academic language use and track their learning of academic language. Students keep a portfolio with examples of their academic language use, and analyze and assess their own progress over time, using evidence from their portfolios, including video clips and writing samples. In the current unit, Ms. Irving is having students write short articles that argue for or against traditional accounts of a famous event in U.S. history. She models with several articles and has students pick out the language used and the organization of ideas. She highlights the importance of using evidence (CCSS.ELA-Literacy.RH.6-8.1), especially for accounts that challenge commonly accepted ideas. In an article on the bombing of Pearl Harbor, she deconstructs claims and evidence regarding the U.S. government's knowledge of the attack. She has students point out where there is weak or a complete lack of supporting evidence for claims.

Ninth-Grade Science: Focusing on analyzing language of complex text
Ms. Nguyen is teaching students to analyze the sentences and structures of science texts (CCSS.ELA-Literacy.RST.9-10.5). She begins: "I would like you all to focus on the second paragraph of the chapter. I am going to model my thinking as I read this language. I know that the text is about geologic time scale from the subheading. I see fossils on the page so I think it might have to do with life. Let's read: *The appearance and disappearance of different organisms during the course of Earth's history provides scientists with data to mark key changes and events in the geologic time scale.* First of all, I notice that the subject of the sentence is long: *The appearance and disappearance of different organisms during the course of Earth's history.* What does it do? It provides data. And what does the data do? Helps scientists come up with the geologic time scale. The language in this sentence is general and abstract, so I now expect specifics, specific examples that show me what scientists do. In upcoming

text I should expect examples of appearance of organisms, disappearances, and different organisms. I should expect to see a time scale that will be similar to, but different from, typical time lines we see in history class. And I should expect to learn how scientists use the fossils to create the divisions of the time scale."

SELECTIVE MODELING

Then again, we can't and shouldn't model everything. Think about all the language that you know and use. Very little of it was consciously modeled for you. What this means is that we must keep in mind that huge amounts of language, complex and otherwise, come from engaging and authentic listening, reading, speaking, writing, and conversing about real ideas for real purposes. This also means that we shouldn't "sentence-stem-ify" every single response by students, and we shouldn't stop to model our thoughts at every sentence during a read-aloud or other lesson activity. By focusing on working with and constructing ideas for engaging purposes in each discipline, high amounts of complex language will be modeled for students in rich and natural ways. We may never know exactly when or which models of language have an effect, but after several years of language-rich and meaning-filled lessons, the evidence of overall language development mounts.

Guiding Complex Language Learning

Guiding learning is vital because students differ depending on the day, the topic of study, the lunch menu, and a host of other factors. Guiding their learning means providing the right supports at the right times, and taking away the supports over time so that students build independence in the use of skills, content, and language. The teacher also adapts and supports language tasks to match current levels and observed needs. Three main types of support are described in the three strands that follow.

Micro-scaffolding and macro-scaffolding. One challenge of guiding is that it is both a micro- and a macro-skill (Schleppegrell and O'Hallaron 2011; also see Chapter 1). We must be able to guide the language and literacy learning of students in one task during a lesson (micro-) while guiding them to develop language and literacy skills throughout the year (macro-). We cannot just put stars next to language and literacy standards up on the wall or in a grade book and think a student has "mastered" it. The Common Core literacy standards, for example, are lifelong; the text or content becomes more challenging each year, but the skills are similar throughout. A physics professor reading the latest article in a journal, for example, uses many of the skills within the Common Core State Standards for literacy across disciplines (CCSS 2011).

Building independence. Guiding language and literacy learning has three strands, shown in Figure 3.4. An overarching habit needed for each of these strands is building students' independence. This is vital because of the tendency to over-scaffold. For example, we have seen classrooms with the same sentence-starter posters up all year. We have seen students use the same visual organizers for essays in the same way for eight months. We need to gradually take away linguistic supports so that students build their abilities to use complex language on their own.

Coaching. Guiding students' language learning is a lot like coaching. A coach of any sport models what to do and think and provides specific feedback to players in practice sessions. A coach explains strategies and then creates more authentic practice sessions to prepare players for real events. As a football coach might model how to catch a ball, we must model disciplinary thinking and skills to help our students expand their learning. When we see that students fail to understand or use a skill effectively, we increase feedback and support. As we observe that students are learning and applying their learning, we gradually reduce our guidance.

TEACHER REFLECTION TOOL FOR GUIDING LANGUAGE LEARNING

There are three important strands of guiding, shown in Figure 3.4. Feel free to use this tool to reflect on ways to improve your abilities to support, scaffold, assess, and adapt instruction that promotes the growth of complex language and literacy.

FIGURE 3.4

Teacher reflection tool for guiding language learning

STRANDS OF GUIDING LANGUAGE LEARNING	LITTLE EVIDENCE	ACCEPTABLE EVIDENCE	STRONG EVIDENCE
Provide and prompt for use of complex language at appropriate times. (PRO)			
Formatively assess students' use of complex academic language and use information to inform instruction. (FAS)			
Provide specific and helpful feedback on use(s) of complex language. (FBK)			

STRAND 1 OF GUIDING: Provide and Prompt for Target Language (PRO)

Clarifying and modeling complex language are often not enough for lasting learning of complex language. Many students need and benefit from having the language provided to them in easily accessible ways for their use in engaging tasks. Common ways of providing language are verbalized examples, sentence frames, referring to the text, visuals posted on walls, and language written on cards or in student notebooks. Yet even when we make the language visible and usable, we often still need to prompt for its use. Especially in engaging discussions, it is tempting for teacher and students to default to basic, noncomplex language.

We should monitor students' language use so that we can nudge, encourage, and remind (i.e., prompt) students to use the new skills and push themselves to use more complex language to communicate. In discussion settings, we should not correct students as they speak, but instead provide language that students can use before they share. They should be able to choose whether or not to use it. All along, students should realize that this prompting is for improving clarity and expertise in communicating in the discipline, *not to please the teacher or to gain points*. One effective way is having students themselves prompt for and provide language. For instance, in the seventh-grade example that follows one student prompts her partner to use new language that they learned recently.

CLASSROOM EXAMPLES OF PROMPTING AND PROVIDING COMPLEX LANGUAGE

Figure 3.5 includes several examples of prompting and providing language in order to support its development across grade levels and disciplines.

FIGURE 3.5

Classroom examples of prompting and providing language during lessons

CLASS	METHOD OF PROMPTING FOR THE USE OF COMPLEX LANGUAGE	METHOD OF PROVIDING COMPLEX LANGUAGE
Kindergarten science	The teacher is teaching students, in pairs and whole-class discussion, to "communicate solutions that will reduce the impact of humans on the land" (NGSS.K-ESS3-3). She asks students to draw their solutions for deforestation and to explain them using complete sentences from starters that are written on the board. Students practice with different partners.	Teacher writes starters on the board: *In order to . . . we need to . . . One way to solve the problem of . . . is to . . .*
Fourth-grade history	The teacher, listening in on pairs, hears a student say, "I don't like what they did to the Native Americans." The teacher says, "Remember, how might a historian say what you said? Look at the language we said we would use from the text: In my opinion, the missions treated the Native Americans poorly. For example, . . ." The teacher also prompts students to use this language in their written exit tickets at the end of the class period.	Taking language from the book, the teacher puts *In my opinion, the missions treated the Native Americans . . . (adverb) . . . For example, . . .* under the document camera.
Seventh-grade math	The teacher has students prompt one another to use the language of justification as they solve problems together. Araceli hears her partner say, "We should use that table way." Araceli prompts, "OK. Can you explain why? And the teacher wants us to try starting with 'Because . . .'" The partner responds, "OK. Because we need to graph it, like, to see where the points intersect, we should use a table."	Students write in their notebooks several stems for complex sentences used for justifying answers: *Because . . . , we need to . . . ; In order to . . . ; Given that . . .*
Tenth-grade English	After looking at essay drafts, the teacher notices that many students are not linking their sentences in logical ways. She does a mini-lesson on cohesion and transitions. Working with a student, she says, "For example, let's look at these two sentences: *There is a desire to be organized and the desire to be like animals. This is a part of human nature.* Readers might not know what the 'This' is for. Are you saying that the tension between being organized, or civilized, and being savage is human nature? So, to be clearer, you might write *There is a tension . . . This aspect of human nature is represented by . . .* You can finish them. Notice that we clarified the 'This' in the second sentence for readers."	Guides students to use writing strategy shown in the frame: *This _____ is represented by . . .* and key vocabulary: *civilized, savage, tension, aspect.*

THE STRATEGIC USE OF SENTENCE STARTERS AND FRAMES

Sentence stems, frames, and starters (SSFs) have become popular in recent years. We have a like-dislike relationship with SSFs. In many classrooms that we have observed, SSFs can be useful, just there, overused, and misused—even in the same lesson. Several negatives are that they can interrupt a speaker's thought process; they are sometimes not understood by students, even when students say them; and they tell a student which words to use, even though we are promoting authentic and original communication. Some students have learned to robotically repeat them and then tack on a few words at the end to appease the teacher.

Thus, as we prepare to use frames to fortify output, we must think about if, when, and how to use frames to keep the messages as genuine and engaging as possible. Often, we must make the activity as engaging as we can. Therefore, we strongly advocate the "use as little as needed and remove as soon as possible" approach to using SSFs over time. This means that we use SSFs at strategic times and take them away ASAP so that students can make the language of the SSFs their own.

STRAND 2 OF GUIDING: Formatively Assess Language Learning to Inform Instruction (FAS)

Students are never the same from one year to the next, or even from one day to the next. We must be diligent in our assessment during each lesson, with one ear and eye always on students' abilities to use complex language and literacy to learn and accomplish tasks. Even though formative assessment is related to the checking for comprehension (CHK) strand at the beginning of this chapter, this strand (FAS) is more focused on assessing students' use of complex language to communicate and interact.

We can formatively assess by asking guiding questions, observing student work, having conversations with students, observing their conversations and presentations, and so on. Usually, like it or not, we find that we need to adjust and adapt our instruction. Common ways to adapt instruction are remodeling, giving more time, adjusting student pairings, connecting to previous texts and lessons, relating to student backgrounds, using different activities, and explicit explanation.

CLASSROOM EXAMPLES OF FORMATIVELY ASSESSING COMPLEX LANGUAGE USE

Figure 3.6 provides several examples of formative assessment strategies used to support complex language development across grade levels and disciplines.

FIGURE 3.6

Classroom examples of formative assessment and instructional adaptation

CLASS	FORMATIVE ASSESSMENT	INSTRUCTIONAL ADAPTATION
Third-grade science	The teacher is observing small groups that are arguing for and against the value of animals forming communities for survival. She observes each group and notices that students are citing examples, but not explaining how they support their ideas.	Gives a mini-lesson on explaining the examples that they come up with. Uses a visual organizer to show how the explanation strengthens the example.
Fifth-grade history	A pair is looking for biases in primary and secondary sources on the time leading up to the American Revolution. The teacher observes that they are not noticing bias terms in the text.	The teacher puts his arms out and becomes a balance scale. As students slowly read aloud, he leans to one side when he hears a term such as *evil, unfair, massacre, inevitable,* and *tyranny.* He lightens up when he does not hear examples to support (give weight to) ideas. He also asks students what was not included in the texts.
Eighth-grade language arts	The teacher circulates as students color-code features of their persuasive letters and notices that many students are not explaining how evidence for their side (underlined in green) outweighs opposing evidence (underlined in orange).	She pulls an expert group that will teach the class groups. She has them analyze a model letter to notice how the author explained how the "apples outweighed the oranges" using persuasive appeals and comparisons.
Eleventh-grade geometry	The teacher is having students explain how to derive the formula for the volume of a sphere using Cavalieri's principle of indivisibles and intersecting planes. Students are practicing their explanations and having trouble with the logical flow of their arguments.	Provides students with a visual organizer and sentence stems such as *Given that . . . Cavalieri's principle states that . . . Therefore, by the Pythagorean theorem, the plane . . .*

STRAND 3 OF GUIDING: Provide Specific and Helpful Feedback (FBK)

One of the most powerful ways to guide and solidify the learning of complex language is to provide specific, helpful, and timely feedback (Hattie 2009). You might be thinking that *helpful* is unnecessary in the previous sentence, but it is needed. *Helpful* (in this section) refers to how well the feedback supports the language needed at that moment to communicate. A teacher might provide specific and timely feedback in pointing out to a student the need to use the five vocabulary terms for the week in an essay, but if it is organized in a confusing way, the vocabulary feedback doesn't *help* improve the communication nearly as much as feedback about its organization.

Most of our feedback to students should be positive! Students, like adults, need positive reinforcement when they are trying new things and taking risks. Language is highly personal and often influences a person's self-perception of academic identity and even of intelligence. Academic English learners, in particular, have a wide range of ideas, often negative, of how others view them because of their language use. For these reasons, we must look for and highlight when students use and even try to use challenging forms of language to communicate.

Many of the complex language skills that benefit from feedback are found in this and other chapters. Several key skills include logically linking sentences, organizing paragraphs, using visuals along with the text, using evidence to support an idea, explaining how parts relate, explaining how apples outweigh oranges, using complex sentences, using appropriate transitions, using modals to soften messages, and using nonbiased language.

CLASSROOM EXAMPLES OF PROVIDING EFFECTIVE FEEDBACK FOR BUILDING COMPLEX LANGUAGE

Figure 3.7 shows several examples of providing helpful feedback during a lesson in order to support complex language development across grade levels and disciplines.

FIGURE 3.7

Classroom examples of providing effective feedback for complex language learning

CLASS	COMPLEX LANGUAGE FOCUS	FEEDBACK ON USE OF COMPLEX LANGUAGE
First-grade ELA	Linking sentences to create cohesion in oral messages	The teacher notices that several students are asking one another questions about the topic of transportation. Karla asks, "Why do people take trains?" The teacher compliments Karla on asking questions beyond just "Do you like trains?" The partner, Julio, was answering with multiple sentences so the teacher complimented him by saying, "Great job, Julio. You made your ideas clear with several sentences."
Fourth-grade math	Supporting arguments in writing with evidence and synthesizing key points from multiple ideas	The teacher notices that several students aren't supporting their arguments in their written explanations of how two different methods for solving a fraction word problem are related. She has two students argue how they are related and then another student synthesize their points. She asks students to include the points and connect them with the language of comparison. For example, the teacher says, "In order to explain how they relate, you can start with, 'The picture method is similar to the numerical methods in several ways. First, . . . '"
Sixth-grade science	Using content terms and ideas from the text in oral output and illustrating them with examples	Students are reading about erosion in order to describe different types of erosion and its importance. After students engage in an oral pro-con activity on the positives and negatives of erosion, the teacher asks students to do the activity again, with different partners, using additional language from the textbook sections, such as *process, gravity, deposition,* and *prone to*. The teacher encourages students to provide specific examples of these terms or point to pictures to support their ideas.
Ninth-grade history	Building up ideas with evidence in academic interactions	The teacher observes as students discuss their overarching question, Why does history change—and not change? They are applying it to what they are learning about social classes and castes around the world, in history and today. One student argues, "All this caste stuff is because humans need to feel superior. This means that . . . " Melissa says, "I wonder if this need has lessened or grown." The teacher provides the following feedback: "Great thinking! I love the connection to our overarching question. One way to clarify is to use more cause-effect language, like up on the board. You can also use several examples to explain how the human need to be superior has caused certain conditions and beliefs in the past and now. Build up this idea. Then—and Melissa, I loved that you posed it as a question—you all can build up her idea of whether this need has diminished or not."

Summary

This chapter outlined the three crosscutting practices that support the high-impact practices in Chapters 4, 6, and 8. As you can see from the many examples in this chapter, the use of crosscutting practices also cuts across all disciplines and grade levels. In every lesson we must clarify the new language that students will need to use to learn and show their learning. We must also model how they should use the language and guide their use of it during the lesson and during the entire school year. Now that the foundational and crosscutting practices have been "covered," we turn to Chapter 4, which describes the nitty-gritty of helping students develop complex language from complex texts.

Using Complex Texts

The voltage and wattage of one's language increases exponentially by reading.

One of the main purposes of having students read in school has been to get content into their heads. Texts have been used as quiet ways to transmit the facts and concepts of a discipline. Yet this chapter's practice of using complex texts helps students get much more out of texts than content. This practice emphasizes using texts as tools and models for building disciplinary language, thinking, and literacy.

The Common Core State Standards emphasize the need to teach students to understand "complex texts" (CCSS 2012). A *complex text* can be any written, visual, audio, or multimedia message that conveys information or ideas for learning purposes. Complexity varies, of course. A text can be complex for some students and not complex for others. More often than not, grade-level texts in school are complex for academic English learners and others who have not been exposed to the wide range of ways that authors of school texts use text structure, syntax, and vocabulary to communicate their messages. Many students lack academic background knowledge and language that comes from having hundreds or even thousands of books read to them, from listening to academic oral language (e.g., documentaries on TV), or engaging in rich conversations outside of school (Wong-Fillmore and Fillmore 2011).

While many educators have simplified texts or just used easier ones, complex texts are the very thing that academic English learners need. Written texts, in particular, provide high concentrations of complex academic language (Wong-Fillmore and Fillmore 2011). As a reader processes the language and creates meaning from it, the mind stores up new terms, syntax, ways of organizing knowledge, and ways to describe thinking skills. Most of this "storage" is subconscious, meaning that not even the reader has control over what types of language the brain holds on to as it creates meaning. What is certain is that when students read and understand large quantities of academic texts, their academic language abilities increase, across the board, for reading, writing, listening, speaking, and interacting.

Figure 4.1 provides a few Common Core standards that illustrate the language and literacy implications that we need to address when teaching academic English learners.

FIGURE 4.1

Selected Common Core State Standards related to using complex texts and their implications for teaching academic English learners

CCSS	IMPLICATIONS FOR TEACHING IT TO AELS
Describe characters in a story (e.g., their traits, motivations, or feelings) and explain how their actions contribute to the sequence of events. (CCSS.ELA-Literacy.RL.3.3)	Students can lack exposure to a wide range of stories, characters, and conversations about character traits and motivations with more proficient readers (e.g., parents). Many students' backgrounds and cultures differ from those of the characters in commonly used school texts.
Determine a central idea of a text and analyze its development over the course of the text, including its relationship to supporting ideas; provide an objective summary of the text. (CCSS. ELA-Literacy.RI.8.2)	Students with diverse backgrounds and literacy experiences can have ideas of what is "central" in a text that do not neatly align with the ideas of teachers and test materials.
Make sense of problems and persevere in solving them; start by explaining to themselves the meaning of a problem and looking for entry points to its solution. They analyze givens, constraints, relationships, and goals; consider analogous problems; monitor and evaluate their progress; and change course if necessary. (CCSS.Math.Practice.1)	Students can have difficulties visualizing the wide variety of scenarios that word problems present in one sitting. They might not know the key terms that signal operations or relationships; many of these terms are often not even typical math vocabulary: *submerge, ascend, another, distribute, pretax, decay*, etc.

Challenges of Using Complex Texts

In addition to the implications in Figure 4.1, there are significant challenges associated with the teaching of new reading standards to academic English learners. Here are two of the most pressing that are addressed in this chapter.

How do I teach grade-level texts to my academic English learners who are reading "several levels below" grade level? The Standards emphasize independent, analytical listening to and reading of grade-level texts. This means training students how to mentally prepare themselves for a text and modeling how readers should put the pieces together to comprehend it. Students are supposed to build independence as they wrestle with the text. Unfortunately, some educators have de-emphasized the use of prereading activities and the teaching of reading strategies, arguing that the overuse of such activities and the focus on isolated strategies enable students to avoid the hard work of wrestling with a text. However, to understand and use grade-level texts, academic English learners often need extra supports, which will be in the form of pre-, during-, or post-reading activities and comprehension strategy mini-lessons. Along the way, of course, we must strategically reduce supports to avoid fostering students' dependence on the teacher or simplified texts, while moving students toward more independent use and comprehension of complex texts.

How do I authentically assess students' comprehension of complex texts? Many factors of text complexity conspire against a reader's comprehension. A firm knowledge of these factors and how comprehension works is an important start for being able to generate formative assessment strategies such as asking questions, listening to student conversations, analyzing text-based writing, and the like. This chapter contains many activities that help teachers formatively assess comprehension.

Formative Assessment of Students' Acquisition of Complex Language from Texts

Figure 4.2 is a tool for assessing three key areas that are not often emphasized with respect to reading in school. The tool helps teachers to roughly assess (1) students' abilities to construct a "message-level" framework of a text before and while reading it; (2) students' complex language development resulting from reading complex texts; and (3) students' growth in their abilities to acquire complex language from text. This last one is vital for building students' independence in learning beyond K–12 school settings.

FIGURE 4.2

Student observation tool for using complex texts

SYMBOL	3	2	1
	Takes a wide-angle look at every text to predict and form its purpose, use its structures, and create a mental framework	Looks at text features but does not fully predict or form a purpose, use structures, or create a mental framework	Pays little or no attention to purpose or structure; does not create a mental framework
	Analyzes the text for how the author uses organization, syntax and vocabulary to communicate complex ideas	Uses some analysis of organization, syntax, or words to see how author is communicating	Uses little or no analysis of organization, syntax, or words to see how author is communicating
	Uses language from the text for real oral and written communication	Uses some language from the text for real oral and/or written communication	Uses little or no language from the text for real oral or written communication

TEACHER REFLECTION TOOL FOR USING COMPLEX TEXTS

Like the other essential practices in this book, we have identified three important strands within the practice of using complex texts. The teacher reflection tool in Figure 4.3 contains the three strands. You can use this chapter, the lessons in Chapter 5, and your own experiences to help you clarify the levels of evidence for each strand in your setting and for your purposes.

FIGURE 4.3

Teacher reflection tool for using complex texts

STRANDS OF USING COMPLEX TEXTS	LIMITED EVIDENCE	ACCEPTABLE EVIDENCE	STRONG EVIDENCE
Use complex texts to support the learning of content (CON)			
Use complex texts to develop students' disciplinary literacy skills (LIT)			
Use complex texts to build disciplinary language and thinking (BLT)			

Notice that comprehension of content is only one strand of this practice. As the reflection tool in Figure 4.3 shows, there are two other strands that we emphasize in this chapter: using texts to develop disciplinary literacy skills and using texts to build thinking and language. These two strands, in particular, are vital for teaching academic English learners because these students need more than content comprehension. They deeply need texts to build the sophisticated language, literacy, and thinking skills that will help them tackle increasingly challenging texts and ideas in the future. Notice also how these strands support several of the AEL shifts mentioned in Chapter 1, such as moving from piece to whole skills, focusing more on ownership of complex language, and moving from just content learning to language-thinking-literacy-content development.

WHAT MAKES AN ACADEMIC TEXT EXTRA COMPLEX FOR ACADEMIC ENGLISH LEARNERS?

The CCSS documents describe text complexity with factors that fit into three categories: quantitative, qualitative, and reader and task. Because of the overlap and complexity of considering all three categories at once, we synthesized the factors into one list and placed them in the first column of the tool in Figure 4.4.

We included the more qualitative factors first because they require more analysis and thought. We included the quantitative factors, the ones that are more "measurable" with visual inspection of the text, on the bottom of the chart. Most teachers don't have the time to use readability formulas or do computer-based analyses, and even if they do, these measures can be misleading. A very sophisticated text might use common words and short sentences, or a very unsophisticated text might use uncommon words and long sentences. Therefore, we must use a large amount of professional judgment as we "measure" the complexity of any given text.

The second column of Figure 4.4 allows a teacher to give the factor a very rough score for how difficult it makes the text for one or more students. We must keep in mind that these ratings will never be completely accurate: numbers will be wrong at times and change depending on the students and the context. The third column provides practical teaching suggestions and strategies, some of which are described later in the chapter, for what to do for academic English learners if the factor in that row "scores high" for making the text extra complex and challenging for students. Like many tools in this book, this is only a sample to get you started. The ideas in each area may or may not apply to your students and setting. Eventually, you will be able to do this type of "scoring" quickly in your head.

FIGURE 4.4

Sample tool for addressing the various complexity factors of texts

Text complexity factors	How difficult the factor makes the text	If the rating is high, we can develop students' complex language and thinking for and from comprehension by doing the following:
Task complexity (What students need to do with the text)	1-2-3-4-5	Modeling the task with different texts and showing models of finished tasks Explaining how the task builds certain thinking skills Highlighting the language that students should use to succeed in the task
Background knowledge (BK) required (compared with students' existing BK and experiences)	1-2-3-4-5	Providing just enough content background knowledge to help students comprehend with little or no support Meta-analyzing important or language techniques commonly used by author
Inferential and sophisticated meaning(s) (e.g., abstractness, satire, irony, metaphor, perspective, dialog, multiple themes)	1-2-3-4-5	Using multiple examples of similar texts Using graphic organizers to show abstract and figurative relationships Using close reading analysis questions and discussion of text strategies that require inference and taking different perspectives
Lack of clear or familiar text structure, connections between ideas, or transitions	1-2-3-4-5	Using graphic organizers that illustrate text structure (e.g., sequence, cause–effect, claim–support, narrative with themes, argumentation, etc.) Modeling for students how to recognize text structures and take notes based on them Modeling for students the thinking that is triggered by cohesive devices and text features
Quantity of thinking skills required in text	1-2-3-4-5	Modeling for students how to use thinking skills to comprehend Modeling how to code texts with thinking skills (e.g., with different-colored sticky notes)
Lack of textual aids that illustrate and summarize	1-2-3-4-5	Having students work in pairs to write summaries that use language from the text and create illustrations for the text
Text length	1-2-3-4-5	Using graphic organizers and note taking to break down the entire text into chunks that relate to one another Analyzing how the author connects ideas in long texts through use of headings, transitions, and references
Paragraph length	1-2-3-4-5	Close reading of each long paragraph: taking notes on its main idea, supporting ideas, and its purpose in the text. Having paired "long paragraph workouts" in which partners read long paragraphs silently and one partner orally summarizes it for the other partner without looking at it

Sentence length and structure	1-2-3-4-5	Having students discuss and explain the role of a long, crucial sentence in the text Modeling for students how to break down sentences into main and supporting information
Quantity of new, difficult, abstract words and terms	1-2-3-4-5	Identifying several of the most important new terms and having groups become experts on a term in their first read of a text Having students use two terms in one sentence (or all terms in one paragraph) that summarizes a key aspect of the text Modeling how to figure out words using word parts and similar words

For example, the following excerpt from *Roll of Thunder, Hear My Cry* (Taylor 1976), might receive high difficulty scores for background knowledge about racism in that setting, sophisticated use of dialog and metaphor, multiple themes, and text length. Thus, to address the factor of students' lack of knowledge of racism, the teacher might refer to other stories they have read and show images from that time period. To address the factor of the author's use of metaphor, the teacher might use a graphic organizer that shows how the fig tree and its elements relate to the events in the book and its themes.

> You see that fig tree over yonder, Cassie? Them other trees all around . . . that oak and walnut, they're a lot bigger and they take up more room and give so much shade they almost overshadow that little ole fig. But that fig tree's got roots that run deep, and it belongs in that yard as much as that oak and that walnut. It keeps on blooming, bearing good fruit year after year, knowing all the time it'll never get as big as them other trees. Just keeps on growing and doing what it gotta do. It don't give up. It give up, it'll die. There's a lesson to be learned from that little tree, Cassie girl, 'cause we're like it. We keep doing what we gotta, and we don't give up. We can't. (156)

At this point we would like to emphasize the importance of using whole novels—not the novel excerpts like those found in many thick language arts textbooks. While it is cheaper and less time-consuming to use small portions of novels for lessons and test preparation, we must teach students how to read entire novels. There are many language and thinking skills that are developed only by reading longer and more complex narratives (Dickinson and Neuman 2006). Reading novels trains the brain to visualize, develop, prune, and remember key ideas as the story progresses. Novels are whole. They allow for authentic and complete development of settings, characters, events, side plots, and literary devices.

Students must also learn to read increasingly complex informational texts. Take a moment to score the complexity factors in Figure 4.4 for the following excerpt from *If the World Were a Village: A Book About the World's People* (Smith 2002), an informational text used in a fifth-grade classroom. The lesson task is to generate and support an argument for why the author wrote the book and how reading the entire text will accomplish the purpose.

> *Earth is a crowded place and it is getting more crowded all the time. As of January 1, 2002, the world's population was 6 billion, 200 million—that's 6,200,000,000. Twenty-three countries have more than fifty million (50,000,000) people. Ten countries each have more than one hundred million (100,000,000) people. China has nearly one billion, three hundred million people (1,3000,000,000).*
>
> *Numbers like this are hard to understand, but what if we imagined the whole population of the world as a village of just 100 people? In this imaginary village, each person would represent about sixty-two million (62,000,000) people from the real world.*
>
> *One hundred people would fit nicely into a small village. By learning about the villagers—who they are and how they live—perhaps we can find out more about our neighbors in the real world and the problems our planet may face in the future.*
>
> *Ready to enter the global village? Go down into the valley and walk through the gates. Dawn is chasing away the night shadows. The smell of wood smoke hangs in the air. A baby awakes and cries. (7)*

Evaluating text complexity is a complex process. This informational text, for example, requires the reader to think mathematically about many numbers and ratios, abstractly view the huge world as a small village, and infer why the last part suddenly puts the reader into what seems like a story. And the task is more complex than just summarizing the content; it is to argue why the author wrote the text in the way that he did, and to figure out how this text might help readers "find out more about our neighbors" and solve the problems that we might face in the future. A teacher could come up with a wide range of activities for a text like this; we emphasize choosing the ones that best address the highest ranking complexity factors and those that will build students' language and thinking at the same time.

The rest of this chapter provides ideas for strengthening each of the three strands within this practice, starting with using complex texts to teach content understandings.

STRAND 1 OF USING COMPLEX TEXTS: Use Complex Texts to Teach Content (CON)

The Standards emphasize the need to help students build independence in their comprehension of complex texts in each discipline in order to learn content concepts. In many lessons, teachers have summarized texts or used simplified versions in order to save time and clarify the content that will show up on tests. Such practices can be even more prevalent in classrooms with high numbers of academic English learners. Yet the over-scaffolding and simplifying of texts, year after year, has enabled students to get by without the intense mental "practice and conditioning" needed to develop grade-level disciplinary language and comprehension skills. Therefore, one area in which we need to push ourselves is developing our abilities to design engaging literacy experiences that help students comprehend the content of complex texts.

❖ Close Reading for Content

Close reading is a broadly used term for describing reading activities that involve analyzing and rereading key parts of a complex text. Close reading usually consists of asking "text-dependent" questions, which means that their answers require the use of the text rather than just one's background knowledge. We provide several versions of close reading in this chapter.

This first version of close reading focuses on understanding key disciplinary concepts presented in a text. We can use Figure 4.5 to help build our habits of asking high-quality content-focused questions during close reading activities. Notice that the complexity of the questions increases the further down one goes on the chart. These content-focused questions can and should be used in combination with questions and activities in the other two strands.

FIGURE 4.5

Types and examples of close reading prompts

TYPES OF CLOSE READING (TEXT-DEPENDENT) QUESTIONS FOR UNDERSTANDING THE CONTENT IN COMPLEX TEXTS	SAMPLE QUESTIONS AND PROMPTS
Clarify key details and concepts that support the topic, plot, or theme.	What is the main problem in this story? How is the main character changing? Where and when is the story set, and why?
Prompt students to consider why the author chose to include certain parts of the text; determine their importance.	Why did the author choose to include the part about . . . ? How is or might this part be important?
Prompt students to infer unclear or uncertain parts of the text.	Even though the author doesn't state it directly, what can we infer about . . . ?
Examine arguments and evidence in the text.	In this persuasive article, what is the claim and how does the author support it? How does the author explain the value of the evidence?
Make connections within the text and to other texts.	How does the part where _____ connect to another part in the text? How does this text compare with other texts that we have read, such as . . . ?

It can be tempting to generate many "text-dependent" questions during a lesson, but not all of them are worth the time. Sets of questions should have focused purposes beyond just filling time, covering a list of facts, or checking for comprehension. Goals include helping to clarify and build essential ideas in preparation for a conversation, a written product, or a performance task. *Answering questions should not be used in place of using the information in meaningful and authentic ways.* Questions can play a role, but a hyper-focus on them can promote students' belief that school is about memorizing information and answering questions to score points or please a teacher who knows the answers.

CLASSROOM EXAMPLE

Here is an example from Ms. Ashton's second-grade classroom, reading a book on ladybugs:

Ms. A: What is this book about? How do you know?

Paul: About bugs. Ladybugs. Cuz of the pictures.

Ms. A: Is it a story or does it teach us information?

Ada: A story!

Ms. A: Why?

Ada: Cuz it has pictures and something happens.

Lisa: I think both cuz I learned about it laid eggs. But also there is a baby and I think it will grow.

Ms. A: Yes, the author is using a story to make it interesting, but also to teach us about life cycles of insects. Now, I wonder something. Why might the mother not stay around to care for her eggs and babies?

Manny: Some bugs don't need mothers. They born knowing what to do. They eat other bugs.

Ms. A: Hmmm. I wonder if this story will teach us this. I also wonder how this is like other stories or science texts.

Zach: Like that story 'bout salmon. The fish lay eggs and die. Babies swim down and then come back. The cycle.

Ms. A: Nice. So we learn about the ladybug but also more about life cycles. What is a good question I could ask right now?

Manny: What's a life cycle?

❖ Reading from Different Perspectives

This activity guides students through repeated readings of a complex text and helps them to discover alternative ways to interpret it. As students go beyond single interpretations and become aware of the multiple interpretations that exist, they develop critical reading skills and gain new insights into concepts. Reading from different perspectives also provides students with meaningful and interesting reasons to reread a selection, an important consideration in light of the Common Core emphasis on multiple interactions with text.

PROCEDURE

1. Select a story, article, or book in which you can identify different perspectives on important concepts and ideas. The sample chart in Figure 4.6 is based on an article about the reintroduction of wolves into the United States.

2. Select the specific perspectives you would like students to take when reading the text. For example, a novel could be read from the perspectives of different main characters. A political pamphlet could be read from different ideological positions such as Democratic, Republican, or Libertarian.

3. Have students do a first read of the text to get the gist of the material.

4. Then show students a list of the perspectives and model how a person from one of these perspectives would react to the materials the students have just read. For example, in the "Reintroduction of Wolves into the United States," you might model how a farmer, hunter, national park visitor, or environmentalist would react.

5. Divide the class into small groups and assign each group a perspective to take as they reread the selection. Students can also choose the perspective they want to use.

6. Provide each group with a perspective chart like the one in Figure 4.6 and direct students to define their perspective. In the example that follows, a farmer has a need to ensure the safety of his livestock and would be concerned about whether or not his sheep are safe from the wolves.

7. Two groups get together and share their perspectives.

8. Discuss with the entire class the insights they gained through their perspective reading and discussions, and then have students write a final summary position statement from that perspective.

CLASSROOM EXAMPLE

Students read an article on the reintroduction of wolves into the United States and take notes on the chart in Figure 4.6 from the perspective of a farmer, hunter, national park visitor, or environmentalist. At the end they write a summary paragraph.

FIGURE 4.6

Sample multiple perspectives chart and summary

Farmer Perspective			
Potential advantages	**Supporting text**	**Potential negatives and concerns**	**Supporting text**
Restore natural balance?	As wolves disappeared, the populations of their prey grew.	I think that they will attack my pets and livestock.	Stories abound of wolves attacking domesticated animals.

Sample Summary Statement

As a farmer, I am worried about the success of human coexistence with the increasing wolf population in the United States. Although most of these wolves are in national parks, there have been incidents of wolves crossing the boundary lines and posing a threat to livestock.

I am in favor of the rights of the wolves to live in the United States, but believe that as a person trying to earn a living, I have rights also. Does the environmentalist value the rights of the wolves over the rights of the farmer? I am a person, and a wolf is an animal. As the population of these animals increases, I will be working toward a balance of rights for wolves and farmers.

❖ Reading Multimodal Texts

As members of the digital age, our students spend a great deal of time sending, receiving, and comprehending visual and text messages as well as listening to music, playing games, and using the Internet. As teachers, we can leverage these different genres to help students build skills for forming clear academic meanings and messages. Multimodal activities can also deepen students' critical thinking abilities as they engage with the multiple sign systems used for constructing meaning (Jewitt 2008).

PROCEDURE

1. Ask students to look at topic-focused pictures and with a partner discuss the answers to these questions:

   a. What information are you able to infer from each picture?

   b. What specific items in the pictures led you to each inference?

   c. What do you think the people in the pictures have in common? Why?

   Distribute the written passage and have students read it silently.

2. Students work with a partner to identify and record three important things they have learned about that topic in the written text and prepare to explain why they chose each item.

3. Provide a copy of a topic-related song or poem and follow along as the song is played or the poem is read aloud. Students take notes in the margins on key ideas that come up, especially if they relate to the ideas from the written text.

4. Students synthesize the most important ideas from all three texts. They respond to prompts such as these:

   - How can we summarize what we discussed?

   - What conflicting ideas came up?

   - How can we bring these ideas together?

CLASSROOM EXAMPLE

During a Civil War unit of Ms. Pitta's eighth-grade history class, she wants to make her students aware of the role African-American soldiers played in support of the Union forces. In preparation for her lesson on Buffalo Soldiers, she identified three different types of texts: a series of pictures depicting soldiers of the era; a written passage providing background information about Buffalo Soldiers and the contributions they made to the war effort; and the lyrics from a Bob Marley song entitled "Buffalo Soldiers." Ms. Pitta engages students in a discussion about the pictures, and then she has them read the written text silently and identify key points in pairs. Finally, she provides students with a copy of the lyrics of the song and tells them to follow along while they listen to it. Before starting the music, Ms. Pitta tells students to record in the margins any questions they would like to discuss when the song ends. Students write synthesis paragraphs at the end.

❖ Coding the Text

As proficient readers, most of us have ways of marking or coding text that we want to remember. Some of you have already written notes in the margins of this book, while others of you have highlighted important passages or underlined unknown words or phrases. By responding to and marking portions of text, we stay focused on meaning and are better able to return to the text when we need to provide evidence to support an argument or information to answer a question.

Effective coding of text is, however, something many of our students must be taught to do. When done correctly, coding encourages students to slow down their reading and become actively engaged with the text while they monitor their comprehension and identify key concepts. Yet without a systematic coding process and an understanding of its benefits, coding can become a mindless activity that results in countless paragraphs covered in yellow highlighting or sticky notes and students with only a shallow understanding of the text.

In school, of course, our students are often prohibited from marking directly in a text. When this is the case, we can rely on other means of coding, such as writing on sticky notes, making notes on separate pieces of paper or into a smartphone or tablet, or completing a graphic organizer.

PROCEDURE

1. Establish a coding system for students to use when reading in your class. They can help you come up with ideas. Here are some examples.

A	Agree	!	Surprising or hard to believe
F	Figurative device	√	Confirms what you thought
?	Confused / question	X	Contradicts what you thought
D	Disagree	Hmmm	New or interesting
E4	Evidence for	CE	Cause/effect
MP	Main idea/Purpose	B	Bias
*	Important	WA	Weak argument
VIP	Very important	Q	Quotation to use or think about

2. Introduce the codes to your students before they read.

3. Model how you would like them to use the coding system by thinking aloud while you code a passage on the front screen.

4. Distribute a different short text and ask students to try out the coding system for themselves. Circulate to formatively assess their coding skills.

5. When they have finished, have students work in pairs to discuss those parts of the text they marked before you engage them in a whole-class discussion of the process.

6. Optionally, develop coding bookmarks that contain the codes. These bookmarks can be distributed to each student to use when they read and in the lower grades can even be laminated and taped to each student's desk for easy reference.

STRAND 2 OF USING COMPLEX TEXTS: Use Complex Texts to Teach Disciplinary Literacy Skills (LIT)

Students won't learn much content or language if they don't know how to use discipline-specific literacy skills to read the texts. Many students don't realize how much skill it takes to comprehend a complex text. Try as they might, they can't just say the words of a text and expect them to magically make sense. A reader must weave together background knowledge, language knowledge, comprehension strategies, and thinking skills—before, during, and after reading a text—to comprehend it. Figure 4.7 roughly shows how readers tend to construct meaning from a text.

FIGURE 4.7
Reading comprehension processes diagram

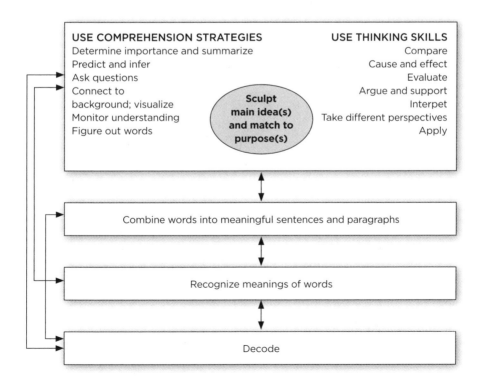

Proficient readers tend to start comprehending by beginning to sculpt the main idea and purpose of the text (Duke and Pearson 2002). Visuals and conversations can contribute to this initial sculpting. Then the reader decodes the letters on a page into sounds in order to recognize the meanings of the words. If the reader doesn't recognize a word, he or she tries to figure it out or skips it if it is not deemed to be important. Then the reader puts the words together into sentences and paragraphs for meaning. To decide if a sentence has enough meaning to move on, the reader monitors his or her overall understanding based on evolving cues in the text and how well the text is confirming expectations. The arrows in Figure 4.7 show this complex process of creating meaning.

The reader also puts the meanings of each sentence and each paragraph together by using comprehension strategies and thinking skills. Eight important comprehension strategies used for most texts are figuring out new words, predicting/inferring, questioning, connecting to background knowledge, visualizing, summarizing, sculpting the main idea, and monitoring understanding (Keene and Zimmerman 2007; Zwiers 2010). There are also many additional thinking skills that readers need to use, depending on the text. These include comparing, categorizing, identifying cause and effect, problem solving, persuading, empathizing, synthesizing, interpreting, evaluating, and applying. Authors expect readers to use these skills and use complex language in a variety of ways to describe them.

Following are several activities that teachers can use to develop students' comprehension abilities that they need to use to master Common Core State Standards.

❖ Wide-Angle Reading

The term *wide-angle reading* emphasizes the broader discourse and message-organization level of reading that sometimes gets skipped as students and teachers jump straight into the "close reading" of key parts of a text. For example, students might know what a word or sentence within a text means, but they might fail to see the overall meaning(s) of a text. They might be able to answer a "text-dependent" question, but not be able to relate the answer to the author's purpose. Students, especially academic English learners, need to have a set of "whole-text habits" that kick in as they begin to read any text. Proficient readers use these big-picture wide-angle reading habits without even knowing it. Look, for example, at the visual organizer in Figure 4.8. As you first began to read this book, your brain prompted itself to begin building meaning, adding on the many ideas that you encountered until now in the text.

The prompts in Figure 4.8 form a framework on which readers can attach the many details and ideas of the text as they read. Imagine being brought to a construction site, shown a pile of materials, and told to build a house. Without plans or a framework, the task is nearly impossible. And yet, without teaching and letting students "build real houses" of meaning from texts, they won't learn how to build up their knowledge and reading skills to use in lasting ways.

An important piece of this strategy is training students to recognize the purposes of texts. Texts have different purposes depending on the genre and discipline. For example, in math, two challenging types of text are explanations and word problems. The purpose of math explanations, which are often in textbooks, is to explain how to solve problems in that section of the book. The purpose of most word problems is to (1) teach students how to apply math skills and ideas to real-life situations, providing them with practice in "translating" verbal ideas into mathematical processes; and (2) build mathematical practices and thinking skills. The purpose of most science texts is to inform us about and clarify biological and physical phenomena. Students need to see and remember the many connections, causes and effects, and relationships in the text. The purpose of history textbooks is usually to explain what and how history happened. Yet the purpose of primary sources can vary: the author wrote it for one purpose yet the student, reading like a historian, might use it to support a position not emphasized in secondary sources. Finally, the purpose of literature is often to teach the reader lessons about life. The reader needs to read the story while interpreting character actions and words, events, and symbols. The better and more quickly a student can sculpt an accurate purpose for text, the better that student's comprehension will be.

Each step in the procedure begins with "Have students . . . ," yet in the initial presentations of the activity, large amounts of modeling are required. Finally, the procedure describes how to guide this activity for students, but eventually these prompts need to become internalized, automatic, and independent habits that students use for all texts in school and beyond.

FIGURE 4.8 Wide-angle reading framework

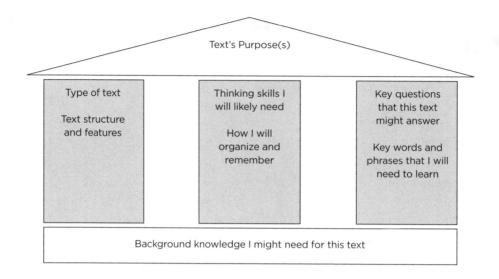

PROCEDURE

1. *Have students look at the title and all other visual clues such as pictures, charts, subheadings, and boxed texts.* Prompt them to think about a possible main purpose for reading the text. They can share with partners and start with expressions such as "To inform me of . . . ," "To persuade me to . . . ," and "To entertain me by . . ." Also, tell them to keep the title stored in their minds and to be on the lookout for references to it and reasons for which it was used for the text.

2. *Have students read the first paragraph.* After reading the first paragraph, have students write their ideas for the text's purpose in the top triangle of the visual in Figure 4.8. They can have more than one purpose and can write their "most likely" purpose in larger print. They should also write in pencil, because the purpose will probably change.

3. *Have students think about background knowledge they might need for the text.* In the bottom rectangle, students put the knowledge that students think they will need to use to understand this text.

4. *Have students identify the type of text, its features, and how it is structured.* Prompt students to look for clues about whether it is narrative, fiction, history, descriptive, persuasive, etc., or combinations (some textbooks use narrative anecdotes to support ideas). For the type of text, they might put informational history textbook, informational science article, narrative fiction, poetry, informational autobiography, persuasive article, etc. For text structure and features they might put subheadings, maps, time line, bold words, sequential, arguments supported by evidence, etc.

5. *Have students identify possible thinking skills* needed for the type of text identified in Step 2. What thinking will I likely need to use? For example, they might put cause/effect, persuasion, explanation, interpretation, and so on. Under the question that asks for the language that signals this thinking, they might put "as a result" signals cause/effect or "a major challenge" signals problem-solution thinking.

6. *Have students identify possible ways to organize and remember* the crucial information for this type of text. They might put techniques such as outline, semantic map, chart, diagram, sticky notes, and so on.

7. *Prompt students to ask questions* using the title that they think the text will answer. They can skim the text, subheadings, and visuals to form the questions and predictions about the text. The questions should relate to the purpose, key information, and thinking skills already on the framework.

8. *Prompt students to identify key words and phrases* that they think they will need to learn in order to understand the text and in order to describe their understanding of the text. They might put terms such as *content vocabulary* or general terms such as *analogous, compensate, paradigm, ephemeral,* and *myopic,* to name a few.

CLASSROOM EXAMPLE

In Ms. Radovic's fifth-grade ELA class, she asks wide-angle reading questions as students walk through the text. She starts with "How is this story organized?"

After some think time, Miguel says, "It's about people telling stories on a porch."

Ms. R. then asks, "What might I ask next in response to Miguel?"

Kara answers, "Why do you think the author wrote a story about people telling different stories?"

"That will work," responds Ms. R. "Now why don't you share your ideas in pairs."

After conversing a few minutes, Abby raises her hand to say, "For thinking skills, we say compare and contrast, because there are three separate stories and we need to put them together, like to see how they connect and what they teach us."

"We think it is about how memories are important," says David. Several other students write his idea down.

"OK. You are starting to build a nice framework. It needs to be flexible and you will have to erase at times, but keep thinking as you read so you can add to and edit what you have."

❖ Interactive Annotations

Annotations can take a wide range of forms, many of which focus on content. This activity's annotations, however, should focus on building disciplinary literacy habits. Such annotations help students build skills for reading in ways similar to those used by authors, historians, economists, mathematicians, and scientists as they read texts in their fields (Richardson 2010).

Students take notes on how the author constructed the text and what the author does with certain parts to achieve clear communication. The important part of this activity is to build students' habits of (1) seeing what the author does and (2) inferring why the author uses the strategy or technique. This builds meta-literacy and the critical thinking skills needed for both understanding and producing complex texts. Ideas for literature and nonfiction texts are included here.

- *Literature:* Students have a 3 x 5 theme card on which they put ideas for themes. They can take notes on different-colored sticky notes. For example, they can write down evidence that supports the theme on yellow, character thoughts and emotions on blue, character actions or words on pink, symbols and metaphors that relate to the theme on green, questions on white, and predictions and inferences on purple.

- *Nonfiction:* Students annotate their thinking that results from prereading and reading the text. If it is persuasive, they might put the central point of view on a pink note, supporting evidence on green notes, counterarguments on yellow, etc. If reading an expository text such as a science chapter, students might note the main cause-and-effect relationships on blue notes, analogies used by the author to remember concepts on pink notes, and questions that were answered on green notes. Students can later organize these notes in ways to help them remember the content and language strategies in the text.

CLASSROOM EXAMPLE

A seventh-grade teacher, Mr. Guerrero, has students analyze a website on the environmental issue of deforestation. The site is subtly persuasive and the teacher works with students to annotate, on a chart, how images of large deforested areas are used, how certain words and phrases are used to weaken the opposing point of view, and how evidence and data about the future of the atmosphere is used. Students then use their notes to compare and fortify their ideas in small groups.

❖ Close Reading for Disciplinary Literacy

Close reading can also be used to build important disciplinary literacy skills. These skills include asking expert-like questions while reading, making inferences and predictions, hypothesizing, problem solving, and connecting to previous knowledge about the discipline. Other skills are found in Figure 4.9. You can prompt students to answer questions and generate their own prompts based on these and other thinking skills.

FIGURE 4.9

Sample close reading prompts for disciplinary literacy skills

DISCIPLINE	LITERACY SKILL	POSSIBLE CLOSE READING PROMPTS
HISTORY	Ask questions	What questions might a historian ask when he or she reads this sentence?
	Make inferences and predictions	Based on this sentence, what do you think the author was thinking and feeling during the outbreak of the war?
	Connect to previous knowledge	How does this letter corroborate or contradict what we learned in the textbook chapter?
SCIENCE	Ask questions	What questions might a biologist ask upon observing the behavior described by the author?
	Make inferences and predictions	Based on what you read, make a prediction about how this species might adapt over time.
	Connect to previous knowledge	Which laws of physics does this event seem to break?
MATH	Ask questions	What questions should we ask as we read a long word problem like this one?
	Make inferences and predictions	Estimate what the answer will be and justify it for a partner.
	Connect to previous knowledge	How is this problem like similar ones you have seen this year or previous years in class or in life?
LANGUAGE ARTS	Ask questions	What questions do you have about the author's reasons for including parts of this story?
	Make inferences and predictions	What do you think the themes of this novel might be? What will happen in the story that will teach us about life?
	Connect to previous knowledge	How is this article similar to texts you have already read? What do you need to already know to understand this article?

CLASSROOM EXAMPLE

In Mr. Wilson's third-grade classroom, students read a textbook section on magnets. Mr. W. asks them to generate questions as they read. He says that two questions have to begin with *How* and *Why*. Then he has students relate what they read to the activity that they did with magnets before they read the chapter. He then lifts up two magnets and asks, "As you read the text, what scientist questions did you come up with?"

"Why the two same sides not stick together?" asks Sofia.

"That's a helpful *why* question. Did anyone else have one like it? What does the text say?" asks Mr. W.

"It says that 'two poles with the same charge will repel one another.' They won't stick."

"I know that, but why?" Sofia asks again.

"Let's take a closer look at the text and see what it says," responds Mr. W.

❖ Multiple Reads

Multiple reads, just as it sounds, emphasizes rereading of a complex text. With each reading of a text, students have a different focus or filter. They remember and use information from previous readings. This approximates what many good readers do when they read a challenging text or part of text. The first read, for example, might be for the overall topic or stance of an author. The other reads dig into the details and extended thinking processes sparked by the text. And, even though this activity is under Strand 2, you will also find uses for it to support content and language development (Strands 1 and 3).

Here are some examples from teachers across disciplines.

- First-grade social studies (nonfiction text on transportation)
  - First read: Read text and pictures for the main topic and author's purpose
  - Second read: Read for important facts and ideas to remember

- Fourth-grade science (textbook chapter on energy transfer)
  - First read: Read for main topic and author's purpose
  - Second read: Read to make up questions about headings and key terms
  - Third read: Read for cause-and-effect relationships

- Sixth-grade math (unit rate word problem)
  - First read: Read for what's happening in the problem and what's asked for
  - Second read: Read for type of word problem and to estimate the answer(s)
  - Third read: Read for key words, phrases, and numbers to set up solution process (e.g., a drawing, chart, or equation that shows relationships between the givens and unknowns)

- Eighth-grade language arts (short story)
  - First read: Read for setting, plot, and character development and changes
  - Second read: Read for themes and symbols

- Tenth-grade history (historical argument article)
  - First read: Read for the topic and author's position
  - Second read: Read for opposing position(s)
  - Third read: Read for own position on the topic

There are many other focuses and filters that students can use during their different readings. Students can read for highlighted thinking skills in the Common Core standards such as comparing, evaluating, synthesizing, interpreting, and analyzing. They can also read for certain types of language and organization strategies used by the author. They can first read independently with no focus; for the second read you can model a reading skill, and then students can read the text a third time, practicing the skill or strategy. You can also have students use visual organizers during any of the reads, as described in the classroom example that follows.

CLASSROOM EXAMPLE

In Ms. Ellis's ninth-grade history class, students are learning about the inspirations and influences of utopian and hero literature in history. The current article is about Shangri-La, the mythical valley in the novel *Lost Horizon* (Hilton 1933). Students use their first read to sculpt an idea for the article's purpose and main idea on a pink square sticky note as well as key supporting ideas on smaller yellow sticky notes. They then place the pink note in the center of the comprehension target visual, shown in Figure 4.10 (Zwiers 2010). During their second read, they revise the pink purpose and main idea note as needed, and evaluate the importance of the yellow support notes, placing them around the pink note. The more helpful or relevant the idea is for clarifying and supporting the main idea or purpose of the text, the closer it is to the center.

FIGURE 4.10
Reading comprehension target

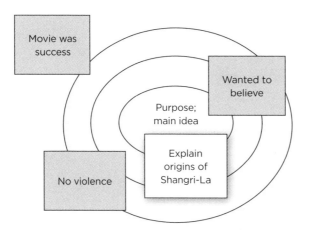

STRAND 3 OF USING COMPLEX TEXTS: Use Complex Texts to Build the Language of Disciplinary Thinking (BLT)

Given this book's focus on teaching complex language and literacy, the emphasis in this chapter leans toward this strand of using complex texts to build the language of the discipline. The activities highlight *using* the text as a resource to build students' complex language of the discipline's concepts and thinking skills. We liken it to training art apprentices. To train art apprentices, we would use a variety of paintings as examples of how master artists use color and media to create messages. But we want our apprentices to do more than understand what the paintings mean or just copy them—we want students to acquire and use the ideas, shapes, and colors to create their own messages and masterpieces.

Each text that we teach can be a rich resource for developing students' discipline-specific language and literacy. The Standards emphasize the value of building students' independence in understanding and creating texts using complex language. Thus, schooling must offer wide ranges of experiences with text language so that students can fluently use the language beyond the text of today for the many texts that they will read and produce in the future. In other words, students must embrace and own the language landscape, not just view it.

Comprehension and language development are symbiotic. The more complex content students comprehend, the more language they acquire; and the more language they acquire, the more they comprehend. And the language that develops from wrestling with complex texts will better equip students to independently read similar texts in the future.

Following are several activities that help to build students' complex language through text.

❖ Close Reading of Key Paragraphs, Sentences, and Words

Close reading can be used to highlight important disciplinary language. One version of close reading that is encouraged by authors of the Common Core State Standards focuses on analyzing a key ("juicy") sentence in a text (Wong Fillmore 2012). This type of analysis helps students to think not only about sentences, but also about how paragraphs and words convey meaning.

PROCEDURE

1. Choose a sentence or paragraph that is both important for the meaning of the text and is valuable for teaching students how authors tend to use language to communicate how experts think in the discipline.

2. Create questions that highlight how the author uses language in the sentence to connect to previous or future ideas in the text; and/or . . .

3.   Create prompts that have students identify the thinking that the author expects readers to do for the sentence. For example, if the sentence contains phrases such as *led to, consequently,* or *ramifications,* students would have to recognize that they are supposed to use cause-and-effect thinking.

4.   Now tell students it is their job to find a different key sentence for the text. They work individually. They need to be able to argue for the sentence they chose, and identify the thinking that a reader needs to do for it.

5.   Students do Step 4 for a key paragraph. Students should be able to explain its importance and how its sentences connect within the paragraph.

6.   Students also identify two of the most key words for the text.

7.   In pairs, students negotiate and agree on a paragraph, sentence, and two words to share with the entire class, explaining why they are key to understanding the text.

8.   Record what students share and try to come to an agreement as a whole class. You can even have them rank the importance of paragraphs, sentences, and words.

CLASSROOM EXAMPLE

Back in Ms. Radovic's fifth-grade classroom, she engages students in a close rereading of the story *From Miss Ida's Porch* (Belton 1998). Ms. R. focuses on two key sentences on page 28: "So you see, on that Easter Sunday I saw history being made there at the Lincoln Memorial. I also saw my papa cry with pride and sadness at the same time."

Ms. R. asks, "How was history being made that day? Tell two different people; I will say when to switch partners. Use some of the language from the book in your ideas."

Students share out. One says, "I think the author wanted to make us think about history and the emotions. And that sometimes two, like, strong emotions can be in you at one time. Like crying with pride. He was proud that they had freedom and could sing, but, however, he was sad cuz Marian and others were not treated as equal."

CLASSROOM EXAMPLE

In Mr. Sawyer's tenth-grade history class, he uses a chart to help set up a discussion of a key sentence: "Americans hoped that the French Revolution would transform France into an ally against Britain; on the other hand, the revolution also fostered radical and violent ideas leading to social and political instability that Americans wanted to avoid." He analyzes the sentence and comes up with several prompts in the right-hand column that students discuss.

PART OF SENTENCE	TEACHABLE LANGUAGE OFTEN USED IN HISTORY TEXTS	PROMPT IDEAS
Americans hoped that the French Revolution would transform France into an ally against Britain;	Past subjunctive: "hoped that . . . would . . . Vocabulary: ally	Why did the author use *would transform* and not just *transformed*?
on the other hand, the revolution also fostered radical and violent ideas	Transition that changes direction of sentence.	What two ideas are being opposed? What are on "each hand"?
leading to social and political instability that Americans wanted to avoid.	Cause-and-effect adjective phrase	What was leading to instability?

❖ Borrow and Build

This activity helps students to acquire and practice the language of disciplinary thinking as they read. It is a structured way to do what good readers do naturally: acquire
language and use it for new purposes. To prepare, choose three texts (A, B, and C) that
require a similar thinking skill (e.g., cause–effect, empathize, synthesize, persuade, evaluate, interpret, infer, compare). The three texts could be three parts of the same text, like
three sections of a textbook chapter or three parts of an article. Students will have to
look for sentences in the text that describe a focal disciplinary thinking skill or language
function, and then use the language to describe the thinking or function in another part
of the text. In the examples that follow, the teacher has students look for language used
to describe cause-and-effect in a history textbook.

PROCEDURE

1. With Text A, model for students how to look for sentences and discourse features
    that describe the thinking skill of identifying and explaining causes and effects.
    Extract entire sentences to preserve the syntax. Underline any terms that are
    especially helpful for the thinking skill (e.g., *as a result of, in order to*).

2. Read Text B aloud and then model how you borrow language from Text A (e.g.,
    led to) in order to describe the thinking in Text B. Students can also contribute to
    this modeling.

3. Have student pairs do Step 1 using Text B. They can find different language for
    the same skill, or they can do Step 1 for a different skill. Student pairs should
    work together, stop periodically, and think as they read. They can gather sentences
    and underline extra-helpful language.

4. Students then do Step 2. They read Text C and use the language they borrowed from Text B to describe key ideas in Text C.

5. Optionally, they can create a chart in their notebooks in which they put thinking skill names in one column and terms they find in texts in a second column. This fosters their metalinguistic awareness. You can give them a fourth text, Text D, and use language from Text C (along with A and B), and so on. In this way, they keep borrowing and building ideas and language.

CLASSROOM EXAMPLE

In Mr. Correa's seventh-grade history class, he starts off the modeling with the first of three parts of a textbook chapter on cultural encounters: "Here is a sentence that uses the term *led to* to describe causes and effects. 'The increasing contact between cultures around the world during this era led to various conflicts.' Now I will read the second part and borrow that language from the first part to describe it." After reading, he says, "The voyages of Columbus led to the deaths of many Native Americans. Any others?"

Leonel says, "The need for cheap labor in the Americas led to the rise of slavery and the Atlantic slave trade." Then students reread the second part for language they will use to describe the third part, with less support from the teacher.

To describe the third part, Maritza says, "The atrocious treatment of the enslaved people resulted in many deaths in their journey across the ocean." Students are asked to write down their sentences as exit tickets.

❖ Read-Aloud Protocol for Building Complex Language

Reading texts aloud can and should be powerful experiences for developing students' complex language (Fox 2013). A read-aloud can be used to prompt disciplinary thinking, which is a powerful way to help students practice the language of that thinking. Here we offer some tips for using read-alouds to build language. Notice the large amount of preparation needed before the actual reading aloud in Step 4.

PROCEDURE

1. Identify and clarify the "teaching focus" (e.g., analyze how the message is organized).

    • Knowing your students' language needs, focus on what they should learn from a text. Consider standards, assessments, the text, and previous work. Choose a text that helps you to model the teaching focus (if you didn't start with a text already in mind).

2.   Prepare the text (on sticky notes or in margins).

   - Preview the text and write down examples of model thoughts that support the teaching focus.

   - Create prompts for wide-angle and close reading (analyzing the title, headings, visuals, and text features for discourse, syntax, and vocabulary dimensions).

   - Indicate prompts for whole-class discussions, quick-writes, and think–pair–shares. These must be based on the teaching focus because they are time-consuming. Provide optional sentence frames to get students starting their utterances with academic language.

   - Analyze the text for complex language that you will highlight.

3.   Connect to and build background knowledge, skills, and language.

   - Communicate the teaching focus to students. Create a visual that shows the teaching focus; discuss ways in which students already use the strategy, skill, or language in their daily lives.

   - Use an example of the teaching focus from recent texts or units in class, and/or examples from the real world. Prompt students to make connections.

   - Fill in any background knowledge (content and/or language) that students will need to build meaning within the text.

4.   Read aloud.

   - Preview the text (show title, pictures, headings, etc.) aloud with students and ask them to predict what they think it will be about and why.

   - Read the text aloud, with expression and clear enunciation, stopping to think aloud thoughts that are based on the teaching focus. Refer to the teaching focus visual. Do not stop too often.

   - Stop at sticky notes to prompt students to think and respond as a whole class, on quick-writes, or in think–pair–shares.

   - Check for students' comprehension of message-level features and syntax.

5.   Practice.

   - Create a short task that allows each student to practice the teaching focus on their own. They might take notes or fill in a graphic organizer.

6.   Conclude.

- Finish with a final review of the teaching focus, its usefulness, and a synthesis look at the teaching focus visual.

❖ Evaluate the Evidence

One of the challenges that many teachers face is building students' skills of finding and evaluating evidence that supports an idea (Belland, Glazewski, and Richardson 2008). First of all, many students don't initially understand the fanatic push for using evidence. Second, they often treat any piece of evidence as the best or only evidence needed. They haven't yet been apprenticed into how the discipline decides what is "strong" or logical evidence for a given idea. Third, many academic English learners don't thoroughly understand the terms we teachers often use for supporting ideas: *evidence, weak, strong, position, example, support, outweigh, claim, warrant*, etc.

An English teacher, for example, might use a persuasive article on an environmental issue to teach how to evaluate evidence and explanations (warrants) for claims. Terms for using evidence will not be directly in the article, so the teacher uses the article to show examples of these terms. The teacher even points out that the author often does not necessarily want readers to engage in large amounts of critical thinking; the author simply wants to persuade readers to take the side promoted in the text. The text becomes an effective artifact for fostering student learning of how to think critically about the value of the evidence given. It offers a chance to think about the many abstract "apples and oranges" that we must weigh against one another in the myriad of complex issues that arise in real life.

PROCEDURE

1. Choose a model text that contains positions, and evidence to support the positions.

2. Have students help you discuss how to think about and assign weights or values to evidence presented in the text. You can use the AAA Test to score the different pieces of evidence:

    - Is the evidence APPLICABLE? Is it relevant to the idea that it is supporting? Use a scale of 1 to 5.

    - Is the evidence ACCURATE? How reliable is the source? Does it conflict with other information? Use a scale of 1 to 5.

    - Is the evidence ADEQUATE? Is the evidence solid, weighty, and valid enough to be used in the argument? Use a scale of 1 to 5. Students should take notes on the answers to these questions, because they can be used to explain their reasoning in output and interaction activities.

3. Put the values on a visual organizer such as the Strength of Evidence Bar Graph in Figure 4.11. The graph is a visual way to show (and discuss) how well a piece of evidence supports a point. It also challenges students to explain the values that they assign.

4. The position or idea being supported by evidence goes in the top box.

5. Students then generate two to four types of evidence that make up the core idea being evaluated. For example, the push to pass a law that raises taxes on gasoline might have evidence such as the results of previous tax hikes or current statistics on air pollution.

6. Put students in pairs or groups with the same issue and have them negotiate which evidence to use and their values. Some students will have different evidence and values, which provides great fodder for discussion. They can ask each other, Why did you choose that type of evidence? Don't you think this evidence is more important?

7. Individually, students think about the parts of the idea that relate to each piece of evidence. They can list these in the lower explanation columns, and even include quotations, if desired. They must write notes that are clear enough to give good reason for the bar graph they will fill in above. They will need to explain their evidence to classmates and to you.

8. Students decide how well the evidence supports the idea in the top box, and then they create a shaded bar (can be colored) up to the roughly calculated level (Not at All, Somewhat, Well, Very Well, Completely).

9. Students can meet with one or two others who have the same issue and share their different levels. For example, a student might begin with, "I thought when the main character said that she would 'never forget the lesson she learned from the storm,' it was strong evidence of her desire for revenge."

10. Students can share their results with the class up on a screen. They can use language such as "We found that ___ was strong evidence because it _____" or "On the other hand, one person argued that . . . "

FIGURE 4.11
Strength of Evidence Bar Graph

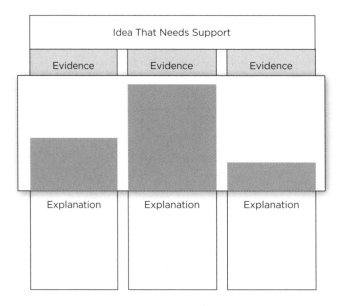

Strengthening Common Activities for Using Complex Texts

The purpose of this final section is to build our teacher habits for strengthening the teaching activities that we already use related to complex texts. Figure 4.12 outlines only a few of the common activities used to develop students' language from texts and comprehension. The purpose of the chart is to get us started in critiquing and strengthening all instructional practices and activities that we see in professional development sessions, resources, and our own lessons.

FIGURE 4.12

Common text-based activities, limitations, and ways to modify them for complex language growth

COMMON PRACTICE OR ACTIVITY	COMMON LIMITATIONS	HOW TO STRENGTHEN THE ACTIVITY TO IMPROVE ITS USEFULNESS FOR BUILDING COMPLEX LANGUAGE
Jigsaw groups (a.k.a., expert groups)	• Students often copy their answers from the book and from team members; they read their answers. • They are focused on filling in the blanks. • It is hard to promote use of target language.	• Make sure that they don't copy or read their answers; they should use their own words with complete and linked sentences. • Have students practice using the language with their expert group before moving to home groups. • Have expert-and home-group members encourage and check for the use of connected sentences and clarity in their responses. • Have home-group pairs practice articulating the information that they heard from members.
Whole-class text-based discussions	• Only a few students get a chance to talk. • It is often overguided by the teacher. • Students often don't know the purpose or direction of discussion.	• Use engaging prompts that require students to refer to the text. • Have student pairs discuss before and after answering in the whole group; have them use language from the text. • Have triads synthesize at certain points. • Have students guide the discussion (e.g., "How might you respond to Kevin's comment?").
Graphic organizers for reading	• Students often focus on filling in the spaces of graphic organizers at the expense of thinking, communicating, and negotiating ideas.	• Have students talk about the ideas before, during, and after they fill in graphic organizers. • Make sure they know why they are using a particular graphic organizer; i.e., what function it serves. For example, they should be able to explain how a Venn diagram shows comparison and how it helps them to think in the discipline.
Role-based and strategy-based reading groups	• Groups of four can be dominated by one or two students. • Focuses mainly on summarizing, predicting, questioning, and clarifying. • Roles can allow students to not practice all skills.	• Coach students to make sure that all students in a group participate equally and that ideas are valued. • Coach students to use additional thinking skills as they read in groups, such as evaluating, taking different perspectives, comparing, interpreting themes, etc. • Clarify that all group members must engage in all the thinking and talking skills of the group. Some teachers use "talking chips" or cards for this.

Summary

This chapter started by emphasizing that academic English learners cannot afford to be sheltered from complex texts. Complex texts are one of the best ways to build students' disciplinary language, thinking, and literacy. But it takes loads of work to support the learning of content and language from grade-level texts. We must strengthen our understanding of the factors that make disciplinary texts complex for our current students. With a clearer idea of these factors for a given text and context, we can design lessons that are fortified by three key strands that make up the high-impact practice of using complex texts: use complex texts to teach content; use complex texts to build disciplinary literacy skills; and use complex texts to build the complex language of disciplinary thinking.

Many classroom examples of specific activities were given, but much more detailed lessons that show ways to use complex text are described in the next chapter.

CHAPTER 5

Lessons Focused on Using Complex Texts

A lot happens in a lesson.

This is the first of three chapters that include annotated lessons showing how to weave complex language and literacy development practices into daily teaching. This chapter describes four lessons from different grade levels and disciplines. Each lesson emphasizes using complex texts to build language and literacy across a variety of settings. All four classrooms have a wide range of AELs from different socioeconomic and language backgrounds. Keep in mind that these lessons are model lessons, not perfect lessons. Even these lessons can be improved. Moreover, many details and dialogs could not fit into the pages of these chapters. As all teachers know, too much goes on in one lesson to capture it all.

Each lesson is the first of three sequential lessons. Chapter 7 describes the next lesson in the sequence for each grade level, with a focus on fortifying complex output. Chapter 9 describes the third sequential lesson for each grade level, with a focus on fostering academic interactions. Please note that, while we have included lessons that emphasize certain high-impact practices in this order (text, output, interaction), the "order" will vary across settings and preferences. For example, you might have lessons that start with an emphasis on interaction or end with an emphasis on output. Most lessons, of course, have all three practices woven into them in varying degrees. Lastly, feel free to refer to the strategic lesson planning section at the end of Chapter 2 to see the "toolbox" that was used to create these lessons.

How to Read Chapters 5, 7, and 9

The lessons in Chapters 5, 7, and 9 use several features to help you understand how to strengthen the teaching of complex language and literacy.

- *Annotations in the margins:* The annotations describe why and how certain lesson activities are used to support AELs at different stages of each lesson. These annotations include references to the AEL paradigm shifts in Chapter 1, as well as to the activities and practices in previous chapters. Some annotations highlight additional standards being reinforced in the lesson.

- *Transcription excerpts:* Often the only way to see what is happening in a classroom is to analyze the actual discourse. Each lesson provides snippets of whole-class, small-group, and paired talk. These samples show both exemplary and "typical" conversations in order to provide reflection opportunities.

- *Standards and objectives:* At the beginning of each lesson there is a description of the standards and objectives being taught. Many standards are often taught and learned (and these might be different) in one lesson. This is messy work, with substantial overlap and reinforcement between different standards. We include additional standards that tend to support the main objective of a lesson. A WIDA English Language Development standard, for example, might overlap with and/or support a Common Core Anchor Literacy standard, which may even support a key NGSS eighth-grade science standard. There are also many "disciplinary practice" standards in each content area, which are the everyday skills that should be used in tasks and in the real world. This section of each lesson is simply meant to (1) better familiarize you with additional standards and (2) show ways to integrate them into effective lessons that emphasize language and literacy development.

- *Codes for practices:* In the interest of space and clarity, we did not put the many codes for the practice strands of Chapters 2, 3, 4, 6, and 8 into the annotations. However, we include them here because coding can be a helpful way for you to analyze the strands of these and other lessons in future chapters. So, if inclined, grab a pencil and jot down the codes from Figure 5.1 where you see practices in these lessons—or your own.

FIGURE 5.1

Strand codes for language and literacy development practices

OBJ: Identify language demands to create language objectives	FBK: Provide timely and useful feedback
AUT: Design authentic language activities	CON: Use complex texts to teach content
BLD: Build on students' backgrounds	LIT: Use complex texts to develop literacy skills
CLR: Use clarification methods	BLT: Use complex texts to build language and thinking
DIF: Differentiate to clarify	ORL: Develop complex language for and by oral output
CHK: Check for comprehension	WRT: Develop complex language for and by writing
MLZ: Model in the learning zone	MMM: Develop complex language for and by producing multimedia messages
FOC: Use focused and thorough modeling	COM: Use interactions to teach academic communication skills
DEC: Deconstruct language and have meta-language discussions	TNK: Use interactions to build disciplinary thinking skills
PRO: Prompt for and provide language	UND: Use interactions to develop content understandings
FAS: Formatively assess complex language learning	

Second-Grade Math: Lesson 1

OBJECTIVES

Ms. Stevens is teaching students how to understand word problems and use multiple representations to solve them. The focal CCSS math standard is "Use addition and subtraction within 100 to solve one- and two-step word problems involving situations of adding to, taking from, putting together, taking apart, and comparing, with unknowns in all positions, e.g., by using drawings and equations with a symbol for the unknown number to represent the problem" (CCSS.2.OA.A.1). Today's content objective is to solve one-step problems with unknowns in the middle position, and describe reasons for the methods used. Ms. S. also highlights two mathematical practice objectives of the day: Reason abstractly and quantitatively (CCSS.Math.Practice.MP2) and Model with mathematics (CCSS.Math.Practice.MP4).

Because her class has a wide range of English learners, Ms. S. uses the 2012 WIDA ELD Standards (Grade 2, Standard 3, p. 60): "Students at all levels of English language proficiency will ANALYZE text of word problems." Ms. S. uses the five different levels to help her differentiate the challenges that she gives to students as they read problems. The five levels of performance indicators include functions of matching, finding, sequencing, locating clues, and categorizing. These functions are woven into the lesson's prompts and tasks.

Ms. S. plans to use the texts as examples of how authors use language to present math scenarios. The main language objective is for students to be able to use the parts and language of word problems as examples for their explanations of how to understand and solve word problems.

INTRODUCTION

The day before, Ms. S. had noticed that students were just looking at the numbers in word problems and adding them or subtracting them without thinking about what was happening in the problem. So instead of launching directly into a problem, Ms. S. decides to build habits of looking at the "bigger picture" of each problem before the students begin to solve it. She uses a variation of wide-angle reading (Chapter 4).

Ms. S.: Remember the word problem yesterday about the spider's eggs.[1] Let's look at it. What are you usually asked to do in a word problem?

> [1] Ms. S. connects to an example from yesterday.

Miguel: Find the answer.

Ms. S.: What usually happens in a math word problem?[2] What do they tell us? Share with a partner. *(Waits and calls on Lara.)*

> [2] Ms. S. prompts students to think about message-level features of the texts (word problems).

Lara: What is happening? Numbers of things. How things go up or down.

Ms. S.: Yes, the author of the problem usually tells us enough information to solve it, so we can use it to figure out how to solve it. The author gives the beginning, which are the numbers in the beginning, then the middle, which is how the numbers might change. And then we must figure out the answer. That is how we read a math problem. And there is lots of language we use to figure out how the numbers change. For addition, what might we see?

Sam: More, *más*, plus, add.

Ms. S.: For subtraction?

Ana: Take away, less, minus, disappear, sell.

Ms. S.:   Yes, we have to be looking for words that tell us how things change.[3] And often the obvious words aren't there. They don't tell us to subtract or add. We must picture what is happening in our minds and put it into our own words to understand it.

[3] Ms. S. highlights how language is used in math problems. This helps students locate clues in the problem (WIDA Level 4).

LAUNCH

In this stage of the lesson, the teacher provides an initial "launch problem" to begin the new learning for the day. Ms. S. uses the launch problem to teach the math skills and the complex language of solving and explaining word problems.

Ms. S.:   Here is the problem. Ana found 17 coins as she was walking to school. Unfortunately, she had a hole in her pocket. When she got home she counted her coins. She had only 9 left! How many coins did she lose that day? *(She hands out cardboard coins.)* Picture what happened. Tell your partner what happened. Tell your partner the beginning of the problem and what changed.[4]

[4] Ms. S. has all students produce oral output to make sense of the problem. They can use real objects to help them (WIDA Levels 1–5).

Vera: *(To partner)* She start with 17. Hole in pocket means she lost coins; and 9 coins is not big as 17.

Alex: Then we gotta subtract.

Ms. S.:   Can you explain why you need to subtract? Say, "We need to subtract because . . ."[5]

[5] Ms. S. asks for math reasoning and prompts and provides a sentence stem to scaffold a response. This prompting also relates to the language objective.

Alex: We need to subtract because it need to be . . . *menos que* 17. It's 9 at the end.

(Back in the whole-class discussion format)

Ms. S.:   So what do we do? And why? Take a moment to think. Start with "In order to . . ."

Pedro: In order to find the answer, I tore up paper into coins and figured it out by counting and taking away till I got 9.

Nora: I used a number line and counted down from 17.

Ms. S.:   Great! You have shown different ways to *represent* the problem. Now, how can we write this mathematically and solve it? Tell your partner. Use the language of the problem like *lose, lost, left* to explain why you are doing what you are doing.[6]

[6] Ms. S. prompts students to use CCSS mathematical practices: making sense of problems, using abstract reasoning, and modeling.

EXPLORATION

In this stage the students work together to solve the problem and justify their methods and solutions. They practice their math language in order to come up with ideas in preparation for discussion.

Kayla: *(To partner)* We can start with 17. She only had 9 left,[7] so she lost coins, so we gotta minus. We don't know how many to minus yet, so a box here. Then equals, then 9 cuz that was the final number of coins. (17 – □ = 9) What do you think?

[7] Kayla "translates" nonmathematical language (left) into math terms (minus), which sets up Rafael's question of how to solve for the unknown.

Rafael: I think is OK. But how we find the box number?

Kayla: We can add it to the 9, maybe?

Rafeal: But how can we add it? We don't know it. Not a number. Nine plus box?

DISCUSSION

In this stage, the teacher brings students back as a whole class and asks students to share. This starts a discussion on possible methods and why to use them. She asks Elia to share, and Elia describes her method.

Ms. S.: OK, usually the answer box, which we call the unknown, is at the end and we know what to do. Now, how might we solve this one with the unknown answer box on the left side of the equals sign? Try it on your own. *(Ms. S. waits.)* Any thoughts?

Elia: Make 17 circles for coins and cross them out one by one till you get 9. Count the crossed ones. That is what goes in the box.

Ms. S.: Hmmm. Let's try Elia's idea.[8] Here are 17 coins. Crossing the first one gets me 16, 15, 14 . . . How many are crossed out? Eight! So 8 goes in the box for our unknown number. After I model, you will tell your partner what happened in the problem and use the answer, 8, in your explanation. I will model how we can think about this.[9] In the problem Ana started

[8] This was not the method Ms. S. wanted, but she adapted and connected the visual representation to the math expression.

[9] Ms. S. models math thinking and reasoning language; this supports the language objective.

with 17 coins and lost some. *Lose* means subtraction and the box represents the unknown answer we are looking for. She ended up with 9 so I put the equal sign, then 9. We found the answer by taking away little drawings, but I want to know another way,[10] especially if the numbers are higher. What if Ana had 200 coins? Would you want to draw them all? What is a more mathematical way to solve it, without drawing?

[10] Ms. S. reinforces the idea of considering additional methods for solving the problem.

Ruth: Well, if you take away the 9 from 17, you get 8.

Ms. S.: Great observation! But we should see if that method works for other numbers. Let's see. Let's try smaller numbers to make it easy to test out Ruth's idea. Five minus box equals 2. Try it.[11] The answer is . . . 3. And 5 minus 2 equals . . . 3. It works! Now you and your partner choose two other numbers and see if it works. (*Ms. S. waits.*) Does it work?

[11] Ms. S. builds an aspect of MP1: trying simpler forms to confirm a possible strategy.

Pablo: Yeah. We did 8 minus box equals 5. We did 8 minus 5 and got 3.

Ms. S.: But does it work for big numbers? How about 90 minus our unknown box equals 20. So, 90 minus 20 equals 70. Does 90 minus 70 in the box equal 20? . . . Yes! What did we just do?

Laura: We tried out other numbers.

[12] Ms. S. describes the metastrategy and highlights that it can be used in many math situations.

Ms. S.: Yes, Ruth proposed a strategy and we tried it out with different numbers to see if it worked. Then we used it to solve our problem.[12] This is what mathematicians do.

PRACTICE

In this stage, the teacher allows students to practice in groups, pairs, and individually. The teacher guides and supports students in groups and individually, pushing them toward independent practice and language use.

Ms. S.: OK, now you are ready to practice your word problem skills on your own. Before you start reading the problem, explain to your partner how we should read word problems. You can use the first problem as an example. You can say, "For example, in this problem . . ."

or "This looks like a subtraction problem because I can see that . . ."[13]

Brian: (To partner) First we look for the beginning numbers. For example, in this problem, Zoe has 14 frogs. Then we look for changes. For example, in this problem . . . some frogs jump away. That's prob'ly subtract. And she has 5 frogs at the end.

Asha: So we put the box after 14 and count down to find the number.

Brian: Or we can do 14 minus 5, like we did with marbles.[14]

Asha: Why?

[13] Ms. S. prompts students to think about math literacy skills for a word problem and being able to categorize types of problems.

[14] Brian refers to a math strategy that they just learned in the whole-group session to help them solve the problem.

CONCLUSION

In this stage, the teacher synthesizes her observations from student practice and reminds students of the objectives learned today.

Ms. S.: Great job, everyone! We learned how to read word problems and we came up with different ways to solve them. We used drawings and we even wrote equations to describe the problems. Tomorrow we will do more work on word problems and you will even write your own problems!

Fifth-Grade Language Arts: Lesson 1

OBJECTIVES

Ms. Flores is teaching her students how to identify and explain themes in short stories. The focal standard is CCSS ELA-Literacy.RL.5.2: "Determine a theme of a story, drama, or poem from details in the text, including how characters in a story or drama respond to challenges or how the speaker in a poem reflects upon a topic; summarize the text." The content objective of this lesson is to determine the theme of a short story based on character actions and words, and to support ideas from the text.

Ms. F. also uses the California ELD Standards (2012) focused on supporting ideas by using the text: Grade 5/Section 2: Elaboration on Critical Principles for Developing Language & Cognition in Academic Contexts/Part I: Interacting in Meaningful Ways/11.

"Support opinions or persuade others by expressing appropriate and accurate reasons using textual evidence" (CA-ELD.5.2.I.11).

Ms. F. reflects on the thinking and language that is needed for this objective. She realizes that students need the language of interpretation and of supporting ideas with evidence. Language demands might include recognizing figurative language and symbols, breaking down paragraphs in the text, and using terms such as *infer, represent, theme, illustrate, message,* and *symbolize.* The story she uses is "Inside Out," a chapter from *The Circuit: Stories from the Life of a Migrant Child* (Jimenez 1997).

INTRODUCTION AND CONNECTIONS

After presenting the objectives, Ms. F. connects to students' prior knowledge by reviewing what they remember about the strategy of wide-angle reading. She reviews the hand motions for each wide-angle reading prompt: for the type of text, she makes a big T with her arms; for thinking skills, she points to her head and looks up; for author's purpose, she puts her hands together in a circle to look through a telescope; for questions, she raises both hands palms up; and for ways to remember the information, she acts like she is putting files into a folder. She then has pairs look at the story's title, the book's cover, and the first paragraph. Students then ask each other the wide-angle reading questions in the visual organizer (using the motions, if needed).[1] They take notes on the visual. Ms. F. reminds them that they will need to update their notes as they read more closely. Students then share out.

Julia:	I think the purpose is to entertain us. Or maybe teach us about his life as a migrant child, like in the book title. But "Inside Out," I don't know.
Brenda:	I think "inside out" means inside of school and outside of school. He doesn't like being in school, but maybe learns more outside of school?
Julia:	For background maybe know about school, about migrant workers, about how it feels to not understand English.
Brenda:	I agree. And for text type, it's a story but not like talking animals. What is it?
Julia:	Real-life fiction, maybe. He uses "I" so maybe autobio, with true stuff but in a story, like when he talks to Roberto.

[1] Ms. F. has students consider the message dimension of the text by talking about their wide-angle reading ideas.

Brenda: And for thinking, we need to inter-pet (i.e., interpret) themes, like the teacher said.

Julia: And metaphors and symbols can be in stories, too.

Brenda: What about to organize the information?[2] We can take notes, I guess.

Julia: Yeah, and questions? I got one. What does "inside out" mean for this story?

Brenda: And what will we learn about life from this? Will we learn about migrant kids' lives?

(Whole class)

Ms. F.: OK, let's see what our wide-angle thoughts about this story are. *(Students share ideas and Ms. F. synthesizes them on the organizer.)* Great job. It is important to do these things every time you read anything. Many are educated guesses, but they are vital for helping you to build meaning of a text as you read.[3] And will you use this visual every time you read in your life? No. These need to become automatic habits for reading.[4]

[2] Students use the wide-angle visual to co-construct a framework for reading the text.

[3] Ms. F. emphasizes that taking the time to preread will help students learn content.

[4] Ms. F. highlights that these strategies and habits should eventually become automatic. They are not just for school.

NEW LEARNING

In this stage, the teacher models and provides input for the new concepts and skills of the lesson. She models effective reader thinking as she reads the first four pages of the text aloud. She stops at times to highlight word choices, literary devices, and events in the story. Then she focuses on a certain part of the text to do some close reading that emphasizes literature literacy, specific skills for reading stories, and the language needed to express literature thinking skills.

Ms. F.: OK. Tell a partner what we should look for in every story. *(Students talk and then share.)* Yes, characters, how they are on the inside and outside, how they change, big problems, and how the problems are solved. Remember the story about the boy and the tiger? The boy changed during the story. And character changes often give us ideas for themes that teach us about life. So, before I read the next part, remind me why authors choose to include symbols and metaphors.[5]

[5] Ms. F. builds on background knowledge and explicitly prepares students to look for elements that contribute to themes.

Mina: It might be like in that story 'bout trees. They grew and Tom grew. So it could help us see the theme, like it shows a lesson we need to learn.

Ms. F.: Great. Now think about why the author put the next part in.[6] *To my left, under the windows, was a dark wooden counter the length of the room. On top of it, right next to my desk, was a caterpillar in a large jar. It looked just like the ones I had seen in the fields. It was yellowish green with black bands and it moved very slowly, without making any sound. I was about to put my hand in the jar to touch the caterpillar when the bell rang. All the kids lined up outside the classroom door and then walked in quietly and took their seats. Some of them looked at me and giggled. Embarrassed and nervous, I looked at the caterpillar in the jar. I did this every time someone looked at me.* Now share why this part might be there. Share with a partner. Remember, it might even relate to the title of the story.

Alicia: So Francisco didn't like school. And he didn't understand any of it. Maybe he liked the caterpillar cuz it didn't talk.

Nico: Maybe he . . . Caterpillars turn into butterflies, right? So maybe Francisco wants to turn into a butterfly. He wants to learn English.

Alicia: But "inside out"? Maybe he is like the caterpillar inside a jar, like in school, and wants to get out.[7]

Ms. F.: So you are saying that the caterpillar is a symbol for . . . Tell me using the word *symbol*. And use evidence from the text.[8]

Alicia: I think the caterpillar is a symbol for Francisco. He wants to get out of school and the caterpillar wants to leave the jar.

(Whole class)

Ms. F.: I heard some great conversations! Let's hear some ideas. *(Students share ideas.)* Now we keep reading to see if our ideas for themes, symbols, and predictions are confirmed or changed. I will read a little more and we will discuss an important part: *But when I spoke to Arthur*

[6] Ms. F. zooms in to do a close reading (focused on literacy) of a portion of text that describes what will become a symbol in the story.

[7] Students collaborate to analyze the text and discuss abstract ideas around the symbolism of the main character and a butterfly. They have space to create, own, and communicate their ideas.

[8] Ms. F. prompts for and provides a term that she wants students to use and learn. She also reinforces standard for supporting opinions.

in Spanish and Miss Scalapino heard me, she said "No!" with body and soul. Her head turned left and right a hundred times a second and her index finger moved from side to side as fast as a windshield wiper on a rainy day. "English, English," she repeated. Arthur avoided me whenever she was around. I think this is an important paragraph for the story. Can you describe why?[9] When we talk about literature, we can start with, "Perhaps the author included this part in order to show . . ." Say it with me . . . Now share in pairs.

[9] Ms. F. engages students in a close reading that builds disciplinary literacy skills and meta-analysis of text.

(In pairs)

Victor: Perhaps the author included this part to show how mad the teacher got when he spoke Spanish.

Jorge: Perhaps author included this part to show the problem of Francisco. That's hard, ordered not to speak your language. And not to have friends because of it.[10]

[10] Students can still communicate strong ideas and develop thinking skills without perfect grammar.

Victor: Maybe that's the big problem. But what about the caterpillar?[11]

[11] Students are engaged enough to ask their own questions about text concepts at the message level—not just word meanings.

PRACTICE

In this stage, the teacher encourages students to practice the day's focal thinking and literacy skills as they continue to read the story. They have a 3-by-5-inch theme card on which they put their ideas for themes. They take notes on sticky notes: character actions or words evidence that supports the theme (yellow), character thoughts and emotion evidence for the theme (pink), symbols and metaphors that relate to the theme (green), and questions (blue). Some students work in pairs on their own, and some students are supported by Ms. F.

Ms. F.: OK. Now you will read some more on your own. You probably won't finish the story. I want you to reread sections if they are confusing or if you think they help you to sculpt the theme. Use the sticky evidence notes to build up your ideas for the theme.[12] And you might have more than one theme. Use our theme chart if you need to, but remember that we are always looking for new and exciting themes to put up on it. Let's have it quiet.

[12] She provides various visual scaffolds such as note cards, sticky notes that stick on the cards (i.e., interactive annotations activity), and theme ideas on the wall to choose from, if needed.

(Ms. F. circulates for several minutes and then gathers several students who need extra support to provide more guided reading.)

Ms. F.:   OK, can I get a quick summary of the plot up to this point?

Victor: Francisco went to school first day and only speaks Spanish . . . *(continues with summary)*.

Ms. F.:   What about ideas for theme that you are sculpting in your minds. If you can argue for it from the text, you aren't wrong.[13] What might this story teach us about life? You can start with, "A possible theme in this story is . . ."

[13] She prompts students to create knowledge, using ideas from the text, not just trying to find right answers.

Alba: A possible theme in this story is to be respect others.

Ms. F.:   What might we ask Alba?

Kim: Why do you think that?

Alba: Because his dad asks him to respect the teacher and he does it. Even though she is mean to tell him to not speak Spanish.

Ms. F.:   That's possible. You will have to keep looking for ideas that support that theme. What about the caterpillar and the chapter title, "Inside Out"?[14]

[14] She guides students to consider additional key ideas from the book, without being overly explicit.

Tony: Oh, I think the caterpillar is like Francisco. They are both quiet.

Kim: And both are trapped, kinda. Francisco can't be himself or even talk his language. And the *orruga*, I mean caterpillar, is not a butterfly yet.

Alba: The caterpillar is maybe a symbol.

Ms. F.:   Hmmm. A symbol for . . . ? I will let you four talk about this. Then keep reading and look for evidence and theme ideas. Remember to put symbol and theme ideas on theme cards and evidence on sticky notes. You will use this structure to help you talk and write your paragraphs.[15]

[15] She prompts students to structure themes and their evidence using the cards.

CONCLUSION

To conclude the lesson, the teacher refers to the objectives of the day and wraps up the lesson, connecting to the learning that will happen tomorrow.

Ms. F.: OK. We did some great work today. We sculpted ideas for themes in our minds and looked for evidence. For example, Alba suggested that the caterpillar was a symbol for the changes happening in Francisco. A symbol is something that represents a theme in a story. We also used some author language to describe how authors write stories. We will continue tomorrow to think about the story and talk and write about our ideas.[16] Finish the story at home and take your note cards and sticky notes with you.

[16] She concludes the lesson by focusing on a student's idea (from Alba, a shy student), referring to the language and content objectives, and connecting to tomorrow's lesson.

Eighth-Grade Science: Lesson 1

OBJECTIVES

Mr. Escobar is teaching his eighth-grade students what energy is with a focus on understanding kinetic and potential energy. The focal Next Generation Science Standards are "Develop a model to describe that when the arrangement of objects interacting at a distance changes, different amounts of potential energy are stored in the system" (MS-PS3-2); and "Construct, use, and present arguments to support the claim that when the kinetic energy of an object changes, energy is transferred to or from the object" (MS-PS3-2). In addition, Mr. E. wants to develop in his students the following NGSS science practices: asking questions and defining problems; constructing explanations and designing solutions; engaging in argument from evidence.

Given the large number and range of English learners in his class, Mr. E. uses the 2012 WIDA ELD Standards (Grade 8, Standard 4, p. 97): "Students at all levels of English language proficiency will ANALYZE energy transfer." Even though this standard focuses on speaking, Mr. E. uses the five leveled performance indicators to help him differentiate the challenges he gives to students as they use the texts.

To support the learning of literacy and content, Mr. E. also teaches the following CCSS anchor literacy standards (grades 6–8): "Analyze the structure an author uses to organize a text, including how the major sections contribute to the whole and to an understanding of the topic" (CCSS.ELA-Literacy.RST.6-8.5). The main language objective is to explain how science authors organize and clarify cause-and-effect relationships in science texts.

INTRODUCTION AND CONNECTIONS

Mr. E. starts by going over the content and language objectives for the day's lesson. He explains to students that they will be learning about the forms of energy and how they can change.

Mr. E. then reads aloud the following challenge for the three lessons on potential and kinetic energy: *You are part of a small team of engineers who have been hired to design a new amusement park ride called FreeFall. Your task is to evaluate the most energy-efficient way to power the lifting of a cage with riders that weighs 1000 kilograms. The cage is a cube with sides measuring 3 meters. The cage will drop 100 meters in a free fall. You will also write a proposal to an amusement park company.*[1]

Mr. E. points to several guiding questions for the next three lessons: What is energy? What are the different types? How do we measure energy? How do we harness it? He has students think about these questions as they watch the demonstration.[2] He holds a baseball at the top of a 1-meter stick and drops it on a lever that propels a small beanbag into the air. He next drops it from 2 meters and the beanbag is propelled higher. He asks students to explain the difference in the two drops.

(In pairs)

Alicia: The higher drop had more energy cuz it was higher.

David: It was heavier from being higher so it made the beanbag go higher.

(Whole class)

Mr. E.: Three, two, one. All right, the ball helped me do some work, right? Did the ball get heavier when I dropped it from 2 meters? No. But it did more work. It had more energy, which is the ability to do work.[3] Now take a look at the textbook section about energy. First, do a quick wide-angle reading with a partner.[4] You have done this before. Alternate the questions to each other.

(In pairs)

Leo: What is the purpose of this text?

Sherie: I think to teach us about energy. What do you think?

Leo: I think its purpose is to show what energy is, maybe where it comes from . . . and different types of it.

Sherie: What do we need to know already?

[1] Mr. E. uses an overarching design challenge to motivate and frame the learning about energy. Students get to directly apply and use new concepts and vocabulary, rather than just memorize.

[2] Mr. E. uses guiding questions and a live demonstration to get students interested in the topic of the text.

[3] Mr. E. uses the demonstration to introduce new terms that they will encounter in the text.

[4] Mr. E. has students engage in wide-angle reading to set up a mental framework for comprehending the text.

Leo: Like the energy in things like cars, planes, lights, and . . . So, how is this text organized?

Sherie: It has titles and pictures. It has a chart with the two types of energy. What thinking do you think we will need to do?

Leo: Usually cause and effect, cuz it's science, but we might compare types of energy, like on that chart . . . (*conversation continues*).

NEW LEARNING

In this stage, Mr. E. models how to read closely for helpful ideas in the text and to analyze how the author is using visuals and language to clarify ideas.

Mr. E.: I usually read textbook sections twice. With this section on kinetic energy, I first read for the section's purpose. (*Reads section aloud.*) I think the purpose focuses on defining kinetic energy and showing how to calculate it with a formula. Now let's all do a second read, silently, zooming in on how the author used visuals. (*Class reads silently.*) Share what you noticed with a partner. Like most of you, I noticed that the author used a picture of a bowling ball, a soccer ball, a baseball, and a golf ball to show how greater mass and speed gave an object more kinetic energy. The picture helped me compare the different masses and speeds as they related to kinetic energy.[5] OK, now I want you all to do a double read like I did with the next section on potential energy. (*Students read.*) Now I have a close reading question for you all: What is gravitational potential energy and what does it depend on? Take silent time to form connected sentences in your own words.[6] Share with a partner. (*Pairs talk.*) Three, two, one. Kristi?

[5] Mr. E. models his thinking used for his first read. He allows students to share the second read, focused on using visuals. He is using the text not just for content, but to show how science authors use language and visuals to communicate complex ideas.

[6] Mr. E. has students reread, and then uses a close reading question to focus students on a main idea of the section. He then encourages students to form multisentence answers in their own words.

Kristi: Gravity potential energy is stored energy. It depends on the weight and how high it is. Like in the pictures. The bigger biker on the same hill has more, and the higher biker on the other has more energy.

Mr. E.: Yes, gravitational potential energy is stored energy with the potential to do work. All right, all types of energy fit into either kinetic (*he moves*), which is the energy of motion, or potential (*he holds the ball up*), which is stored. Now I think it helps to make a T-chart. *(He hands out cards.)* Take a moment to talk with your team members about what category the type on the card fits into.[7] Give reasons! Some are tricky. For example, nuclear energy seems active but it's energy stored in the bonds between protons in an atom, so it is what? Yes. Potential.

(Teams work.)

Liam: Uh, this card has *Geothermal* on it,[8] like in volcanoes and geysers, it says. Is geothermal stored?

Elise: It says that molecules move so I think it's kinetic. What about *Nuclear*? Bombs explode and that's a lot of motion.

Liam: But before it blows up, it's stored, I think.

Shaun: OK, potential for now. And *Radiant* energy, like sunlight?

Elise: I don't know. I remember something about light waves. Waves move, so I say kinetic. . . .

(Mr. E. helps the class create a master T-chart and discuss why the types of energy belong in each category.)

Mr. E.:   Now let's think about how all this information might be helpful for designing the new FreeFall ride. Use this chart to make a list of possible ways to use or generate or save energy. On my list, I put pluses next to energy that I might gain, and minuses next to energy I might use (and pay for). For example, I put a minus next to "Electricity for lifting the cage up 100 meters" and a plus next to "Wind power harnessed from the wind as the cage falls."[9] With your team, come up with other ideas.

(Teams work.)

Natalie: We could put solar panels on the top of the cage for kinetic.

[7] After clarifying terms with movement, Mr. E. uses a graphic organizer to help students immediately do something with what they learned from the text. This helps them to start building abilities to improve on WIDA ELD Standard 4.

[8] The cards provide new language that students can and should use in their interactions with partners to accomplish the task.

[9] Mr. E. has students start to think about how to use the ideas from the text in their designs. He models the language he used for his ideas, some of which came from the text.

Alemu: Why is light kinetic? I thought it has to be movement.

Natalie: I think cuz light is waves and waves move. So it's a plus.

Alemu: OK. I put a plus by the height of 100 meters. It's very high up, you know. And it has potential energy up there.

Amy: I put minus by gasoline for motor for to lift it up. Kinetic.

Alemu: But gasoline is a chemical, right? So *(looking at the chart up front),* that is potential energy.[10]

> [10] Students use the chart to think and argue about categories of energy types as they begin to come up with ideas for their designs.

PRACTICE

Mr. E. then asks students to turn to the textbook section on the transfer between kinetic and potential forms of energy. He first has them focus on generating a clear and complete purpose and on understanding how the visuals help to clarify the purpose. *(Silent reading time)*[11]

Mr. E.:   As I milled around, I heard Abel say that the author used visual examples to show transfer of one type of energy to another: a boy throwing a baseball, a pendulum on a clock, and a waterfall. I also thought about the baseball I let drop from 1 and 2 meters. Quickly share with your team how energy transferred in these cases. Try to use the words *transform, potential energy,* and *kinetic energy.*[12]

(Teams work.)

> [11] Mr. E. releases more responsibility to the students to work on their own and more quickly to wide-angle read the next section and focus on the use of visuals.

> [12] Mr. E. positively reinforces Abel's (a shy student) idea and then connects the text to the opening demonstration. He has students orally process the connections and use several academic terms.

Gabriel: Balls fall. Movement. That's kinetic. Water up high, potential.

Sierra: Yeah. The water at the top has potential energy and it transfers into kinetic energy when it falls. Like you said, the balls fell, too. Same thing. But the pendulum. It has energy when it moves.

Gabriel: When up here it stops. It's most high. Kinetic into potential here.[13]

> [13] Gabriel, despite his lower proficiency in English, helps Sierra to understand how the pendulum uses energy. He is comparing energy using graphic supports.

Sierra: Yeah. And down at the bottom it doesn't have potential energy, but it's going its fastest. So it's kinetic at the bottom.

(Whole class)

Mr. E.: Three, two, one. All right. Can someone share their ideas of how these relate? Remember to refer to the text and borrow language from it.[14]

Abel: We said that all the things have something up high and stopped. That's potential energy. Then they fall and they have kinetic energy. When they hit the ground or stop, the energy transfers. But in the pendulum, it turns back into potential.

Mr. E.: Thank you, Abel. Now, as an engineer, I wonder how this concept of transfer from potential to kinetic or vice versa might help me with my desire to reduce loss of energy or recapture the amount of energy for my new ride design. Read the section again with this in mind. Take a close look at the visuals and think about how they compare with your design challenge. *(The class reads silently.)* Now share your thoughts with your team. Be creative![15] Wild ideas welcome here!

(Teams work.)

Kyle: Well, we use lots of energy getting the cage up to the top. But then, I don't know.

Raul: Then we can use it when it falls. Like that ball falling. It has energy when it hits the ground. We can use that, I think.

Than: I guess. That's kind of like a dam. It is energy from falling water.

Raul: Yeah, so with the cage, the potential energy at the top transfers. . . . It changes to kinetic when it falls.

Kyle: But how do we catch it?

Than: The energy or the cage?

[14] Mr. E. has students use the text and borrow its language to compare and explain what is happening scientifically.

[15] Mr. E. encourages students to be creative and innovative, as designers must be in the real world.

Kyle: I guess both. We have to stop it slow to not kill the people. Maybe like a big rubber band?

Mr. E.: Interesting. So what kind of energy would that be when the big rubber band was stretched to its max? It's in the book.[16]

Than: Elastic potential energy?

Kyle: But then we need to reuse that energy, right?

Mr. E.: I see a direct way and an indirect way to use it.[17]

Raul: Direct. Oh. Maybe just have the rubber band lift the cage back up, like a bungee jump. So then we don't have to lift the cage as far to get it back to the top. It just stops halfway up and people get off.

Kyle: Yeah. But the indirect? So it stretches the rubber band, then the rubber band turns—what are those things in dams?

Mr. E.: Turbines.

Kyle: So the rubber band turns a turbine to make electricity and it charges a battery that helps us lift the cage.

Mr. E.: Do you think it will create enough electricity to lift the cage all the way back up?[18]

(Conversation continues.)

16 Mr. E. validates the idea and points students into the book to further inform their idea and show them how to describe the energy.

17 Mr. E. pushes students to think about two different ways to use the energy from their design idea.

18 Mr. E. uses a question to get students to think about energy loss throughout the process, which will lead to them comparing the energy losses of different features.

19 Mr. E. has students gather and organize their thoughts with a final written task. He models language that students can use to begin their writing. He encourages them to elaborate, be clear, and use examples from demonstrations, the text, and the real world.

CONCLUSION

Mr. E. asks students to share their brainstormed ideas for using the concept of energy transfer to minimize energy use for the new ride that they are designing. He then has them fill in an "I'm glad you asked" card to respond to people, such as parents, when they ask what students learned in school. For the card, Mr. E. has them finish the prompt, "In order to design an energy-efficient amusement park ride, I had to learn about several ideas in the book. One important concept is . . ."[19]

Mr. E. finishes by connecting his observations of students' ideas and work to the content and language objectives for the day's lesson. He reminds students to think about what they did today and not lose their notes because they will use these ideas in tomorrow's lesson, which will be focused on designing real models to test and describe their designs.

Eleventh-Grade History: Lesson 1

OBJECTIVES

Before this lesson, Mr. Rodríguez's students learned about the dynamics in Europe and the United States after World War I, as well as Hitler's decision to invade Poland in 1939. Mr. R.'s content objective for this lesson focuses on developing students' knowledge and analysis of the origins of U.S. involvement in World War II, with an emphasis on U.S. reaction to the attack on Pearl Harbor. Mr. R. will teach students how to analyze how a complex primary source is structured to determine its central ideas.

In the three-lesson sequence, Mr. R. also focused on New York's ESL Standards 3.9-12, "Students will listen, speak, read, and write in English for critical analysis and evaluation," and 3.9-12.1, "Develop and present clear interpretations, analyses, and evaluations of issues, ideas, texts, and experiences; justify and explain the rationale for positions, using persuasive language, tone, evidence, and well-developed arguments."

Focal Common Core anchor literacy standards are "Analyze in detail how a complex primary source is structured, including how key sentences, paragraphs, and larger portions of the text contribute to the whole" (CCSS.ELA.RH.11-12.5) and "Determine the central ideas or information of a primary or secondary source; provide an accurate summary that makes clear the relationships among the key details and ideas" (ELA-Literacy.RH.11-12.2). In this and the next two lessons he will also continue to teach historical reading skills such as sourcing, contextualizing, and corroborating. He used these standards and focuses to create the lesson's language objective: "Students will be able to explain how a political speech's organization features and word choice combine to create meaning."

INTRODUCTION AND CONNECTIONS

After presenting the objectives, Mr. R. builds students' knowledge of the attack on Pearl Harbor by having his students read an eyewitness account written by a Japanese commander who led the first wave of the air attack. His students are asked to compare and contrast this account with one from their textbook that they read yesterday.[1] As they read, students highlight in yellow any information that is consistent with the information in their textbook. When students finish reading, Mr. R. begins the discussion by asking students to share what they have highlighted.

Eva: In this one he talks about Wheeler Field and Hickum Field and the bases at Ford Island being bombed . . . just like the book yesterday did.

Irma: He says the battleship *Arizona* was bombed.

[1] Mr. R. begins by building students' knowledge of the attack and developing basic skills for comparing and questioning the differences between primary and secondary sources.

Diego: Yep, and he also says that he thinks he hit the battleship *Maryland*.

Eva: And he talks about all the antiaircraft fire and how it got stronger.

Alan: And that he could see all eight battleships in the harbor through his binoculars. We also read about that yesterday.

Mary: But he doesn't say anything about the other ships being hit.

Mr. R.: So why do you think the other ships weren't mentioned in the commander's account?

Diego: Maybe because he couldn't see them from where he was.

Mr. R.: That's what an eyewitness account does. It tells us what that person sees and nothing else. Remember that all secondary sources are based on the perspectives from primary sources.[2] Now reread the account and highlight in blue any ways in which it differs from the information in the textbook.

[2] Mr R. highlights the importance of considering the perspective of a primary source author.

NEW LEARNING

In this stage, the teacher models and provides input for using close reading as a way to uncover key details, arguments, or evidence in the complex history text, Franklin Delano Roosevelt's Pearl Harbor Speech to Congress, on the day after Pearl Harbor was attacked.

Mr. R.: Today we are going to listen to and read one of the most famous speeches in U.S. history. As you read, identify what the president claims about the attack on Pearl Harbor and then we're going to evaluate the evidence or reasoning he uses to support his claims. We will also look for how Roosevelt's choice of words helped communicate his message and accomplish the purposes of the speech. First, as we do with any text, we think about the purpose.[3] Even before listening and reading, tell a partner what the purpose might have been. *(Mr. R. waits as students converse with one another.)* Now follow along with the text of the speech while we listen to this audio-recording. As you listen, think about whom he was addressing and what the president hoped to accomplish. Adjust your purpose as you

[3] He prompts students to build their "message-level discourse" habit of thinking about a text's purpose even before reading or listening to it.

follow along. *(Students listen to and read the speech.)* Now tell a partner what you think the purpose of the speech was and what information in the speech makes you think that.[4] *(Students talk and then share.)*

Diego: In the very last sentence he asks Congress to declare war, so that must be the purpose. "I ask that the Congress declare . . . a state of war has existed . . ."

Eva: Wait. Can't the president declare war?

Ana: No, only Congress can declare war, so he had to get Congress to make the declaration.

Mr. R.: Was this the only purpose?[5] Remember that it was on the radio, so lots of people in America were listening.

Trini: There wasn't TV or news channels back then, so people were still learning about the attack. So I think he was trying to inform them.

Gil: Or get them mad. He probably also wanted the American people to support his decision to go to war. I heard about Vietnam and lots of Americans didn't support it.

Mr. R.: So it sounds like we have identified two purposes for this speech: to urge Congress to declare war on Japan and to rally the American people to support the war effort. Now let's think about some of the arguments the president makes and some of the evidence he uses to try to convince Congress and the rest of the country. Listen while I read a few sentences.[6] "It will be recorded that the distance of Hawaii from Japan makes it obvious that the attack was deliberately planned many days or even weeks ago. During the intervening time, the Japanese government has deliberately sought to deceive the United States by false statements and expressions of hope for continued peace." Now, with your partner identify the claims the president makes in these sentences and what evidence he cites to support those claims. *(Students talk.)* OK, now share starting with "One claim that he made was . . . And the evidence he gave to support it was . . ."[7]

[4] He has students collaborate to find evidence to support their ideas for purposes of the speech.

[5] Mr. R. brings up the possibility of an additional, less obvious purpose for the speech.

[6] He gathers the two main ideas and uses them to model the skill of finding claims and evidence to support the purpose(s) arguments.

[7] Mr. R. provides "linked sentence frames" to help students use connected ideas in their conversations about the text.

Diana: One claim was that the attack was planned for a long time before it happened.

Mr. R.: And . . . ?

Diana: And the evidence he gave to support it was Hawaii is a long way from Japan, so it had to take time to plan.

Mr. R.: OK. What's another claim the president made?

Kara: That the Japanese lied to us.

Mr. R.: How did he tell us that?[8]

[8] He has students look at the language used in the text to evoke responses and convince listeners.

Kara: Here: "the Japanese government has deliberately sought to *deceive* the United States by *false* statements . . ." So they lied on purpose to trick us, right?

PRACTICE

In this stage, the teacher uses a close reading of a key sentence in the text. This analysis is designed to help the class understand how sentence structure, word choice, and text structure can affect our understanding of and our reaction to a complex text in history.

Mr. R.: OK. As Kara showed us, words are very powerful. Now we're going to focus in on a key sentence that FDR used: *Yesterday, December 7, 1941—a date which will live in infamy—the United States of America was suddenly and deliberately attacked by naval and air forces of the Empire of Japan.*[9] I'd like you to work with two other people and discuss the following questions: Why is it the first sentence? Why does he use the word *infamy*? Why do you think he chose to use *Empire of Japan* instead of *Japanese forces* or the *Japanese government* or *Japan*? Why might he have used *suddenly and deliberately*? Reread it several times.

[9] Mr. R. has students analyze a key sentence to identify and deconstruct its role in the text.

Randy: Using it in the first sentence also tells what is coming in the rest of the speech. It lets us know that he is going to explain what the evil was.[10]

[10] Students think about the placement of the sentence and what it does.

Hilario: *(To Randy)* I think the president choose *infamy* cuz it is something evil. And that's what he wanted Congress and the people to feel about the Japan . . . that attacking Pearl Harbor was evil.

Randy: Why do you think he used *Empire of Japan* instead of one of the other names?

Hilario: *Empire of Japan* sounds bigger and more important.

Randy: Yeah, it sounds worse, like they want to take over the world.[11]

[11] Student builds on partner ideas to co-construct content understandings.

Hilario: I think he used *suddenly and deliberately* to make it look like we didn't know. But maybe we did know and we wanted to get attacked so we could go to war.[12]

[12] Student poses a novel hypothesis as a result of the discussion time.

(Whole-class discussion)

Mr. R.: OK, how did your discussion build up your understanding of how language is used in speeches?

Hilario: Randy said that it was a good, like, topic sentence for the whole speech. It was emotional and told you what he was going to talk about.

(Discussion continues.)

CONCLUSION

To conclude the lesson, the teacher reviews the standards and objectives for the lesson and recaps the strategies they used to read and analyze the complex texts.

Mr. R.: Well done, everyone! You have done an excellent job of analyzing how President Roosevelt used language to have an important impact on people's understanding of and reaction to what happened at Pearl Harbor.[13] We read a variety of materials during this lesson, and all of them were challenging. One of the things I've noticed was that you are improving at preparing to read the texts, identifying the purposes, and understanding why it's important. Being able to analyze how certain language influences communication is key. In the future we're going to practice these skills on a different type of text: posters that were developed during World War II to recruit people to fight as well as to do other things associated with the war effort.[14]

[13] He recaps the key skills of the lesson, referring to the objectives.

[14] Mr. R. provides general feedback on the learning of the day and connects it to future lessons.

CHAPTER 6

Fortifying Complex Output

*Let's build bridges where we
need to cross the river.*

Many students have learned to play the "game" of school, answering with one-word answers or just enough language to get the teacher to move on to someone else. Many just say, "I don't know," even if they do know. Or, students are asked to use a sentence starter that they might not fully understand to answer a question to which the teacher already knows the answer. The opposite needs to happen: language is meant to bridge information gaps, to communicate ideas and information to others who don't already know them—to be used to get things done. Students' language doesn't need to be perfect or even correct, but it needs to communicate. If it is fake or just for show, it won't grow.

For the Common Core and other new standards, students need to learn how to use language to clearly communicate whole messages that are valued in the discipline. This means that we must help students produce clearer and more complete output. A major aim of this chapter, therefore, is to equip teachers with ideas for helping students increase both the quantity and the quality of their oral, written, and multimedia messages.

To get a taste of this chapter's focus, Figure 6.1 includes several CCSS standards related to output and their implications for teaching academic English learners. This is also an example of charts that you might create in your setting.

FIGURE 6.1

Sample output-focused Common Core State Standards and their implications for teaching academic English learners

CCSS	IMPLICATIONS FOR AELS
Students adapt their communication in relation to audience, task, purpose, and discipline. They set and adjust purpose for reading, writing, speaking, listening, and language use as warranted by the task (CCSS Introduction 2013).	AELs need to understand how to select and use complex language appropriate for the purpose of the task and the audience. They need models of how to address different audiences.
Introduce a topic clearly, provide a general observation and focus, and group related information logically; include formatting (e.g., headings), illustrations, and multimedia when useful to aiding comprehension (CCSS.ELA-Literacy.W.5.2a).	AELs often lack high amounts of feedback on their writing, thus needing clear notions for knowing what is "clear" to others, what is a worthy "focus," and what are "logical" descriptions and formats for an audience's comprehension.
Adapt speech to a variety of contexts and communicative tasks, demonstrating command of formal English when indicated or appropriate (K-5 CCRAS Speaking & Listening).	AELs differ widely in their knowledge of what constitutes formal English and when it is appropriate to use it. Students need extra modeling and practice with tasks and settings in which formal English is to be used.
Students analyze and explain the process of solving an equation. Students develop fluency writing, interpreting, and translating between various forms of linear equations and apply related solution techniques and the laws of exponents to the creation and solution of simple exponential equations (CCSS Math Appendix A 2013).	AELs need to understand and apply the complex language needed to explain a process; understand and apply specific academic terms and phrases; and be able to express their understanding on both oral and written output that uses appropriate complex language.

Students retain more language and content concepts when they create and communicate original messages (Swain 1985; Walqui 2006). Organizing and articulating thoughts for real people provides students with much-needed practice for complex language growth. Constructing authentic messages requires students to coherently put two or more sentences together to form an original message. This pushes students to use academic vocabulary, syntax, and message-construction strategies in ways that disciplinary experts do in order to clearly communicate complex ideas. If we want students to be prepared to produce output that is sophisticated, appropriate for the discipline, and authentic, then we need to provide them with multiple and extended opportunities to practice these skills with tools and linguistic supports to facilitate the process. And over time we help them build their skills to construct these messages independently.

In this book we differentiate output (this chapter) from interaction (Chapter 8). We consider output to be messages that do not depend on the receiver's ongoing responses for the shaping of subsequent sentences by the speaker or writer. A good example is the difference between giving a speech and having a conversation with a person about the same topic. Both are challenging. In a conversation, a person can respond to the other(s), but participants never know where the conversation will go and lots of improvisation is required. For the speech, a speaker needs to meet the needs of a broad audience with only one chance to get the message across. To help students maximize the clarity every time they communicate with oral, written, and multimedia output, read the rest of this chapter.

Challenges of Fortifying Complex Output

In our work in classrooms with teachers and students we have identified various challenges that teachers face when shifting from an environment where the teacher does most of the communicating to one in which students have multiple opportunities to produce complex academic language in meaningful ways. The following questions illustrate the most common challenges. Under each question we have provided some suggestions for addressing these challenges. More specific ideas for addressing these challenges can be found later in this chapter and in the sample lessons in Chapter 7.

HOW DO I ENSURE THAT ALL OF MY STUDENTS ENGAGE IN HIGH-QUALITY ORAL OUTPUT?

There are several routines and structures that teachers can use to encourage and ensure that all students engage in activities that require oral use of academic language. First, when designing tasks and activities for pairs, you can assign A and B roles to students and design the task so that each role is central to completing the task. Second, have students rehearse what they might say in a whole-class discussion with one other student. If students have an opportunity to rehearse an answer using the appropriate language, they will less likely feel intimidated when called on to talk during a whole-class discussion. Third, give students linguistic supports and starter language that they can use in oral responses.

HOW DO I BALANCE ORAL AND WRITTEN OUTPUT, EVEN THOUGH I FEEL LIKE I NEED TO FOCUS MOST OF THE TIME ON DEVELOPING STUDENTS' WRITING SKILLS?

There is a strong connection between students' use of complex language in oral output and their use of this language in written output (Williams 2008). One approach is to design tasks in which students are engaged in whole-class and small-group discussions about a topic or a text in preparation for writing. Such discussions, when properly prompted and guided, prepare students for writing and provide them with opportunities to practice the use of complex language orally before using it in writing. Some teachers do the reverse: they use writing to prepare students for discussions and presentations. And several teachers with whom we work look at the standards for writing to give them ideas for oral output activities. Such overlap and reinforcement between oral and written work is vital given the limited amount of time that we have with students.

Formative Assessment of Complex Output

Having several criteria can help us assess and improve the quality of output that we want students to produce. First of all, the output should be as relevant as possible and pertain to the prompt or topic of discussion. Each message should be as clear as possible. This doesn't just mean correct grammar and spelling. We have all read grammatically correct texts that we didn't understand at all. Clarity means that for a certain audience, be it one person or a large crowd, you have crafted the language such that the least amount of misinterpretation or confusion will happen. Each message should also be as memorable as possible. Unlike many learn-it-for-the-test-then-forget-it approaches, lessons should be set up such that students value ideas enough to remember them. If my audience (partner, teacher, readers) wants or needs to remember my message, I will try to make it memorable. I might use an analogy, visuals, repetition, or well-chosen words. The message needs to have coherently linked sentences and use the complex language being learned in the lesson. Finally, the output should show evidence of disciplinary thinking skills, which you can code as CE = cause/effect, CC = compare/contrast, SU = support, EM = empathy, and EV = evaluation.

Using Figure 6.2, you can create summative, formative, and peer assessment tools for oral output. You can use such tools to show students what you are looking and listening for as you observe them and their work in whole-class or group settings. Students, in pairs and small groups, can use tools like this to coach and encourage partners to produce higher-quality output, not just minimized language for basic answers. When students do this, you have many mini-teachers out in the class helping you to improve their complex language abilities.

FIGURE 6.2

Student observation tool for using complex output

SYMBOL	3	2	1
	Relevant to the topic or task.	Related to the topic or task.	Not relevant to the topic or task.
	Clear, original, whole, and memorable	Partly clear, original, whole, and/or memorable	Not clear, original, whole, or memorable
	Coherent with logically linked sentences	Partly coherent with partly linked sentences	Not coherent and without logically linked sentences
	Uses target language and language of text(s)	Some use of target language and language of text(s)	Little or no use of target language or language of text(s)
	Shows disciplinary thinking (CE, CC, SU, EM, EV)	Shows some disciplinary thinking	Shows little or no disciplinary thinking

Most of the formative assessment ideas should come from the lesson activities themselves. Several general ideas for formative assessment are as follows:

• Present students with different tasks and audiences across disciplines and observe the language used in each.

- Give writing and multimedia assignments that are read by and assessed by multiple people who offer feedback; compare the feedback.

- Record paired conversations where students explain a concept or process to each other, and analyze the conversations for appropriate use of language.

- Ask students to use index cards and explain their understanding of key terms and phrases using text and images. Allow students to also use their primary language.

- Schools and students have come to think of oral and written output mainly as ways to assess content learning. True, oral and written responses are effective ways to formatively and summatively assess the learning of content; however, producing output (via writing, talk, production of multimedia) is also a highly valuable skill *for* the building of disciplinary ideas, language, and thinking skills. Producing authentic language is a huge factor in creating engaged learning and in the building of disciplinary literacy.

TEACHER REFLECTION TOOL FOR FORTIFYING COMPLEX OUTPUT

Similar to the other essential practices in this book, we have identified three important strands within fortifying complex output. The reflection tool in Figure 6.3 contains the three strands. You can use this chapter, the lessons in Chapter 7, and your own experiences to help you clarify the differences between the levels of evidence for each strand in your setting.

FIGURE 6.3
Teacher reflection tool for fortifying complex output

STRANDS OF FORTIFYING COMPLEX OUTPUT	LIMITED EVIDENCE	ACCEPTABLE EVIDENCE	STRONG EVIDENCE
Develop complex language abilities for and by oral output (ORL)			
Develop complex language abilities for and by writing (WRT)			
Develop complex language abilities for and by producing multimedia messages (MMM)			

STRAND 1 OF FORTIFYING COMPLEX OUTPUT: Develop Complex Language Abilities for and by Oral Output (ORL)

This strand focuses on structuring, strengthening, and supporting the quantity and quality of students' oral messages using complex language. Oral production skills support content learning, but they are also important in and of themselves for success in many domains of life. Students not only need to learn to know and think; they need to be able to clearly articulate their knowledge and thinking. Often, by articulating thoughts for someone else, they are clarifying thoughts for themselves.

Oral and written uses of language in school are both similar and different in their complexity. Written texts tend to use more embedded clauses, prepositional phrases, nominalizations, and long sentences. Oral language valued in school tends to use intonation, repetition, and conjunctions to link ideas within a message (Halliday 1989). There are many variations of oral language used by students beyond classroom walls that are highly complex. We must value such variations and use them as resources for cultivating additional language skills and genres.

In school, the most common forms of oral output are answering teacher questions, giving oral presentations, doing jigsaw activities, and sharing with a partner. We can use these forms and others as ways to beef up students' oral skills. Even though we do see some value in certain "repeat after me" and echo-reading activities, we see more power in helping students build their abilities to organize and verbalize their own thoughts into clear and complex messages for others. One of the fascinating aspects of language is that, compared to all the sentences and paragraphs used each day in the world, very few are exactly the same. People must create each one anew. And the process of taking topics and ideas that swirl around in our heads and quickly putting them into organized sentences in real time is a major skill that demands loads of practice and loads of support.

The teaching activities in this chapter have several principles that guide them:

- *Emphasize authentic communication.* We need to remember that our goal is to build students' abilities to use complex language to construct and communicate authentic messages. These are the skills used by advanced-level students and professionals in college and in the workplace. To reach advanced levels (including in first grade), our students need multiple opportunities to construct authentic messages across disciplines. When designing classroom activities and tasks, we must think through how we envision the types of output we would like to hear from students and the language we want them to use.

- *Emphasize whole-message skills.* Through our teaching, we reinforce for our students the importance of whole messages. Although we might use some instructional time to build academic vocabulary and to strengthen students' syntax skills, we must emphasize that these are the building blocks for communicating more sophisticated messages.

- *Build a classroom mind-set of using practice time to build language skills.* This means, from the start of the year, that we encourage students to use the talk time that we give them to improve their oral language. This can happen most often when an activity is structured such that students get to share with a second or third partner about the same topic.

Whole-Year Message and Syntax Focuses

This is not a lesson activity, but rather a strategy for the entire year. Instead of randomly teaching language skills as needs arise throughout the year, it can be effective to focus on certain complex language skills across all units of study. For example, the CCSS include standards on crafting logically connected messages, taking different perspectives, arguing with evidence, and explaining causes and effects across subject areas.

A grade-level team (or teacher), for example, might choose to pick several *message*-dimension skills to work on in each unit of study across the year, such as crafting

- a descriptive paragraph with appropriate ordinate and subordinate ideas (oral and written);
- an opinion or argument-based paragraph that includes appropriate reasons, evidence, and explanations (includes response to literature writing); or
- a cause-effect paragraph with appropriate cause/effect language (in science, history, and narratives).

All the preceding paragraphs need to have appropriate topic sentences, supporting sentences, transitions, and cohesive devices such as sequence markers, pronouns, and nominalizations. For each unit, teachers, depending on the grade level, will want to have students also expand ideas from paragraphs into larger output pieces such as essays, reports, articles, web pages, and the like.

A grade-level team (or teacher) might also decide to pick several *sentence*-level skills to work on in each unit across the year such as crafting sentences that

- begin with subordinate clauses such as *Because* . . . , *In order to* . . . , *Due to* . . . , *Even though* . . . , *Unlike* . . . ;
- use relative clauses (starting with *which, that, who*); or
- use gerunds and participles.

In order to improve in using these kinds of sentences and paragraphs, students need to see and hear plenty of models throughout the year(s) across the disciplines. We can look for text structures, paragraphs, and sentences in texts and oral messages to use as models. Students can also help us out by producing models.

❖ Linked Sentence Starters

One way to use sentence starters to support message-dimension skills is to provide sentence starters that link together. This helps students to logically connect two or more sentences as disciplinary experts might do. So, instead of just letting students get away with one sentence, have them put two or more together to push their thinking and increase their abilities to connect ideas in order to communicate them. Paragraph frames are a variation of this practice, but they are usually too long to use for oral responses without making students sound like robots. Consider the following linked starters.

- The _____ for several reasons. First, . . .
- A key theme in the story is . . . One example of . . .
- The _____ and _____ are similar in many ways. The most important similarity is . . .
- Even though . . . , I believe that . . . A key piece of evidence from the book is . . .
- Evidence suggests that . . . This conclusion is important because . . .

You can use linked sentence starters to support complex output in a variety of activities, such as answering oral questions, writing, and even thinking, as described in the next activity.

❖ Mental Sentence Duos, Trios, and Paragraphs

One of the focal shifts of this book is placing more emphasis on building students' abilities to use connected sentences to communicate logical, complex, and real ideas in a discipline. The common discourse format in many classrooms is asking questions to which students answer with a word, phrase, or single sentence. By contrast, this strategy has students pause to put more than one sentence together. This, by the way, also provides more wait time. You can start with two connected sentences, work up to three, and then have them generate full oral paragraphs. They can use the linked sentence frames in the previous activity description, if needed. This strategy can be used at any point in a lesson when you are asking students to answer a question or respond to a prompt.

When you get to the level of having students think in paragraphs, model for them how a typical paragraph has a topic sentence with sentences that support it. While this is not new to anyone who has taught writing, the new part here is the focus on building in students the mental habit of automatically "thinking" in paragraphs before they speak or write. The more that students organize knowledge into logically connected sentences and paragraphs in their minds, the better they speak, read, listen, write, think, and learn. An effective way to work on this habit is through oral output exercises.

PROCEDURE

1. Explain to students the rationale for mentally connecting sentences and constructing paragraphs.

2. Practice with just-learned topics and previously learned content.

3. Model how to think about an idea and generate a strong topic or initial sentence. This is one of the most challenging stages because topic sentences are often about more general and abstract ideas. They need support with details and examples. You can show examples of topic sentences and support sentences, several of which are found in Figure 6.4. Have students notice the more general and abstract nature of the topic sentences versus the specific "example" and concrete nature of the support sentences. Discourage sentences that start with "I like . . ." or "My favorite . . ."

FIGURE 6.4
Examples of topic sentences and support sentences

INITIAL AND TOPIC SENTENCE EXAMPLES	SUPPORT SENTENCE EXAMPLES
Many animals have adapted to camouflage themselves from predators.	The fur of many rabbits changes from white in the winter to brown in the summer.
Living on the frontier was very difficult.	Roads were bad, which made it hard to transport products back east.
Bullying is bad for everyone.	In the book, Ana doesn't like who she was becoming as she realized she was bullying others.
The choice depends on how many books you are buying.	If you buy fewer than twenty books, then you should buy from ABC Books because the cost line is lower on the graph.
The arrival of Columbus was like when someone comes and takes over your house.	Columbus came and took the Native American lands and their gold.

4. Show students how to use support sentences to support the topic sentence. You can do this by drawing or writing the sentences as models, but then emphasize that you eventually want students to do this supporting mentally, without anything to look at or read.

5. Model oral examples. Have students "toss out" a topic to you and model for them how you generate a topic sentence from it and support sentences. For example, they might shout out, "Soccer" and you might respond with, "Soccer is a popular sport around the world for several reasons. One reason is that all you need is a ball, a field, and something to make goal posts. Another reason is . . ."

6. In pairs, have the "listener" say a topic or ask a question to a partner, either randomly (easy topics) or from prepared cards (lesson-based topics). The partner then takes a moment to think of a topic sentence and possible support sentences. The listener helps provide ideas for improving the topic sentence and adding any support sentences along with cohesive devices (*first, second, in addition, another, moreover, however, for example, if,* and so on). The talker then practices a final version.

Partner A: Why do you think we should study viruses?

Partner B: We should study viruses in order to understand how the diseases work. If we know how viruses live and die, then we can prevent lots of viral diseases. For example, science has produced many vaccinations, such as the one for smallpox, to prevent illnesses. In addition, knowing about viruses helps us see . . .

7. Talker and listener switch roles.

8. Pair off students with new partners to share their oral paragraphs again: "My topic was _____. My mental paragraph is . . .

9. The listener then paraphrases the paragraph.

10. Talker and listener switch roles.

11. Variation: An extra challenge that you can add to this and other pair activities is to time the utterances. Tell each student they must talk for a minimum of thirty seconds, a minute, and so on. Increase the time over the year and have them work on the coherence of the message.

❖ I Am . . . Monologues

Improvisation can help students practice real-time formulation of ideas for oral output in engaging and extended ways. In this low-prep activity, students become a person or object (or anything else) and describe who they are and what they do from a first-person point of view. You can give cards out to organize who people are, or you can let students decide. You want students to prepare their monologues and then present them in pairs or triads to others who are different from them. They should not memorize the monologue. They can use note cards. You can also do this improvisationally, with little preparation other than a moment to prepare the first sentence. Sample categories and topics are provided here.

- **Famous Person.** My name is Paul Revere. I am a silversmith who organized an alarm system to watch the British military. I am famous for warning the people in Lexington and Concord about the approach of British forces.

- **Witness to an event.** My name is Huitzillin. I am an Aztec warrior hiding outside the city of Tenochtitlan. I am here because Cortes and his army have taken over the city.

- **Thing.** I am a white blood cell. I have an oval shape. I travel through the bloodstream and take care of problems such as bacteria that invade the body. They usually get in through cuts or food.

PROCEDURE

1. Model the process using a person or thing that students would not use. That is, don't model with ideas that would be good for students to use.

2. A student is given a card with the person or object written on it, or the student chooses the topic.

3. The student briefly studies the topic to pick out the key components or traits to include. The student can take notes on a note card or sticky note. The easiest ideas to include are the following:

   a. What I am like (physical or personality traits)

   b. What I do or did that makes me important

4. Remind students to teach as much about the topic or person as possible through the monologue. Remind students to include various functions and parts of the topic, purposes, problems, motivations, effects, desires, events, and any humor that might make it more entertaining.

5. The student then practices the monologue with a partner or two. Students can use notes for the first and second practices, but not for the third. The student can then present to a small group of different partners or in front of the whole class. The teacher can provide certain types of sentence frames for practice in pairs and triads, but they should not pause to look at frames the third time.

6. Listeners should listen during and take notes after the presenter is finished. Listeners can also ask questions. If the actor doesn't know, he or she can say something like, "It has been a long time since that event, so I can't remember clearly." Or "The event was very traumatic so I am trying to forget the details."

❖ Pro-Con Improv

Too many academic English learners are adept at saying the minimum to scrape by in school. The Pro-Con Improv (adapted from Dennis, Griffin, and Wills 1981; Zwiers 2008) and its variations can be used to help students to craft and say extended messages with connected sentences, use academic cohesion devices in speech, and build abilities to see two sides of an issue. You can have students practice with familiar topics like those in Figure 6.5. For academic topics, teachers often have students create T-charts with information for both sides that helps them prepare for the activity.

FIGURE 6.5

Pro-con poster

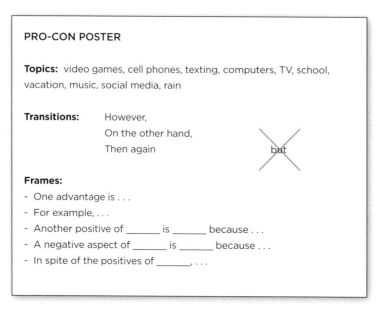

PRO-CON POSTER

Topics: video games, cell phones, texting, computers, TV, school, vacation, music, social media, rain

Transitions: However,
On the other hand,
Then again   ~~but~~

Frames:
- One advantage is . . .
- For example, . . .
- Another positive of _____ is _____ because . . .
- A negative aspect of _____ is _____ because . . .
- In spite of the positives of _____, . . .

PROCEDURE

1. If needed, have students prepare a two-sided T-chart before the activity to provide students with more ideas for what to say. They shouldn't look at it during the activity.

2. Students form pairs, and one partner in the pair is the "director" who names the topic (e.g., rain) and claps while saying, "Pro!"

3. The other person (the speaker) thinks of positive aspects of the topic and says them. The speaker might say, "Rain is important because it waters the trees and plants such as crops and gardens. It also cleans the air and . . ."

4. Then the director, after hearing two or three points, finds a good time to interrupt with a clap and says, "Con!"

5. The speaker starts with an academic transition from the board (e.g., *However, On the other hand, Then again*) and follows it with the negative aspects of the topic. (Students should not use the word *but* because it is so common in speech and writing.) For example, "On the other hand, rain can ruin people's plans for weekend activities. For example, last weekend I went to . . ." Speakers can use sentence starters (based on CCSS) such as those in the poster. Moreover, students can be asked to use complex sentence frames and language such as *Because . . . , In order to . . , In spite of the . . . , likewise, in a similar way, similarly, as well, in the same manner, in contrast, even though, nevertheless, yet, unlike, however, on the other hand, despite, conversely, whereas, therefore, consequently, given that, for this reason, thus, this led to, in addition, moreover, equally important, furthermore, and finally.*

6. After going back and forth three times or so, you can stop them and have the director decide which side of the issue the speaker favored, based on what the speaker said. They can also write this down.

7. Partners switch roles and choose a different topic. Or, students switch partners and talk about the same topic, but without looking at their notes.

8. Directors tell the speaker which side they think the speaker leaned toward, citing evidence from the speaker's performance.

VARIATIONS

- A variation is a whole-class version in which the teacher has students stand up and respond back and forth as he or she calls their names (e.g., "Mario, pro!"). They need to use the academic transition to contrast with the previous student's comment, or start with a response such as "I agree with Mario's point about . . . because . . . I would like to add that . . . "

- To emphasize thinking skills, student directors can also say "Cause!" and "Effect!" or "Compare!" and "Contrast!" or "For!" and "Against!" or "Fortunately" and "Unfortunately" (like the children's book by Michael Forman [2011]). An American history teacher, during a unit on the Civil War, had directors clap and say "Union soldier" and "Confederate soldier" to contrast different perspectives (e.g., two different characters, historical figures, authors, animals, objects).

- In a pro-con fishbowl, two students model in front of (or in the middle of) the rest of the class, who listen and need to decide which side the actor favors at the end.

Authentic-Augmenting Repetition Activities

You might recognize these activities, especially if you are familiar with second-language teaching methods. A common theme in this book is making language exchanges authentic. That is, there should be an information gap: the listener doesn't know what the talker is going to say, but wants or needs the information. This book uses the term *augmenting* to emphasize that we must encourage students to improve the quantity and quality of what they say each time they say it. Students are often adept at just getting by with the minimum, or just repeating the same basic response, especially in oral activities. We must model and emphasize that for each successive partner, they must borrow language and ideas from previous partners, and improve and augment their responses with each new partner. It can help to model a non-example by just repeating, for instance, "I think that living in the city is more advantageous" in monotone voice to three students in a row. Then model how you might augment your answer the second and third times.

Following are several authentic-augmenting activities that can be used across grade levels and disciplines.

❖ Face-to-Face Lines and Circles

Facing lines and moving circles are often used by language teachers to increase the amount of language produced by students. Even in high school, it helps for students to get up and move around a bit to get the learning wheels spinning. Split the class in half and have the inner circle facing out and the outer circle facing in, each with a partner. Ask an important question, indicate which circle should begin, and have students share their answers. You can have them start with sentence frames. After both have had a chance to share, have the inner circle shift two people over. With conversation lines, have one line move by having the end person(s) go to the other end of their own line. Remind students to augment their answers with each turn! Observe a student or two to watch for augmentation and to provide support.

❖ Interview Grids

Students create a simple chart like the one in Figure 6.6 to record their classmates' answers to a prompt or two. They paraphrase partner responses in the blank spaces. Emphasize to students that you will be looking for evidence of thinking skills, complex language (connected sentences and academic vocabulary), and content understanding. You want notes only on the spaces, and no one should be reading their fine print. They should meet with just one other student and have good eye contact in each exchange.

You can follow a student around and see if his or her language gets longer and stronger throughout the activity.

FIGURE 6.6
Interview grid sample

NAME	WHAT CAUSES EARTHQUAKES?	HOW CAN WE REDUCE DAMAGE FROM EARTHQUAKES?
Me		

❖ Opinion Continuum

Students use a continuum like the one in Figure 6.7 with two opposing ends of an opinion to articulate and gather ideas and language from other students. First, the asker asks the opinion-giver where his or her opinion is on the continuum. The opinion-giver then signs his or her name on the asker's continuum at the appropriate point where it matches the level of his or her opinion. Students should not be directly in the middle. The asker then asks why. The asker can ask clarifying questions as a teacher would do. The opinion-giver then explains and justifies his or her opinion with examples. The asker can put notes down underneath the opinion-giver's name. Students then switch roles and repeat the first three steps. Remind students that they should have much stronger and longer responses on their last turn. At the end, students share their augmented ideas with the class.

FIGURE 6.7
Example of an opinion continuum

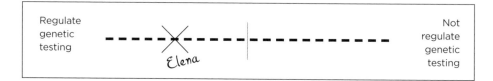

❖ **Opinion Formation Cards Café**

In this authentic-augmenting activity, students build up their opinion on a topic as they listen to the ideas of others. This approximates real life because students hear different people share their opinions and need to negotiate multiple points of view. .

PROCEDURE

1. Choose texts that illustrate or support two different sides of a controversial issue and put excerpts from the texts on small cards or strips, as in Figure 6.8. These can come from the same or different texts on the topic. Try to have at least six different colors, three for one side of the issue and three for the other. Six sheets of different colors are usually enough; just print a table that includes the same excerpt in each cell on each colored sheet and then cut them up. And don't tell students which sides are supported by which colors.

FIGURE 6.8
Evidence cards

A study showed that children who watch TV engage in more violent behaviors.	A survey showed that children who watched educational shows began to read sooner.

2. Tell students the topic and have them read their own card. After they read, have them clarify their own opinion on the issue to themselves. This opinion might conflict with the evidence on the card, which is fine, but they will have to tell others why.

3. Students have successive paired meetings with other students who have different pieces of textual evidence (cards with different colors). They read cards to each other and both state their current opinion on the issue with reasons and evidence. They build on the ideas and language of previous partners each time that they meet with a new partner. They can also ask questions and prompt for elaboration.

4. They can use frames such as these:
   "In my opinion, _____ because _____. Yet I also . . . Given the points that I have heard so far, such as _____, I think I lean more to the side of _____ because _____. The answer depends on . . ."

5. Students can share out their final opinions at the end.

VARIATION: INFER THEMES FROM PARAGRAPHS

Pick several paragraphs from a fiction text, write them on different colored paper, and distribute them to students. Have students infer or predict what the theme of the entire text will be about, based on the paragraph and the title of the text. They meet with several conversation partners who have different paragraphs and build up (or prune away) their ideas of what the theme might be.

STRAND 2 OF FORTIFYING COMPLEX OUTPUT: Develop Complex Language Abilities for and by Writing (WRT)

Output also includes producing written texts such as essays, articles, letters, and literature. We must help students develop their abilities to use appropriate vocabulary, syntax, and message construction strategies to produce written texts that communicate clear, meaningful, and original academic messages in each discipline.

While it is more common to focus on developing complex language *for* writing, we turn things around a bit and highlight activities in which writing helps to build language. Expository writing in the Common Core, for example, focuses on disciplinary thinking and reasoning such as having a clear thesis, creating paragraphs that support the thesis, using topic sentences for each paragraph, using specific evidence and warrants, using varied sentences and transitions, and so on. Because we tend to focus on the more tangible products of writing, we must be extra intentional in our uses of writing to develop students' complex language. The following activities can help us do this.

❖ Back It Up

This activity gives much-needed instruction and practice in supporting one's reasons with solid evidence. It shows students the different types of evidence that exist and lets them evaluate the relative strength of each. It builds students' abilities to communicate and question the support of ideas in an argument.

PROCEDURE

1. With the help of students, come up with criteria for good evidence, such as the AAA Test (see Chapter 4): Is it applicable? Is it accurate? Is it adequate? You can have them remember the test and even make up hand motions.

2. Put samples of persuasive texts up on the overhead and/or in the hands of students and model how to find the types of support shown in Figure 6.9 for backing up reasons. You can underline or highlight, or even create a table where students need to find the type of support and fill in the table with the appropriate one.

FIGURE 6.9

Types of support chart

TYPES OF SUPPORT TO BACK UP REASONS IN PERSUASIVE TEXTS	
Fact/statistic	The World Health Organization [WHO] announced a 17% increase in deaths by malaria last year.
Quote from expert	Ultimately we must address the issue presented by Marianne Stevens, chief spokesperson for the WHO: "It is getting increasingly difficult to reduce mosquito populations without using more toxic prophylactic substances."
Quote from person involved	A traveler to Nepal said, "We don't want to get malaria, but we keep getting crazy nightmares and other weird side effects."
Citation from credible source	In a recent WHO report, researchers estimated that certain strains of malaria will become totally resistant to current preventative medicines within the next five years.
Example	Last November, a high number of travelers with strange symptoms were brought to local health clinics. All had been using Larium.
Anecdote	On a recent trip to Nepal, I contracted malaria even though I was using the latest prophylactic medicine.
Hypothetical situation	Imagine a world with just mosquitoes flying around.
Rhetorical question	Will the mosquitoes win? Are we smart enough to defeat them?
Analogy	Can mosquitoes be spies? It seems like every attack strategy we have, they have prepared for and quickly adapt.
Comparison	This is similar to using certain types of radiation to cure cancer. The radiation often does unforeseeable harm to certain parts of the body.

3. After students are familiar with different types of support and finding them in texts, they are ready to create their own reasons and support for their position. Model how to choose a position on a controversial topic and fill in the chart in Figure 6.10.

FIGURE 6.10

Position and reasons chart

My position/side:					
Reason 1		Reason 2		Reason 3	
Support	Type	Support	Type	Support	Type

4. Now have students consider the counterarguments, also called *concessions, counter-reasons,* or *opposing points*. Have students think about what the opponents would argue, and put these reasons in the spaces provided in Figure 6.11. Then, if they have supports for the counterarguments, put them below those, along with the type of support. Knowing the type of support is helpful because if they only use quotes from people involved and analogies, this likely will be a weakness to mention in the responses to counterarguments.

FIGURE 6.11

Counterargument chart

Counterargument 1		Counterargument 2		Counterargument 3	
Support	Type	Support	Type	Support	Type
My response to this		My response to this		My response to this	

5.   Students think about the counterarguments and prepare logical responses that acknowledge and validate the counterarguments, but then go on to explain that the counterarguments are not as strong as those that support the students' position. Typical ways to respond include comparing statistics, questioning the validity and date of the statistics, questioning the cause/effect explanations given by the counterarguments, questioning the credibility or value of the people or sources of information, challenging an analogy or comparison, or even exploiting the analogy to one's own side.

6.   Students create conclusions that synthesize the points made and leave the reader with the main argument presented in the thesis, without straight-up copying the thesis. It is often effective to work on clever and powerful closing statements that will make the reader think about the issue.

Note: A kinesthetic extension of this activity is the hand-motion-accompanied chant called Claim-Support-Explain, which is described in the fifth-grade lesson in Chapter 7.

Argument Scale Graphic Organizer

This hands-on activity (Zwiers 2010) is an effective next-level activity to apply the skills developed in the previous activity, Back It Up. The organizer allows students to visualize and grasp the process of weighing reasons and evidence of two sides of an issue. They can use a two-dimensional visual or a three-dimensional one that they cut up from a template printed on 8.5-by-11-inch paper. Download either one from aldnetwork.org. For the 3D one, cut and fold it so it looks like the picture at the top of Figure 6.12. Cut on the solid lines and fold on the dotted lines. You should model this process with a large replica of the scale made out of construction paper.

PROCEDURE

1.   Each pair of students has their own balance scale and will add to both sides as they converse.

2.   Students write the issue in the center box and write each opposing position of the argument on each side.

3.   Decide on the most persuasive reasons and their evidence. Put each reason and its evidence on a separate card. Make large and small cards of two colors, one for each side. The larger boxes are for the most important or most valuable reasons and evidence for a side. Deciding which are largest prompts students to prioritize and compare reasons, a key thinking skill within this process. Factors and criteria used to generate reasons might include long-run versus short-run gains, financial

FIGURE 6.12

Argument scale organizer

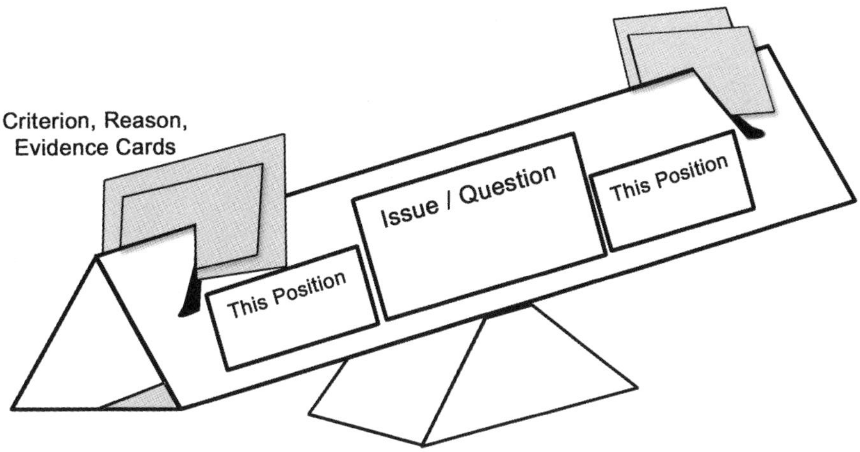

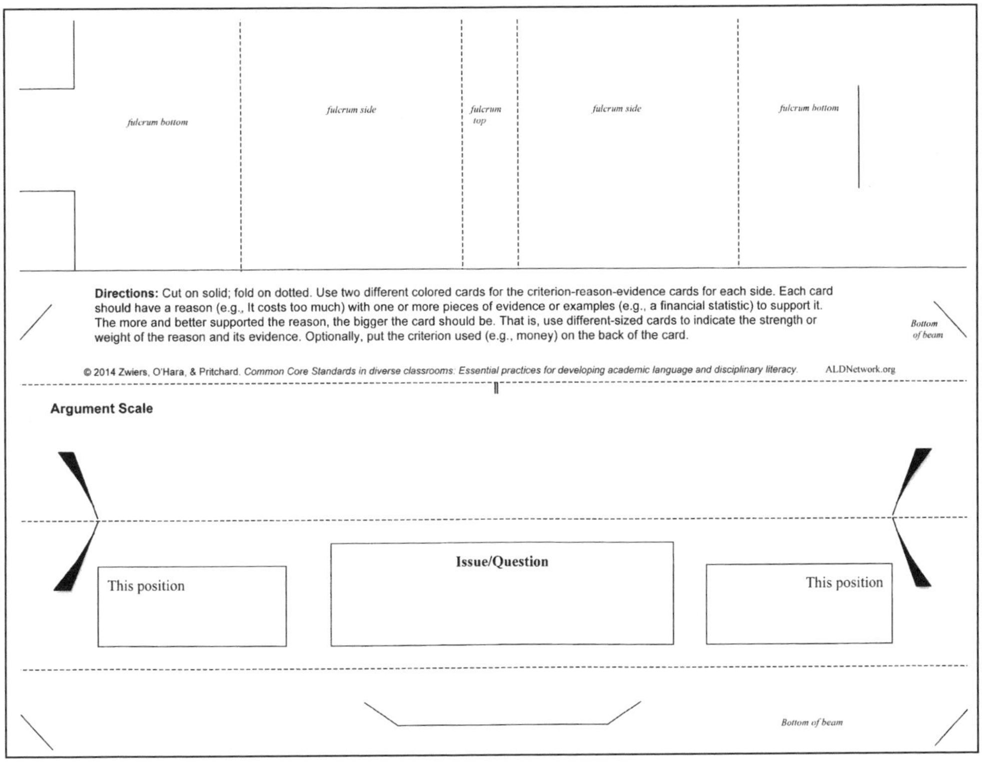

Criterion, Reason, Evidence Cards

This Position

Issue / Question

This Position

---

fulcrum bottom

fulcrum side

fulcrum top

fulcrum side

fulcrum bottom

Directions: Cut on solid; fold on dotted. Use two different colored cards for the criterion-reason-evidence cards for each side. Each card should have a reason (e.g., It costs too much) with one or more pieces of evidence or examples (e.g., a financial statistic) to support it. The more and better supported the reason, the bigger the card should be. That is, use different-sized cards to indicate the strength or weight of the reason and its evidence. Optionally, put the criterion used (e.g., money) on the back of the card.

Bottom of beam

© 2014 Zwiers, O'Hara, & Pritchard. *Common Core Standards in diverse classrooms: Essential practices for developing academic language and disciplinary literacy.* ALDNetwork.org

Argument Scale

This position

Issue/Question

This position

Bottom of beam

cost, risk, lives lost, ethics, freedom, environmental impact, future impact, health, culture, human rights, beliefs, human progress, etc.

4. Have students explain how a reason and its evidence weighs down the side the card is on. For example, if the criterion is money, then the reason might be that it will cost too much according to the evidence of other similar cases and their costs. Students should include the evidence that they have found in texts, which can include quotations and statistics.

5. Have students put the cards ("weights") on the scale, which will make it more or less balanced.

6. Students then compare related reasons on opposing sides and evaluate which one is more convincing and/or has the strongest evidence. For example, a student may have two weight cards with "High cost of incarceration" on one and "Rehabilitation programs are more effective" on the other. She may decide that the cost of incarceration is too high and that the money could be used for other rehabilitation programs. She should have some evidence for each card. If one of the reasons is found to be weaker, the pair might agree to tear a corner off to make it weigh less, thereby showing students that it is weaker.

7. Students come to some agreement and then use the ideas to write a persuasive essay.

Notice that this activity has students using complex texts, producing output, and interacting throughout the procedure (i.e., it could also have been in Chapters 4 and 8, but we just put it here to save paper).

❖ Connecting the Sentences

A student will not communicate well without being able to logically connect sentences. In every discipline we need to teach students how to best create and connect sentences. Here are a few ideas that we can use to help students with this skill.

- *Use transitions for certain text structures.* A transition tells readers what to do with the next piece of information and how to read a whole paragraph. Some transitions mark cause and effect (*therefore, as a result, due to*); some mark sequence (*first, then, later*); and some mark comparisons and contrasts (*on the other hand, then again, although, by contrast*).

- *Support with examples.* Another structure is providing a more general statement and supporting it with examples. For example, you might have just asked for an example as you read the previous sentence, and this sentence provides it. Or a student might write, *Literature teaches us how to live right. In* To Kill a Mockingbird, *Atticus takes the case even though he knows he will lose.* The student does not have to begin the sentence with *For example* if the sentence is specific enough and readers are expecting an example.

- *Use pronouns, nominalizations, and academic "labels."* A common way to connect sentences is with condensed terms that refer to previous ideas. A writer or speaker condenses the previous sentence or ideas into a single term. This technique (*technique* is a good example of a common academic label) allows writers to save space and not repeat ideas in a text. A nominalization, often preceded by the relative pronoun *this*, tends to be a noun created from the action in the previous sentence or paragraph: realization, escalation, misinterpretation, allegation, etc.

- *Use subordinate clauses with linking words.* Students must learn how to use subordinate clauses to link to previous sentences. For example, if a student wants readers to be cautious about using primary sources, she might write, *I think there was a lot of bias in primary sources during the time of the American Revolution.* She might then be coached to follow this statement with a complex sentence that begins with *Even though primary sources help us to better understand what really happened during the Revolution, we need to look for bias.* An easier subordinate clause to teach is one beginning with *Because. Because people were usually taking one side of the war, they wrote to convince others what they believed.* Notice how the subordinate clauses connect to ideas in the previous sentences.

- *Anticipate reader questions.* Another way to connect sentences is to anticipate what the reader will ask about the current sentence and answer it with the next sentence. If a student writes, *The human body is like an amazing machine,* we would want the student to follow this with answers to likely reader questions such as How? Like what machine? What are examples? How is it not like a machine?

Finally, it is very helpful to analyze how professional authors connect their ideas in the texts that we teach. Take a portion of text and go through it with students, looking at how sentences are connected with transitions, references, or other ways. Highlight ways to improve the connections or organization.

And finally, always prioritize meaning over grammar. The bulk of the skills for crafting and connecting sentences will not be learned from direct teaching but from extensive immersion in meaningful texts and conversations. Sure, we can weave in some of the ideas in this activity at strategic times, but they must be used to support clarity and meaning in engaging tasks, such as those described next.

STRAND 3 OF FORTIFYING COMPLEX OUTPUT: Develop Complex Language Abilities for and by Producing Multimedia Messages (MMM)

Output also includes producing multimedia texts such as images, posters, web pages, video, audio, and combinations of these. These days, high amounts of communication are visual or audio; just look at the many web pages that rely on combinations of images, video, audio, and written messages. Using new technologies in instruction can fortify students' communication skills as they produce their own multimodal texts. These tools can also promote the growth of cognitive skills and even metalinguistic awareness.

Through the use of new technologies, students can design digital and multimedia products and access information in interactive cyber learning environments, all of which encourage meaningful applications of new knowledge and language. Moreover, the improved use of these environments develops many of the twenty-first-century technology skills students need as they graduate from high school, enter postsecondary education programs, and work toward future careers (O'Hara and Pritchard 2009; Skinner 2007; Zhao 2003.)

Several effective applications of technology include the use of interactive whiteboards, podcasts, video, multimedia presentations, mobile technologies, and Voicethreads. Teaching students to use these technologies to communicate can provide academic English learners with the following:

- Contextualized, authentic, engaging ways to learn and show learning

- New ways for teachers to model complex language

- New opportunities for the formative assessment of complex language use

- Timely feedback

- Opportunities to interact with complex multimodal texts that incorporate linguistic scaffolds

- Opportunities to collaborate in the production of complex texts

- Scaffolds for making meaningful connections among text, images, video, sound, animation and annotations

- Tasks that help students to be more strategic learners (Zhao 2003; Hobbs and Frost 2003; Skinner 2007)

The teaching of language through multimedia is highly engaging for students. As a result, various language and literacy development needs can be addressed simultaneously by promoting the use of visually engaging and language-rich technologies. All of the following activities utilize technologies that can build multimodal communication skills to foster academic language and disciplinary literacy, and vice versa.

❖ Using Online Presentation and Feedback Applications

New technologies afford students the opportunities to develop their language skills in engaging activities that integrate communication skills. Interacting with technologies such as Voicethread (a free program available online at voicethread.com) fosters creative thinking, knowledge construction, and the development of innovative products and processes.

Remember that the overall goal should be the integration of complex language, technology, and the communication of content understandings. As you prepare the lesson, consider the following suggestions for selecting the appropriate technology: (1) choose a technology tool that helps students maximize their communication; (2) choose a tool that works within the reality of the technology your classroom, for example, number of computers that are available, Internet access, and so on; and (3) choose a tool that focuses on the overall goal of integrating complex language, technology, and content.

PROCEDURE

1. Show models of the presentations or projects that you are asking students to create.

2. Have groups choose one topic and outline what they want to communicate to others about it (e.g., a persuasive message, a solution to a problem, or its importance). See the classroom example that follows for specific ideas.

3. Ask the groups to work together to create their presentation that communicates the message to others. Encourage students to push themselves to use complex language in their oral exchanges and final product.

4. Have students engage in online annotation and discussions of each group's presentation.

CLASSROOM EXAMPLE

Mr. Dillon's eighth-grade social studies class is studying the origin and history of famous walls around the world. Mr. Dillon has his students analyze the implications that walls have had for global peoples and cultures. Students research a famous wall from around the world and communicate its significance to others through multimedia (e.g., Great Wall of

China, Berlin Wall, Belfast Falls Road Wall). As students work to complete their projects they use the following digital technologies: Internet research to access information about famous walls around the world, online communications to communicate with peers in other parts of the world to ask them about walls in their communities, image capturing and editing to take and edit pictures of walls within the local community, Voicethread design and development to create their final presentations, and video annotation.

Students compare and contrast walls from historical, political, and cultural perspectives. They also engage in online "conversation" by commenting on peer projects. The project allows and requires students to use complex language with one another and apply it within an authentic project connected to their lives.

❖ Hypermedia Authoring

Culminating hypermedia projects can be used to reinforce students' understanding of newly learned language as well as to assess their ability to use this language in authentic ways. Students can create hypermedia products at the end of a unit of study, where they use the key language in explaining the unit's key concepts, and create hyperlinks between these texts and different media used to represent their meaning. Having students work in pairs allows each student to be engaged in the creation of the slides, typing the report, and creating the hyperlinks, and still provides them with opportunities to communicate with another student.

PROCEDURES

1. Ask pairs to start by brainstorming how to create a multimedia product (e.g., web page or slide show) that explains each of the target concepts using images, text, scanned diagrams/drawings, and recorded sound bites. Before they continue, they share and explain their plan to you for input and feedback.

2. Ask student pairs to create hypermedia presentations incorporating multimedia components to represent their understanding of each target term or phrase. One idea for doing this is to set up a scanning station, recording station, and printing station for the class.

3. Students create text about their chosen topic to aid the communication. Ask student pairs to check in with you and provide them with feedback and suggestions for editing their project. They can also team up with one other pair of students and edit each other's work.

4. Finally, ask each pair to present their final hypermedia products highlighting each main idea and creating hyperlinks to the web pages and slides that further elaborate on and explain supporting idea.

CLASSROOM EXAMPLE

Mr. Collins's fifth-grade class has been learning about ecosystems. At the end of the unit Mr. C. wants to develop some activities to reinforce his students' understanding of the key academic terms and phrases and their underlying concepts. The culminating project for this unit is a hyperlinked report.

He gives the following directions: "You are a member of a research team hired by the World Wildlife Foundation. Your task is to go into the rain forest and research an endangered animal. Your team will create a report about this animal, the animal group it belongs to, its physical and behavioral characteristics, and why it is on the endangered list, and suggest how changes in its physical and behavioral characteristics would help it to survive. You will present the report to the foundation. The members of the foundation do not understand most of the terms and ideas on the list you will be given. When you use these ideas and terms in your report, you must create a link to a page that explains what each one means." Because they are using PowerPoint to create hyperlinks, the process allows them to simultaneously view the highlighted word in their report and the slide with their representation of the word.

❖ Creating Multimodal Texts in Mathematics

Building up communication skills is especially challenging in math class, where texts and teachers have traditionally simplified or avoided using large amounts of explanatory language for describing conceptual understandings. Much of the focus has been solving problems as quickly as possible. In this activity students create a web page that helps other students understand (not just get the answer) an important aspect or concept of math. Students must hone their discourse-dimension skills to put together a message that is as clear as possible for a wide audience of math students.

PROCEDURE

1. Show models of other web-based guides and videos. Highlight how images, videos, and language are combined to explain and clarify complex ideas (or how they can confuse readers).

2. In pairs, students sketch out the processes that they will try to teach with their online guide. You can have them explain the same concept but it is often effective

to have several concepts going on so that there are information gaps that students need to bridge as they learn from one another.

3. Students then write the transcript of the first screencast (video capture of what happens on a computer screen), podcast, or video (e.g., on a smartphone) that will be on the main page. Have them use language and strategies that you covered during the introductory modeling.

4. Students borrow images from the Internet and create their own images and diagrams. They take their own photographs or scan handmade drawings into the computer.

5. Students create screencasts, podcasts, or videos. They edit them and post them on the main page of their guide. This can become part of a larger guide that spans a semester or an entire year.

CLASSROOM EXAMPLE

The topic of study for Mr. Santini's ninth-grade algebra class is quadratic equations. Mr. S. would like for his students to be able to understand and explain the process for using quadratic equations (HSA-REI.B.4b), and apply quadratic equations to solve real-world problems. Academic language demands include using connected sentences, creating paragraphs with a logical order of ideas, and terms such as *equation, variable, squared, exponent, more than, less than, quadratic,* and *equal to.* For the main page of the guide, students will create podcasts explaining what a quadratic equation is and why learning to solve these equations is important. Mr. S. has them address different solution methods such as completing the square and using the quadratic formula. Students first produce a script of what they will record in the podcasts and in them highlight the key vocabulary and message structures that they will use. On linked pages students will explain how to solve other quadratic equations with different methods, creating short podcasts, videos, screencasts and/or written descriptions that provide a detailed account of the process involved.

Digital Storytelling

The development of multimodal stories can be engaging for students and can help scaffold the development of academic writing (Hobbs and Frost 2003; Skinner 2007). As students use images, video, animation, sound, and language to develop their stories, they learn to convey meaning and emotion through narration. Teachers can scaffold the writing of stories by explicitly making connections between the use of sounds, texts, and images, and the appropriate use of vocabulary, syntax, and discourse. As the language proficiency levels of students increase, teachers can require them to incorporate more text into their digital stories.

There are many applications for computers and tablets that help students create and share digital stories. Two examples are Photostory and Toontastic, which allow students to record their voices as they narrate stories and images. It is important to highlight seven key elements of digital storytelling: point of view, plot, emotion, focus, pacing, voice, and sound (Lambert 2002). These elements also help you to generate and clarify the criteria to use in assessing students' complex language development, their understandings of the ELA content, and technology use.

PROCEDURE

1. Model the process of brainstorming ideas for a story. Come up with characters, a plot, etc.

2. Organize the ideas into a storyboard with drawings and words. Explain the rationale for including or excluding certain parts. See Figure 6.13 for a sample template for a storyboard. Remind students about the elements of a story because they are about to become authors of original stories. Remind them that you want to see uses of target language in their stories and explanations.

3. Connect a tablet or computer to your projector or interactive whiteboard. Launch a storytelling application (e.g., Toontastic) and model how to use the technology to navigate through the creation of a story from the storyboard that incorporates images, drawings, text, narration, and sound.

4. Students brainstorm ideas for their own digital stories. Pair students and have them create a storyboard, together with a script, that outlines their personal stories and incorporates some target language. You can have students think about the purpose of their stories: teaching a theme, inspiring the audience, conveying emotion, etc.

5. Students choose the media components (photos, drawings, video, music) that they will incorporate into their stories. Optionally, you can allow learners at lower levels of language proficiency to record their narrated stories first and then use the narrated product as a scaffold for writing it down and adding it to the digital format.

6. In pairs, students can use a digital storytelling application to combine photos, narration, recorded audio narration, video clips, and music to create their

multimodal stories. Young students can go to stations, one of which has the teacher there to guide them in developing their stories.

7.   Students post them to ToonTube or present them to others in the class.

8.   Choose several model stories and engage the whole class in a discussion of how the images and sounds were used in each story to convey meaning and emotion.

9.   Students then work on their own to create their own digital stories.

10. As a part of peer editing, students work in small groups to respond to peers' stories and communicate their ideas of meaning and emotion in the stories.

CLASSROOM EXAMPLE

Mr. Garcia's first-grade students are learning how to describe elements of a story such as characters, settings, and major events (CCSS.ELA-Literacy.RL.1.3,7). After modeling the storyboarding of a story generated by the whole class, Mr. G. models how to use Toontastic to put the story into the tablet and illustrate it. He thinks aloud as he decides on which parts he will include and which parts he will leave out. He goes through the seven elements of digital storytelling. He highlights various language choices he makes, such as when he whispers or yells at times, depending on the part. He describes why he chooses suspenseful music at one point and how it influences the mood of the story. He has a student record her voice and inserts it into the story. He plays the final version and solicits comments and suggestions for editing the narration and the images. Students then produce their own storyboards and digital stories. Pairs share with other pairs and they take some time to edit the stories based on peer input. After they are done creating their stories, they create a final audio clip in which they describe the setting, characters, what they learned, how they changed, major events, and why they wrote the story.

CLASSROOM EXAMPLE

Mr. Johnson's high school English language development class is focusing on the development of figurative language in the context of narrative writing and the elements of compelling stories. Students create digital stories about how their heritage has shaped who they are as a teenager in the United States. Students interview family members about how they came to live in the United States and their experiences. They also collect photographs and/or short video clips from their local community and of their families. After collecting information, in pairs the students create a storyboard that tells their personal stories to one another. Mr. J. then asks students to convey emotions with figurative language. Students also use their selection of images, narration, and music to clarify the story for readers. They use the application Photostory to combine photos, narration, and music as they create their multimodal stories. Upon completion of these projects, students share with the entire class. Mr. J. chooses two student examples and engages the class in a discussion of how the images and sounds were used in each story to convey meaning and emotion. He highlights the figurative language. Students are then asked to work in small groups to generate explanations of figurative expressions used.

Strengthening Common Activities for Fortifying Complex Output

A core purpose of this book is to build the habit of using and modifying existing activities, lessons, and assessments to maximize student learning of complex language and literacy.

Most of the commonly used practices and activities, such as the ones in Figure 6.14, can be effective, but they usually can stand some extra tweaking to maximize students' abilities to produce complex output. For example, many output activities do not bridge information gaps or do not allow enough authentic or augmenting practice of new language. We should always have the lingering question in mind: How can this activity help build students' independence in communicating clear, complete, and complex academic ideas?

FIGURE 6.14

Common activities, limitations, and ways to modify them for higher-quality output

COMMON PRACTICE OR ACTIVITY	COMMON LIMITATIONS	HOW TO STRENGTHEN THE ACTIVITY TO BUILD COMPLEX OUTPUT SKILLS INTO AND FROM IT
Student presentations	• If all read about the same topic, most of the students already know what is being presented. • Student audience has short attention span when only listening.	• Have students present on topics not known to other students. • Have audience take notes on a graphic organizer and/or do something with the information. • Show and analyze the language of model oral presentations. • Students practice multiple times.
Written essays	• Students have seen few good models of student-level writing. • The audience is only the teacher who is grading it.	• Show and analyze models of good student essays. Model how to improve not-so-good essays. • Have students write for peers, parents, other adults at the school, and adults or students outside the school.
Sentence starters and frames	• Looking at sentence frames during presentation or answering questions can make it inauthentic or unoriginal. • Language in them is not always understood.	• Students practice the frames with different groups and the teacher; they then try to use the frames without looking at them. • Analyze the frame for the skill or function that it is communicating and focus on that skill . . . then add the language to it.
Graphic organizers for writing	• Students can focus on filling in the spaces of graphic organizers at the expense of thinking and communicating and developing and negotiating ideas.	• Have students talk about the ideas before, during, and after they fill in the graphic organizers. • Make sure they know why they are using a particular graphic organizer; i.e., what function it serves. For example, they should be able to explain how a Venn diagram shows comparison.
Pair-shares and turn-and-talks	• Pair-shares can lack quality in the use of complex language. • There is often no information gap (no need for listeners to listen).	• Make sure students know the difference between pair-shares, which focus on output, and interactions (Chapter 8), which focus on back-and-forth building of ideas. • Have students take silent time to think of their sentences and how they will connect them, before sharing. • Have them respond to two different prompts and then paraphrase what they heard.

Summary

Fortifying output skills helps students put their ideas into words, sentences, paragraphs, and whole messages. We fortify output not only for the sake of helping students get better at communicating, but also to build their language abilities and content understandings. This chapter has provided many activities that can be strategically woven into lessons across disciplines. The next chapter describes four annotated lessons that more deeply describe how teachers can build students' abilities to communicate through speaking, writing, and multimedia products.

CHAPTER 7

Lessons Focused on Fortifying Complex Output

I learned more than anyone from that explanation—even though I was the one who gave it.

This chapter describes the second lessons for each of the series of lessons started in Chapter 5. The four lessons in this chapter emphasize practices and activities that teachers use to fortify students' abilities to produce complex output. This chapter also focuses on what we might call "short outputs," which means oral and written output that students use to communicate their ideas to accomplish tasks. This is different from long, "end-product outputs," which consist of larger tasks like essays, posters, and presentations that tend to be summative performance tasks at the end of a unit. We wanted to show how teachers can build students' skills for producing meaningful output, with a particular emphasis on clear and complete oral communication, throughout a lesson or unit. These lessons show how teachers help students fortify their output not just to show learning of language and content, but also to reinforce and expand it. So in the following lessons, look for ways in which teachers integrate the three strands (oral, written, multimedia) to develop students' abilities to communicate complex ideas across disciplines.

Also notice how teachers do not overdo sentence frames and starters. When working on academic language development, sentence starters must be used just enough-ly. We need to find the delicate balance between providing models of the language for students to practice and overdoing them so much that it bogs down real communication and engagement.

Second-Grade Math: Lesson 2

OBJECTIVES

In Lesson 1 (in Chapter 5), Ms. Stevens began teaching students how to understand word problems and use multiple representations to solve them. She continues with the focal content standard, CCSS.2.OA.A.1: "Use addition and subtraction within 100 to solve one- and two-step word problems involving situations of adding to, taking from, putting together, taking apart, and comparing, with unknowns in all positions, e.g., by using drawings and equations with a symbol for the unknown number to represent the problem." Today's content objective is to solve two-step problems with unknowns at the end position, and describe reasons for methods used.

Ms. S. continues to develop her English learners' mastery of the 2012 WIDA ELD Grade 2 Standard 3 (p. 60): "Students at all levels of English language proficiency will ANALYZE text of word problems." Ms. S. uses the descriptions of the five different proficiency levels to help her differentiate the challenges that she gives to students as they talk and write about the problems. The five levels of performance indicators are functions of matching, finding, sequencing, locating clues, and categorizing. These functions are woven into the lesson's prompts and tasks.

Ms. S. also highlights the mathematical practice objectives of the day: CCSS.Math. Practice.MP2: "Reason abstractly and quantitatively"; and CCSS.Math.Practice.MP4: "Model with mathematics." Language objectives for these CCSS mathematical practices include being able to connect sentences and describe the drawings using *in order to, equation, describe, reason, compare,* and *visualize.* A final language objective is for students to be able to use appropriate language to clarify math scenarios as they write their own problems.

INTRODUCTION

After briefly going over the objectives, Ms. S. begins the lesson by connecting the key ideas and skills learned the day before. She reminds students of how they used different ways to read problems and looked at how the authors use language to set up math situations. Ms. S. has pairs come up with a simple word problem like they solved yesterday.[1] Ana dictates it and Ms. S. writes it on the board: "A boy had 22 candies. He gave some to his friends. Then he looked in his pocket. He only has 5 now. How many did he give away?"

Ms. S.:   OK, now tell each other how to read a word problem.[2] You can use Ana's problem for an example. You might say, "First you find the beginning numbers. For example, in the candy problem up there, the beginning number is 22 . . ."[3]

[1] Ms. S. has students create a problem that connects to what they did yesterday.

[2] Ms. S. prompts students to explain literacy strategies for math problems.

[3] Ms. S. provides linked language stems to scaffold talk. Both students then use "For example . . ."

(Students converse in pairs.)

Lena: Well, you look at the numbers at the beginning. . . . For example, 22.

Asha: Then you look for what changes. For example, the boy gave away some, but we don't know how many.

Lena: Then we look at the end. For example, the boy ends with 5. . . .

LAUNCH

The launch problem for today connects to yesterday's lesson and provides a more challenging (two-step vs. one-step) problem. There are two changes rather than one, and the problem is longer. The problem is up on the board. Ms. S. reads it, acts it out, and has her students act it out as they all read it again:[4] *David was climbing a rope up a cliff. He was at 50 feet. Suddenly, his hands slipped and he slid back down 20 feet! He climbed another 25 feet up and was too tired to go on. How high was he when he stopped to rest?*

Ms. S: OK, class, picture what happens as you read the problem silently. Think about it for a minute. Think about what you will say. Now tell your first partner what happened. Remember what your partner says, because you can use their ideas and language when you talk to your second partner.[5]

[4] Ms. S. acts out the problem to help students visualize the changes. They act it out to reinforce meanings.

(In pairs)

Carla: I don't know. I think we subtract cuz that's what we did in that candy problem.

Kylia: We are supposed to describe what is happening. So the guy goes up, then slips down, then goes up again. There are two changes. Right?

[5] Ms. S. reminds students that they will augment their ideas and language for their second conversation.

(They switch partners.)

Carla: *(To Kevin)* We need to find out how high he is at the end. Two changes. Maybe going up is add and going down, he slipped, is subtract. You know, minus it.[6]

Kevin: Hmmm. Yes. That sound right. Juan said we just add 'em all up. But I think cuz of slipping down, we can't do that. So to make it less, we gotta subtract.

[6] Carla augments her response in the second exchange based on what she hears in her first exchange.

Carla: But then we need to add again.

(Back in whole-class format)

Ms. S.:   Nice warm-up! Can someone give me their final idea that builds on others?

Carla: In order to find how high he is, we start with the beginning, 50. Then cuz he slips down, we need to subtract. But then he goes up so we add.[7]

Ms. S.:   Great. Carla saw that *climbing* the hill was positive and that meant adding. And *slipping* was[8] . . . *(Students: "Minus, subtraction, less")* What is the opposite of positive? Neg . . . *(Students: "Negative").* And *negative* usually means to subtract. So what do we do in this problem? It is different from the problem yesterday. After thinking for a moment in silence, start to tell your partner with, "In order to find out how high he climbed . . ."

[7] Carla shares a clear explanation with the whole class after practicing with two partners.

[8] Ms. S. points out that words can mean mathematical processes to help solve the problem.

EXPLORATION

In this stage of the lesson, the teacher provides time for students to work on the problem and verbalize their understandings and ideas to others. Students explore and experiment with ways to solve the problem and then give reasons. Students who finish early work on a similar problem or create their own. Ms. S. reminds students to give good reasons for what they think they should do. As students talk, Ms. S. listens in for misconceptions and strong responses.[9] She supports students in putting sentences together to create logical ideas.

Nayra: To find out high he climbed, we draw. Look at this. He's at 50 feet.

Pablo: Then he fall down. We can't add cuz that's, 5 plus 2, . . . 70. He does not fall up. So 50 minus 20, right?

Nayra: That's 30. We're done.

Pablo: No. He climb up after slip down. So 50 plus 25.

Nayra: No.

Ms. S.:   Nayra and Pablo, when you disagree, explain why. Try starting with something like, "I disagree because . . ."[10]

[9] Ms. S. monitors understandings and clarity of explanations throughout the lesson.

[10] Ms. S. intervenes to prompt students to respectfully disagree and justify their ideas.

Nayra: I disagree cuz he slips and is up 30 feet now, not 50. Then he climb up. So we add. So we do 30 plus 25.

Ms. S.: Did that make sense, Pablo? *(Nods head.)* Yes, that was a clear explanation. And you used more than one sentence and connected them with *then* and *so*.[11]

> [11] Ms. S. validates the use of multiple connected sentences to explain math ideas.

DISCUSSION

In this stage, the teacher focuses on helping students generate and understand the mathematical expressions for the word problems.

Ms. S.: If I want to write this with numbers and symbols, what might be the equation for this problem? Remember the numbers and the box we used yesterday? Think about it and then share your idea with a partner. Try to use the language of the problem like *climb, slip*. Explain what these words mean as you point to what you have written.[12] *(Wait time.)* OK, let's do this together.

> [12] Ms. S. focuses students on connecting the words to the numbers and symbols of the equation.

Alex: I put 50 minus 30 plus 25 equals an empty box.

Ms. S.: Do we agree? OK. Now let's write some sentences around Alex's equation. "He started at 50 feet up." *(She draws an arrow from the sentence to the 50.)* "He slipped down 30 feet so we subtract 30" *(arrow to − 30).* "Then because he climbed up again 25 feet, we add 25 feet" *(arrow to + 25). The answer is how many feet up he ended his climb (arrow to empty box).*[13] Oh, and what's the answer? Fifty-five feet, in the box. Great. Now it's your turn.

> [13] Ms. S. models the language and thinking she uses to explain going from the text to the math symbols in the equation; she emphasizes CCSS MP2 and MP4, reasoning abstractly, and modeling.

PRACTICE

Ms. S. provides time for students to work on a new, similar problem and practice speaking and writing their understandings of how to solve it. The new problem is *A leaky fish tank had 15 gallons in it. Karin put 5 gallons in to fill it up. The fish were happy. But when she looked the next day, 12 gallons had leaked out! How many gallons were left?*

Ms. S.: Remember to look at the beginning and the changes in the problem. You can draw it if you want. I also want the math equation and the sentences that point to each part, like we just modeled. Remember to explain your ideas. See if you can read it on your own and think about it before you explain it to your partner.[14]

> [14] Ms. S. pushes students to read and think more independently before collaborating.

(Silent time, then partner shares)

Miguel: The beginning is 15. Here on tank. Not full.

Lisa: Yeah. So 15. Then fill it up. That's add. That's 5. So it's 15 plus 5.

Miguel: But 12 leaked. That is bad, like minus, subtract. Right? So little lines for gallons. 1, 2, 3, 4, 5 . . .

Lisa: No, we need to do the equation.[15] So, 15 plus 5 minus 12 equals we don't know. So a empty box. Now we have to write around it. . . .

[15] Lisa focuses the conversation back on the strategy (generating an equation) that the teacher used.

(Whole-group format)

Ms. S.:   I saw some great thinking and heard some clear explanations. Now when you finish the tank problem, I want you and your partner to come up with a similar problem with different names and numbers and objects. It should have two changes. They can be different, like subtraction and addition, or they can be the same. Remember that it should have a beginning situation, a middle where things change, and a final question about what happened.[16] You will share them with your classmates.

[16] Ms. S. has students create their own problems, using today's problems as models of the math and language, to share with classmates the next day.

CONCLUSION

Ms. S. refers to the content and language objectives of the day and reminds students how they analyzed changes in a problem and used different ways to solve them to get the same answer. She tells students that they will need to use their math skills and their talking skills tomorrow to be able to have effective conversations about math problems.

Fifth-Grade Language Arts: Lesson 2

OBJECTIVES

Ms. Flores continues to teach her students how to identify and explain themes in a short story. The focal standard is CCSS ELA-Literacy.RL.5.2: "Determine a theme of a story, drama, or poem from details in the text, including how characters in a story or drama respond to challenges or how the speaker in a poem reflects upon a topic; summarize the text." The content objective is the same as in Lesson 1: Determine the theme(s) of a short story based on character actions and words, and support ideas from the text.

Ms. F. continues to use the California ELD Standards (2012) focused on supporting ideas by using the text, CA-ELD.5.2.I.11: "Support opinions or persuade others by expressing appropriate and accurate reasons using textual evidence."

With today's emphasis on oral and written output, Ms. F. reflects on the thinking and language that is needed for the output related to this objective. She realizes that students need to practice using some of yesterday's language of interpretation, of supporting ideas with evidence, and of explaining how the evidence is warranted. Target language includes terms such as *infer, represent, theme, illustrate, message,* and *symbolize,* as well as message-organizing strategies such as explaining warrants with relevant and logically linked sentences.

INTRODUCTION AND CONNECTIONS

After presenting the day's objectives, Ms. F. connects to student backgrounds by asking them to look at the lyrics of a popular song and consider the possible theme. She then offers a non-model to show students that support and explanation are needed.

Ms. F.: First, let's connect to what we did yesterday. I want you to get out your theme cards and sticky notes and quickly share with a partner the theme that you interpreted for this story. Say as much as you can in your time slot. Student A, start. *(Waits 30 seconds.)* Student B, go. *(Waits 30 seconds.)* OK, a quick share out—share your partner's idea.[1]

> [1] Ms. F. warms up students' output muscles and connects to yesterday's learning. She uses timed talking to push students to practice putting academic utterances together, and to listen.

Kiera: I think the theme was keep working hard for your dreams. Like Francisco and learning English.

Kim: I think the theme was to be like a butterfly. Like Francisco changed.

(Whole class)

Ms. F.: I heard some themes and some evidence. We should always be looking for themes to help us improve how we live and who we are. Remember that there are themes in all kinds of media: stories like "Inside Out," TV shows, movies, poems, novels, pictures, and songs. Now let's look at the verses of a popular song. *(Reads lyrics aloud.)* What do you think the theme is?

	Tell your partner. (*Wait time.*) Now my turn . . . I think the theme of the song is that love is worth the risks. In verse two she sings, "I might lose my whole world, but a new sun might bloom." *(Waits.)* Now, did I say enough? What more should I add?[2]

[2] Ms. F. models an incomplete example to show students what is often missing in oral and written work on themes.

Samuel:	You could say more, like explain more. Say why you think that.

Ms. F.:	Yes. Yesterday and in previous lessons we worked on supporting ideas for theme with evidence; and today we'll work on ways to make our ideas stronger when we share them with others.[3] We'll work on explaining why it is good evidence for the theme we share. This is the explain part of a new Claim-Support-Explain chant that we will use.

[3] Ms. F. uses the modeling to introduce students to a strategy for overcoming the lack of explanations in many messages about theme or in other forms of argumentation.

NEW LEARNING

In this stage, the teacher models and provides input for the new concepts and focal skills of the lesson, such as explaining evidence and expressing it with oral and written output. She models the use of the theme cards and evidence on sticky notes and explaining them. She has students coach one another to produce high-quality oral and written output. She observes to formatively assess and make adjustments as needed.

Ms. F.:	One way to help us express this like experts is the little chant, Claim, Support, Explain. Chant it and act it out with me.[4] Claim is your idea for the theme or an argument. It is your view or position. Put your fist out and down, like planting a flag, and say it, Claim. Support is the evidence or data that you use to support the claim. Put your other hand under your fist to support it. Explain is your explanation of how the evidence strongly supports your claim. Move both hands toward your face to take a closer look. Let's try it again. Now if I have a theme on my card like—let me borrow Alba's, do you mind? Her theme is: We need to be patient like caterpillars. Now let's look at her evidence: Francisco stays in school; he dreams of becoming a butterfly; he learns some English and feels better; he proudly carries his blue ribbon. I then choose what I think is strong evidence. So, my claim (*fist out and down*) is "The main theme of the story is that we

[4] Ms. F. introduces a chant with kinesthetic motions to clarify the ideas and language of claim, support, and explanation (warrant).

need to be patient like caterpillars. Evidence from the text that supports this is when Francisco stays in school even though he has problems and can't understand. This is my support (*hand under fist*). This is strong evidence because, even though he had many challenges like not knowing English and the fight, he stays and learns. This shows patience (*both hands in close*). This is the key objective of today's lesson, to be able to explain how the evidence supports the theme.[5] Now you try it in partners.

[5] Ms. F. models with a student-generated example and connects back to the language objective of the lesson.

Juan: I think maybe the one about the ribbon is strong evidence. Francisco is proud and he feels good about giving it.

Elia: Evidence is like butterflies show off; they are kinda proud of their colors, right? Francisco was patient and even had a hard time, then came out of it happy, kinda like a butterfly.

Juan: Another evidence is maybe Francisco stays in school. It helps the theme cuz it shows patience. He was like caterpillar in the jar. He waited and then turned into a happy boy.[6]

[6] Juan builds on Elia's idea of patience and the butterfly; he makes a metaphorical comparison to explain the theme.

PRACTICE

In this stage, the teacher provides practice time and support as needed. They engage in the output activity, the interview grid, in which they share and support their ideas for the theme of the story "Inside Out." Students make four columns and four rows. They put NAMES at the top of the first column and THEME at the top of the second column; they put EVIDENCE in the third column and EXPLANATION at the top of the fourth column. This activity also prepares them for the final short writing task.

Ms. F.: OK, now I want you to take a minute and look at your own theme cards and evidence notes to choose your strong evidence. You will describe your claim, support, and explanation of how it supports your theme. Now I would like you to use some academic language here. First, you can start your claim sentence with "An important theme of this story is . . ." Then you might start your support sentence with "Strong evidence of this theme is . . ." For the explanation I want you to connect to the sentence before. You might start with a verb with *–ing, This,* or *When.*[7] OK, if Tony is my partner, here is my model answer for the story, with hand motions: "An important theme of this story is to talk instead of fight (*fist out and down*). Strong evidence is Curtis and the fight (*hand under fist*). When Curtis attacked, he didn't ask Francisco first (*brings fist and hand close to face*)."[8] Tony quickly writes a few words for my theme and checks off when I provide evidence and an explanation in the third and fourth columns. Now Tony shares his theme, I take notes, and then I move on to talk with Alba. This time I share a longer and stronger answer: "An important theme in this story is to avoid fighting by talking things out. Strong evidence that supports this theme is when Curtis starts fighting without finding out how Francisco got his jacket. Not talking about the problem caused the fight, which made everyone upset."[9] Notice that I made "not talking" into the subject of my last sentence. Now, take a moment to organize your own answer. See if you can connect the sentences in your mind. (*Wait time.*) Now, you need to tell three different partners and write the theme they say and check off if they provide evidence and explanation. Help them if they need it. Each time you talk with a new partner, you need to make your answer longer and stronger than the one before. Use the language and ideas from your previous partners to build up your own.[10] And use the hand motions, if you want.

Alexis:	I think the theme is to learn English (*fist out*). Because the kid doesn't know it and needs to (*hand under fist*). Know English . . .
Daniel:	Knowing English.[11]
Alexis:	Oh yeah. Knowing English helped him make friends (*hands in close*).
Daniel:	I think the theme of this story is to be patient and keep trying. He is like the caterpillar, you know. Then he learns some English and flies.

[7] Ms. F. pushes students to connect evidence and explanation sentences; provides authentic oral practice of these.

[8] Ms. F. models the connected sentences with the hand motions to reinforce the abstract idea of explaining how evidence supports claims.

[9] Ms. F. models the connected sentences with two student partners to show how to build up one's oral output.

[10] Another way to organize the switching of partners is to use conversation lines or rotating circles. One line or circle moves.

[11] Daniel, a more proficient speaker, models the correct way to make a verb the subject of a sentence.

Alexis: He doesn't really fly, but he feels happy.

(Partners switch.)

Oscar: I think the theme is don't judge a book by its cover. For evidence, Francisco is smart inside but the kids don't know it cuz they just speak English. When they see he is nice, they like him. Like the title, "Inside Out."

Alexis: I think the theme is being patient for good things. The caterpillar is patient to become a butterfly. Evidence is Francisco waits to learn English and make friends. Wait . . . waiting to learn English helped Francisco make more friends and feel happy.[12]

[12] Alexis borrows ideas and language for a new theme; he learns to use the verb with *-ing* as the subject of the explanation sentence.

CONCLUSION

In this stage, the teacher wraps up the learning by giving students the task of writing their thoughts down using their best language. This written output is a way to solidify and organize the oral output practice.

Ms. F.:   To finish up, we can practice putting our thoughts into writing. I will model this up front, starting with a theme sentence, then an example sentence, then an explanation sentence. I will write these out for us, too: "An important theme of the story 'Inside Out' is to be yourself, even if you are different. An example from the story is when Francisco makes up stories in his mind. Making up stories shows that he is creative and unique, even though he didn't understand what the teacher read out loud." Notice the third sentence where I used the –ing form, the gerund, of the verb from sentence two.[13] . . . Now try it on your own. You can finish it or polish it up as homework. *(She circulates for several minutes.)* And many of you will want to put this theme work on your blog pages.[14] I can see that we improved a lot in our objective of explaining evidence for themes. We will use these skills and ideas tomorrow as we have constructive conversations.

[13] Ms. F. further models how to connect the sentences and pushes students to use gerunds to connect sentences.

[14] Ms. F. does a final formative assessment round and reminds them of an ongoing multimedia use for this work.

Eighth-Grade Science: Lesson 2

OBJECTIVES

Mr. Escobar continues to build on the previous lesson in which students learned about kinetic and potential energy as well as energy transfer. This lesson further reinforces, with the hands-on building of models and data gathering, the focal Next Generation Science Standards from Lesson 1: "Develop a model to describe that when the arrangement of objects interacting at a distance changes, different amounts of potential energy are stored in the system" (MS-PS3-2); and "Construct, use, and present arguments to support the claim that when the kinetic energy of an object changes, energy is transferred to or from the object" (MS-PS3-2). Focal NGSS science practices include asking questions and defining problems, developing and using models, planning and carrying out investigations, analyzing and interpreting data, constructing explanations and designing solutions, and engaging in argument from evidence.

Mr. E. continues to use the 2012 WIDA ELD Standard 4 for Grade 8 (p. 97): "Students at all levels of English language proficiency will ANALYZE energy transfer." Mr. E. uses the five leveled performance indicators to help him differentiate the challenges he gives to students as they build and explain their models.

To support the development of communication skills content, Mr. E. emphasizes two Common Core speaking standards: "Present claims and findings, emphasizing salient points in a focused, coherent manner with relevant evidence, sound valid reasoning, and well-chosen details; use appropriate eye contact, adequate volume, and clear pronunciation" and "Integrate multimedia and visual displays into presentations to clarify information, strengthen claims and evidence, and add interest" (CCSS.ELA-Literacy.SL.8.4-5). The main language objective is to explain the relationships between what is happening in the model and the designs that students are proposing.

INTRODUCTION AND CONNECTIONS

Mr. E. starts the lesson by going over the content and language objectives for the day's lesson. He explains to students that they will be learning more about how energy transfers and then apply this knowledge to their designs of the amusement park rides. They will also be making models.

Mr. E.:   All right. Who wants to fall 100 meters in a cage? Who wants to save as much energy as possible? Today we will make some models but also focus on how to communicate what is going on orally and in writing.

Scientists and engineers, like all of you, are smart, but sometimes they aren't clear and clarity is important, especially if it involves four people in a falling cage, right?[1] So, today you will build models with a metal box like this, and a meter stick. But first, let's do some review. Tell a partner what kinetic and potential energy are, examples of each, and examples of how energy is transferred. Extra credit for a description of where the energy from this lightbulb originally came from. This is a good chance to add information with a *which* clause, which is a strategy we are focusing on this year.[2]

Chelsea: Potential energy is stored, like gravity if you are way up on a hill.

Maria: Kinetic is moving, like a car. So for transfer, drive up the hill and stop. You make transfer kinetic to potential cuz it can roll down *sin* gas. Which is kinetic again.[3]

(Whole class)

Mr. E.: Three, two, one. All right, what did we come up with?

Calvin: The lightbulb shines light. That's a wave, which is kinetic. It comes from electricity, which is kinetic. The electricity comes from turbines run by water at the dam, which is kinetic. The water comes from bein' stored up high, which is potential. It gets up there from evaporation and rain, kinetic, from the sun's rays, kinetic.

Mr. E.: Well done, and nice use of *which* clauses, Calvin.[4] OK. So we see how energy is transformed in a variety of ways. We will now use this knowledge as we build our models. But first I want you to review your notes from our brainstorm design session at the end of yesterday's class. You will also need to talk with your team about which features, like solar power, wind turbines, springs, etc., you want to incorporate into your final design and into the model. I want to see a drawing before I hand out materials for your models.

[1] Mr. E. emphasizes the importance of being clear when describing ideas in science.

[2] Mr. E. reminds students to practice their yearlong focus on adding information with *which* clauses to clarify science explanations.

[3] Maria grasps the content despite her "imperfect" grammar. (Activities like these are effective ways to improve proficiency.)

[4] Mr. E. provides positive feedback on Calvin's use of clauses during his explanation.

NEW LEARNING

In this stage, Mr. E. starts students on their building of models to test and articulate their design ideas. The models should include labels of the areas of types of potential and kinetic energy using appropriate complex language. With the day's focus on output, Mr. E. has students share ideas and rationales in complete and connected sentences. He also uses one group's idea to do a quick mini-lesson helpful to all students.

Mr. E.:	All right. The model. On this meter stick, 1 centimeter represents 1 meter. In your teams, create a scale model of your design. Use materials from this table or ask for anything that might help. Remember that I will be listening for how well you explain the transformations of energy in your model. Sara might explain to Juan, "The kinetic energy from the wind resistance on the turbines is transformed into electric energy, which is also kinetic. This energy then goes to a battery and is transformed into chemical energy, which is potential." Notice how I connected the sentences with *This energy* and how I used *which* at the end of both sentences.[5]

(In teams)

Griselda:	We need to put the trampoline under; we can use rubber bands.
Mr. E.:	So, what happens to the energy?
Griselda:	Oh, it transfers. It's from kinetic to elastic.
Mr. E.:	Which is . . .[6]
Griselda:	Which is potential.
David:	Elastic is potential when it's tight, right? Then it shoots it up so it turns back into motion, which is kinetic.
Mr. E.:	Right, but it doesn't go all the way back up, right? What happens?
Eric:	It loses energy. From wind and sound and friction, I think.
Mr. E.:	I would like you to figure out how much energy is saved by your trampoline, roughly. So what can you do? Hold on. Everyone might benefit.[7] *(He hands out*

[5] Mr. E. models how one student could use connected sentences to explain the energy transformations in the designs.

[6] Mr. E. provides and prompts for Griselda's use of *which* to better explain (and remember) what is happening.

different types of balls to all teams.) All right. Remember the ball drop? Many of you have a way to propel your cage back up to save energy for the next ride, right? The ball drop can help us.[8] Drop the ball from one meter and measure how high it bounces. What happens with the energy?

Darla: Potential then kinetic and then turns into elastic from the bounce.

Eric: Then back to kinetic and then to potential.

Mr. E.: Wow! All that from dropping a ball? Let me draw this on the board. Now, can you be a little clearer in how you describe the transformations? And show us up here as you explain.[9]

Darla: At one meter the ball has potential energy from me lifting it. When I drop the ball, the potential energy turns into kinetic energy. Then, that energy turns into elastic energy when it squishes, just before it starts back up from its bounce, see?

Mr. E.: So now, for some fun, let's figure out the numbers. Kevin, can you explain what you were doing to find the potential energy?

Kevin: In the book, the formula is weight times height. This softball weighs 2 newtons and bounced up to .4 of a meter. So that is .8 joules, right?

Mr. E.: OK, what does .8 joules represent? Connect your sentences. Start with "After dropping the ball from 1 meter . . ."[10]

Kevin: OK. After the ball dropped from 1 meter, it bounced back up to .4 of a meter. This bounce is . . . represents .8 joules, which is energy saved, which is potential.

Mr. E.: Well done. Now I want all groups to figure this out with the different ball that you dropped. *(Group work time)* Now practice what you will say about the energy of your group's ball drop. You will share with three consecutive partners from different groups. You will say your description three different times, so it should

[7] Mr. E. realizes that an extra teaching activity for this group should be shared with the whole class. He refers to yesterday's opening activity and has all students now join in.

[8] Mr. E. is essentially using a model (ball drop) for a model (ride model) and having students compare them.

[9] Mr. E. has Darla fortify her explanation in a more scientific way, using the graphic support to aid the explanation.

[10] Mr. E. prompts Kevin to fortify his explanation by using connected sentences and an academic sentence starter. Notice that Mr. E. prompts and provides, beforehand, but does not correct students' grammar as they speak.

improve over time. And feel free to borrow ideas and language from partners.[11] (*Three successive pair-shares*) What did you end up with? Chelsea?

Chelsea: Our group dropped a basketball. It weighs 6 newtons. It bounces up to 0.6 meters. The gravitational potential energy at the top of the bounce was 3.6 joules.

Mr. E.: OK. Now everyone describe how you might use what you just learned for your designs and your scale models. If you don't have a system that uses elastic energy to propel the cage back up, work with a group that does.

(In teams)

Sherie: We can bounce the box up and measure how high it goes up the meter stick, like we did with the ball.

Alicia: But then we need to multiply, right? For the real thing.

Alemu: Yeah. By a lot cuz the real cage is heavy.[12]

Mr. E.: *(To everyone)* Now continue with your models and calculating the energy lost and gained. Some formulas are in the book. I can help you, if needed.

[11] Mr. E. has students practice their explanations alone and then do an augmenting repetition activity to build up their ideas by talking to three different partners.

[12] Students start to realize and describe the comparisons between the models and what they represent.

PRACTICE

Mr. E. circulates and sees students with solar panels, wind turbines, trampolines, rubber straps, "generators" to produce energy from the fall, and batteries to store energy. One group has a buoyant cylinder that falls into a deep tank of water and floats the cage back up. For this stage, Mr. E. has students prepare the descriptions of their designs. They explain what their cage and other mechanisms will do to use and save energy.

Mr. E.: OK, now that many of you are almost done with your models, it's time to start preparing the presentation. Prepare note cards for your oral presentations to the amusement park companies. Each member of your team will present to a different company, so you must all prepare. Focus the note cards on the energy transformations, their numbers, safety, and thrill factors. Feel free to use graphical representations representing the potential and kinetic energy types in the system. Here is a sample card: "One advantage of our design is the energy saved by our solar panel feature. On a sunny day, the photovoltaic cells produce 900 watts. We store this in a battery to use for lifting the cage. . . ."[13]

(Teams work.)

Allie: What do we put on the card? Like we could put it's a vantage to use the big rubber bands.

Jon: And the gravity energy potential that it saves, like we just did. The box went up to 25 centimeters.

Lupe: Five newtons times .25 meter. It's gravity energy 1.25 joules. It's good energy.

Allie: But this is just the model. What is the real number?[14]

Lupe: We gotta multiply. By what? *(Silence)*

Mr. E.: The real cage is 1,000 kilograms, which is around 10,000 newtons. So if the real rubber band system lifts the cage a similar percentage of the original height as your model, what do you get?[15]

Lupe: It would go up 25 meters, no? So . . . 25 times 10,000. That's 250,000 joules.

Jon: Oh yeah. So we put "A big advantage is our rubber band system for catching the cage and bouncing it back up. We calculate that this will save 250,000 joules for each ride."

Mr. E.: Draw it and clarify to one another what happens with the energy transfers. You will need this to show what you know.[16]

(Whole class)

Mr. E.: All right. As a final step, I want you to meet with your 9 o'clock partner and use your cards to make a pitch for your design. A pitch is a persuasive argument. Don't read directly from the cards! You will trade roles after 2 minutes.[17] For example, you might start with, "I want to show you how our ride will save your company money in energy. An important feature is our trampoline system. It costs 12 dollars to lift the

[13] Mr. E. has students write their ideas with connected sentences on note cards for a real-world-like purpose. This also requires students to evaluate which ones are most convincing and support them. He provides a model card with connected sentences.

[14] Allie pushes the group to use the ideas from the model and apply them to figuring out what the actual number of joules saved would be. Lupe's strong math skills help.

[15] Mr. E. adds an important condition, "if the real system lifts . . . ," to show students how to think about scale and variables.

[16] Mr. E. challenges this group to discuss energy transfers using graphic supports.

[17] Mr. E. then has students use the cards they just created in a real-world-like scenario in which they fortify their arguments face-to-face with another person.

cage each time. At the top the potential energy is 950 kilojoules. When it bounces . . ."

(Role-play work)

Mayra:	I think you should use our ideas for the ride. One feature is a generator. It catches kinetic energy, which we store in a battery, which is potential.[18]

[18] Mayra somewhat uses Mr. E.'s model to start her pitch, and she uses *which* clauses without being prompted.

Alemu: Hmmm. How much energy is lost?

(Pair work continues.)

CONCLUSION

Mr. E. concludes the lesson by pointing out how many groups were comparing the energy transformations in their models to their designs. He has them orally share their ideas for features to make a master list for use the following day.

Mr. E.: Three, two, one. Nice job today. I was focused on how well you explained your ideas orally and on the cards. You used connected sentences and your cards sounded very convincing. Now I would like us to make a master list of features that our design company will use to put together final proposals. Describe your ideas to me from your cards, without reading them aloud.[19] *(Students share the ideas as Mr. E. writes them on the board.)* Tomorrow we will have some interesting conversations about these ideas. Be ready. As homework, I would like you to write down how a scientist might describe the kinetic and potential energy transfers when a person takes a ski lift to the top of a hill and then skis down.[20]

[19] Mr. E. gathers student ideas by having them describe them, without reading, to the whole class. These ideas will be used in conversations tomorrow.

[20] Mr. E. gives a short written output task as homework that applies their learning and language from today to a related real-world situation.

Eleventh-Grade History: Lesson 2

OBJECTIVES

Mr. Rodríguez continues to teach his students about World War II. The focal standard is "Present information, findings, and supporting evidence, conveying a clear and distinct perspective" (CCSS.ELA-Literacy.SL.11–12.4), which builds from the standard, "Analyze how a complex primary source is structured, including how key sentences, paragraphs and larger portions of the text contribute to the whole" (CCSS.ELA-Literacy.RH.11–12.5). The primary source models that Mr. R. is using for this lesson are posters from World

War II, so students will be looking at the structure of the posters (title, word choice, font, image, colors) and how each part contributes to the whole.

Mr. R. continues to focus on NY-ESL Standards 3.9-12, "Students will listen, speak, read, and write in English for critical analysis and evaluation," and 3.9-12.1, "Develop and present clear interpretations, analyses, and evaluations of issues, ideas, texts, and experiences; justify and explain the rationale for positions, using persuasive language, tone, evidence, and well-developed arguments."

Students will be viewing, analyzing, and discussing several posters before creating and presenting one of their own design. With this lesson's emphasis on oral and visual output, Mr. R. focuses students on the language objective of developing their language strategies used for propaganda and for explaining the interpretation of texts.

INTRODUCTION AND CONNECTIONS

After presenting the day's objectives, Mr. R. explains that today they are going to be looking at posters that were used during World War II to persuade people to think or do something to help the war effort. They will learn how to analyze them and look for their visual themes. Then they will create a poster utilizing the same techniques and present it to the class. To connect to previous learning, Mr. R. distributes a chart that lists the eight types of persuasive techniques, a topic the class has previously studied. Mr. R. projects a series of print ads on the board and asks which persuasive techniques they are using.

Mr. R.:	Here is an ad that is familiar to all of you. What is your first impression? What is the theme and purpose?[1]
Eva:	I think they are trying to sell me on the fact that if I buy this car, I will be like that movie star.
Uriel:	Yeah, I will have fans and friends.
Mr. R.:	So which of those techniques is it?
Jenna:	I think it's transfer.
Mr. R.:	What might we ask Jenna?[2]
Tye:	Can you tell me why you think it's transfer?
Jenna:	Because the ad is saying, not directly, that if you drive that car you will be just like that movie star. They know that people want to be movie stars, good looking, rich. So they use them.

[1] Mr. R. engages students' thinking about persuasion and propaganda with an advertisement from a current magazine.

[2] Mr. R. pushes students to help facilitate discussion in order to build independence in their conversation skills.

Mr. R.: Nice and clear explanation. And we need to be ready to give clear and complete explanations without being asked. Usually, for important ideas in life, a short answer isn't enough. So today, we will work on this skill.[3]

[3] Mr. R. emphasizes that he wants students to elaborate and explain without being prompted by him or even other students.

NEW LEARNING

In this stage the teacher models and provides input for the new concepts and focal skills of the lesson. Mr. R. asks the class if they have ever heard of Rosie the Riveter, and a few students raise their hands. He then projects a poster of Rosie on the whiteboard and tells them that this is one of the most famous posters developed during World War II, part of a recruitment campaign called "It's a Woman's War Too!" To get them ready to analyze the text, he asks students to respond in pairs to the prompts: "What was the purpose of this poster? Who was the intended audience?" He has students take notes using a T-chart (title on one side and visual message on the other) so they can keep a record of their ideas to use as a resource when developing their own poster.[4]

Mr. R.: Remember from now until the end of the year that I want us to work on extended and complete explanations. I don't want to have to keep asking you for examples or elaboration. So, what do you think was the purpose of this poster? What are the authors trying to persuade their audience to do?

[4] Mr. R. has students do some wide-angle reading of posters to set up the purpose and audience, and he has them take notes to provide talking points.

Carlos: I think it is saying that women are strong and they can work too.

Mr. R.: *(Waits and then motions with hand for more elaboration.)*[5]

Carlos: My evidence is that she has on a bandana, work shirt, and the shirt is pulled up and she is showing her muscles. That tells us that she is as strong as a man. And look at the words at the top, "We Can Do It!" With an exclamation point. Means business.

[5] Mr. R. nonverbally communicates the reminder to Carlos that he needs to say and explain more.

David: I agree. But she has on mascara, and lipstick and fingernail polish. So they are still saying she is feminine.

Mr. R.: OK. Now, what do we know about the role of women in our society before World War II?[6]

[6] Mr. R. prompts students to access their background knowledge in order to help them comprehend the different layers of meaning of the posters.

Laura: They stayed at home and most of them didn't work like men.

Mr. R.:   OK. Great start. Now I want you all to form your own ideas of what the poster creators were trying to do and how they were persuading people. Each of you now has one of four posters. You will have three conversations with three different partners to come up with a final statement about the purposes and techniques. With each turn, your response should be longer and stronger.[7] Use the ideas, language, and examples from previous partners. I will say when to switch.

(In pairs)

Kira: *(To Lisa)* My poster says they want women to work in factories.

Lisa: What makes you say that?

Kira: The poster says, "Do the job HE left behind."

Lisa: I wonder if the war helped, like, get more respect for women, you know, to work like men. Like, did they prove that they can work in factories so that they got jobs after the war?[8]

Mr. R.:   Switch partners!

Esteban: My poster has "Women in the war: We can't win without them" and a lady working on a missile. Its purpose is to get women to work on war machines. They don't want them to feel guilty about just sitting around. They want to convince them that it is not just man's work. And Eva's poster made people afraid not to work for the war.[9] Lots of propaganda.

Kira: My poster tries to convince women to work in the factories and be part of the war fight. They might be trying to make women feel less guilty about men out fighting. It might be showing respect to women. I think it uses glittering generalities because it says that it will make you proud and help win the war if you work in factories.[10]

[7] Mr. R. has students engage in an augmenting series of conversations in which they build up their ideas as they talk with others about their different posters.

[8] Lisa is inspired to pose historian-like questions that might inspire further learning.

[9] Esteban refers to Eva's poster to add to his own ideas about the purpose of posters and how they are propaganda.

[10] Kira's second, longer response builds from Lisa's idea of respect and Esteban's language (convince) and idea of guilt. It is also more coherent with connected sentences.

PRACTICE

In this stage, the teacher models and supports students in the output activity of making and presenting their own posters related to World War II.[11] They choose real topics besides persuading women to work in factories, such as buying war bonds, conserving fuel, not sharing information, growing food, etc. Before they start working, Mr. R distributes a poster-planning sheet and a rubric (see the Poster Rubric in Appendix B). He discusses it with the class so that they understand the criteria he will be using and how the criteria relate to the features of the poster. He uses one of the primary source posters to show the criteria they will be using for their own posters.[12]

Mr. R.: At the top of the planning sheet you see the four elements that you need to address in your poster: purpose, visual theme, persuasive technique, and slogan. As you and your partner work on your poster, keep these items in mind. Remember, you are trying to communicate as powerfully as possible with a visual and a few words. I will be looking for effective conversations as you work together. And you will need to prepare a clear and complete oral presentation for your poster.[13] *(He circulates and asks questions to keep the pairs focused on the elements of the rubric.)*

[11] Students get a chance to creatively apply and synthesize their ideas into propaganda products based on the WWII posters.

[12] Mr. R. uses a real poster to show how he would evaluate a real poster; he asks students to evaluate the criteria before he shares, and they discuss differences.

[13] Mr. R. emphasizes the importance of the conversations during the work and the oral presentation at the end.

When students finish their posters, each pair stands in front of the class and explains what they were trying to accomplish and how their choice of words, font, image, and colors supported their purpose. They show the visual first and then uncover the text, to add some suspense as the rest of the class "reads" them.[14]

CONCLUSION

In this stage, the teacher wraps up the learning by having the students write a reflection about the lesson, which they will finish as homework. He emphasizes the use of connected ideas and new vocabulary learned in the lesson. Mr. R. prompts students to describe how the lesson's activities deepened their understanding of the various propaganda efforts undertaken during World War II, how they helped them to create realistic posters, and how they learned to be better historians.[15]

[14] Students share their posters and reasons for their design with the rest of the class. Classmates can ask questions.

[15] Students synthesize what they learned and how they learned into a written product. They describe what they learned about propaganda and World War II, and how they used it to create authentic purposeful posters. They also describe how historians might have used these posters.

CHAPTER 8

Fostering Academic Interactions

Enter into each conversation ready to build new ideas, walk in new shoes, and ride new trains of thought.

Interaction is fundamental to identity, learning, and even survival (Rutledge 2011). Yet many educational systems have somehow failed to value the building of students' abilities to understand one another and to build meaning *together*. The focus has often been on individual "achievement," most of which has been measured by multiple-choice tests. The focus has also been on non-complex language, on the pieces and grammar rules that are easily tested. Fortunately, the Common Core State Standards emphasize interaction skills and complex language development. And even if they didn't, we have a duty to provide students at all levels and ages with multiple and well-supported opportunities to interact using original, whole, and academic messages (Cazden 2001; Lemke 1990; Long 1981; Mercer and Littleton 2007).

In too many school settings, large numbers of students could have learned a wide array of standards even better through interactions with other students. Interaction can offer "three for the price of one" learning, so to speak: language, communication skills, and content in one activity. Academic interactions move beyond many surface-level school activities that consist of reciting facts, making up sentences to show grammar rules, and matching vocabulary meanings. In authentic interaction work, students use the facts, grammar, and vocabulary in connected sentences to clarify, fortify, and negotiate complex ideas. And in doing so, learning sticks even better. Granted, this is a major shift in pedagogy (see Chapter 1), a shift from training them to choose answers to helping them pose questions, explore different points of view, and build meanings with others.

The Common Core State Standards highlight the importance of teaching students to communicate in academic ways. Consider the following excerpts from the CCSS documents in Figure 8.1. Notice how these are applicable and necessary across all disciplines.

FIGURE 8.1

Selected Common Core State Standards related to interaction and their implications for teaching academic English learners

CCSS	IMPLICATIONS FOR TEACHING AELS
An important focus of the speaking and listening standards is academic discussion in one-on-one, small-group, and whole-class settings. Formal presentations are one important way such talk occurs, but so is the more informal discussion that takes place as students collaborate to answer questions, build understanding, and solve problems (CCSS Key Points document).	Many AELs are reluctant to speak in front of groups because of their lack of confidence; pairs and small groups allow for less stressful and more oral practice. AELs often need modeling and guiding in what it means to collaborate and build understanding.
Prepare for and participate effectively in a range of conversations and collaborations with diverse partners, building on others' ideas and expressing their own clearly and persuasively (K–5 CCRAS Listening & Speaking).	AELs often need extra instruction on how to express ideas with connected sentences and to use persuasive language strategies in academic ways.
To become college and career ready, students must have ample opportunities to take part in a variety of rich, structured conversations—as part of a whole class, in small groups, and with a partner—built around important content in various domains. They must be able to contribute appropriately to these conversations, to make comparisons and contrasts, and to analyze and synthesize a multitude of ideas in accordance with the standards of evidence appropriate to a particular discipline. Whatever their intended major or profession, high school graduates will depend heavily on their ability to listen attentively to others so that they are able to build on others' meritorious ideas while expressing their own clearly and persuasively (CCSS Note on Speaking and Listening, 6–12).	AELs often need extra explicit explanation and modeling of contributing appropriately to a discussion, comparing abstract ideas, synthesizing ideas in a conversation, and choosing and explaining evidence to support ideas. Many AELs need extra practice in listening, paraphrasing, remembering ideas shared by others, and seeing how to build on or challenge it. Many AELs also need explicit reasons for taking time to talk to peers in a lesson.

Most teachers have seen these or similar standards and have heard the many exhortations to increase the quality of student–student interaction during lessons. Yet what is often missing is the how. How do we begin? How do we improve student talk? How do we foster interaction skills using and supporting the curriculum that we teach? How do we know what a good conversation should sound like? How do we assess interactions and move students forward each day, month, and year? This chapter will not answer these questions completely, but it will provide a platform for diving a bit deeper into the exciting "messiness" that is interaction work.

Academic Interaction Challenges

Fostering academic interactions highly depends on all the other practices in this book. Interaction is challenging to teach because it requires building students' abilities to think on their feet as they respond to and build ideas with others in real time. This practice requires us to assess students' varying conversations while they happen and to provide helpful feedback along the way. We are often not exactly sure what we want students to talk about. And the classroom can get loud.

WHAT DO WE WANT TO SEE AND HEAR?

A big challenge of fostering high-quality interactions is clarifying what we (teachers) want to see and hear in student conversations. What exactly does a great student conversation about plate tectonics or the Industrial Revolution sound like? Unfortunately, this is something each teacher must work on over time for his or her particular setting. A very helpful way to start, however, is to write out a good conversation between two students. This product can be used to gain a better idea of what we would like to work toward with our students. We can also use it as a model to show students where we are going with conversation work. You can use the assessment tool in Figure 8.2 to guide the writing of the model conversation.

HOW CAN WE TEACH STUDENTS THE BEST THINGS TO SAY NEXT?

Another challenge is the unique nature of each conversation. Every student is unique. Put two unique students together and you get a unique conversation every time. You can start them off with a sentence frame or two, but once they get into conversation, you can't control what happens in each turn of their conversation. If you do, it is not a conversation! Students need to manage the conversation themselves. Yet how does a student know what to say next to make the conversation deepen or at least help it to keep going? This is a major purpose of this chapter. We focus on building students' automatic habits during interactions such as knowing when and how to elaborate; how to listen and remember; knowing when to use examples and evaluate the value of the examples; knowing when to paraphrase and how to keep the conversation focused; and knowing when and how to respectfully disagree, negotiate meanings, and value a partner's ideas and thinking.

HOW CAN WE TEACH COHESION IN TURNS AND WHOLE CONVERSATIONS?

In real-time interactions, students can't practice or "edit" their thoughts as they might for an oral presentation or a written essay. They must be able to make their turns clear for a given partner at a given point in the conversation. A core objective that we mention often in this book, especially in Chapter 6, is teaching students to put their ideas into original and connected sentences, paragraphs, and messages. Turn clarity (see Figure 8.2) means that the sentences within a turn use appropriate language and are logically connected, often by using grammatical references to ideas in previous sentences or logical links.

Students must also have conversation cohesion, which means that every turn should build or connect to the topic of the conversation. For example, a student may be able to connect sentences quite well in a turn, but that turn might be way off topic (i.e., good turn cohesion, but not so good conversation cohesion).

HOW DO WE TEACH LISTENING?

A common challenge mentioned by many teachers is that students need to improve their listening. Listening for what? This is the bigger question that we need to consider. Listening in a conversation is complex. In traditional lesson settings we ask students to listen so they can fill their heads with what they hear and repeat it in some form. But in conversations, listening is required to build, challenge, and negotiate ideas. We do not listen to a partner and repeat or write down what he or she said in our own words. We instead use it to "go somewhere," to build on, and to emerge with new ideas or even as new people.

The temptation for most people, including us, is to not listen to the partner's idea as we instead form our own idea and prepare it for sharing. As you listen to a partner, different parts of your brain do different things: one part figures out what your partner is trying to say, another part looks for key points or flaws in the partner's ideas, another part thinks of questions to ask, and still another part forms your own ideas to share when appropriate. We must train students to keep new ideas on mental back burners while listening to the partner's idea and (on our front burners) thinking about ways to build on it.

WHICH CONVERSATION SKILLS CAN WE TEACH?

Yet another challenging aspect of this practice is that most of the skills needed for having productive conversations are not natural to students, nor are they typically assessed or taught in the average curriculum. These unnatural skills include focusing on one topic, responding to each other appropriately, building on someone else's idea, participating equally, negotiating meaning, and listening well.

To overcome these challenges, this chapter outlines practical strategies for assessing and building interaction skills that require and develop complex language and literacy.

Formative Assessment of Academic Interactions

A student once remarked, "This conversation stuff is way more than just talking plus listening." Conversation (a.k.a. discussion, interaction, talk) about academic topics is not the same as listening to an academic lecture or giving an academic speech. Indeed, this chapter treats conversation as a fifth language skill, which is in addition to—and a combination of—the more famous language skills of reading, writing, listening, and speaking. Constructive conversation requires the set of skills and features in Figure 8.2, which can also serve as a formative assessment tool.

FIGURE 8.2

Formative assessment tool for students' academic interactions

	3	2	1
Focus on objectives (disciplinary concepts and thinking)	Students' turns show strong evidence of the target knowledge and thinking skill(s) of the lesson.	Students' turns show some evidence of the target knowledge or thinking skill(s) of the lesson.	Students' turns show little or no evidence of the target knowledge or thinking skill(s) of the lesson.
Build idea(s) in the conversation	Turns build on previous turns to build up an idea, meaning, or understanding; there is shared creation, clarification, fortification, and/or negotiation (CCFN).	Some turns help to build an idea, meaning, or understanding intended in the lesson. There is some shared CCFN.	Few or no turns help to build an idea, meaning, or understanding intended in the lesson. There is little CCFN.
Use clear turns with connected, academic sentences and within each turn	Each turn is clear and, when needed, uses two or more sentences that are logically connected; sentences are academic and original.	Some turns are clear and use two or more sentences; some turns use logically connected sentences; some sentences are academic and original.	Turns rarely are clear; rarely use two or more sentences that are logically connected; sentences are rarely academic and original.
Use appropriate nonverbal behaviors	Partners use appropriate postures, movements, and eye contact to show engagement and listening.	Partners use some appropriate postures, movements, and eye contact to show engagement and listening.	Partners seldom use appropriate postures, movements, and eye contact to show engagement and listening.

As you can see from Figure 8.2, good conversations are complex. While some teachers might be content to hear, "Can you elaborate?" or "Can you give an example?" in a conversation, this chapter is intended to facilitate the teaching of more advanced interaction skills. By apprenticing students in how to converse about academic topics in ways that build and deepen understandings, we can move them into more productive and constructive talk.

Another dimension of assessing conversations is to look for different "levels" of complexity of a conversation. You will often observe multiple levels of conversation around the room, even in one lesson activity. One pair of students might just linger around the first level, the "R" level, of retelling each other summaries, plots, or main ideas. Another pair reaches the next level, the "C" level, in which they compare, contrast, classify, and infer causes and effects. Still another group might reach the "I" level, the level of interpreting themes, predicting, or hypothesizing. A pair in the corner reaches the "S" level, the level of supporting their interpretations with evidence and examples. This level often involves weighing and comparing evidence as they negotiate ideas. Other "levels" of conversation complexity include evaluation, persuasion, establishing relevance, and application of the ideas across time and domains. We must keep in mind where (how deep) we want students to go in their conversations during the year, and plan and push accordingly.

TEACHER REFLECTION TOOL FOR FOSTERING ACADEMIC INTERACTIONS

Similar to the other essential practices in this book, we have identified three important strands within fostering academic interactions. The reflection tool in Figure 8.3 contains the three strands. You can use this chapter, the lessons in Chapter 9, and your own experiences to help you clarify the differences between the levels of evidence for each strand in your setting.

FIGURE 8.3

Reflection tool for fostering academic interactions

STRANDS OF FOSTERING ACADEMIC INTERACTIONS	LIMITED EVIDENCE	ACCEPTABLE EVIDENCE	STRONG EVIDENCE
Use interactions to teach academic communication skills (COM)			
Use interactions to improve students' disciplinary thinking skills (TNK)			
Use interactions to develop students' content understandings (UND)			

Clear and Engaging Purposes for Conversations

Many students don't know why they are talking. Are they conversing just to be in conversation? Just to practice conversation skills? To give or get answers? Is it free time? If the purpose isn't authentic and if it isn't going anywhere, then the talk is not useful. This is why setting up the conversation and knowing its purpose(s) is vital. There are roughly five academic purposes for engaging in classroom conversation: clarifying an idea, building knowledge, creating a product, solving a problem, and arguing a perspective. Granted, all these can happen in one conversation. The problem is when two students are asked to converse but they do not have sufficient purpose, skills, and background knowledge to co-construct ideas.

To strengthen the purpose of conversations, we can include one or more types of purpose in the prompt. The prompt should require the processing and clarifying of the content just learned, and it should move toward a product, idea, or solution to which both partners can and need to contribute their thoughts.

A challenge that can arise in developing conversation purposes and prompts is finding the right mix of personal engagement and academic development. Conversations tend to be more engaging to students as the level of personal and emotional attachment to the topic increases. Yet often, the more engaged they get, the less academically they talk. It is up to us to realize this problem and leverage the engagement while integrating as much complex language into the discussion as possible. The best way to combine the two is to use a strong prompt that includes both. This usually entails adding the engaging part of the prompt to the school-like part. For example, we see many prompts that ask students to compare, contrast, describe, classify, analyze, and identify causes and effects. Why? Just to "do" school? These are usually not particularly engaging things to do for many students, especially as they get older.

We can make purposes and prompts more engaging by having students make a decision or solve a problem similar to what might exist in the real world. For example, if students compare two forms of government, they can do so in order to decide which form a new country should adopt. If students need to identify themes in a novel, they can do so in order to design a website that helps people understand and apply literature themes to improve their lives. Or, if students need to explain how they solve a math problem, they can discuss ways to clarify their ideas in a "guidebook" for helping next year's students in the class. Finally, in science you can have students converse about the variables they would need to control as they design an experiment that would yield the gravity constant for a newly discovered planet.

Ways to Model Academic Interactions

For most of the activities in this chapter, students will need a hefty amount of high-quality modeling. Many academic English learners have not been exposed to models of constructive, academic interactions. Briefly, here are several different ways in which we can model interaction skills, moves, and language.

- *Teacher is student A, and all students work together to be student B.* The teacher models what one person might say in a conversation and asks the class for possible responses. At times the teacher might say to the class, "OK, how might you, as my partner, respond to my comment?" and then ask, "OK, which of the responses we just heard might be best at this point to deepen the conversation?"

- *Fishbowl.* Teacher converses with a student (or two students converse) up front or in the middle of the room to model a conversation. Teacher can stop to "meta-analyze" at times, or ask the watchers to comment or suggest conversation moves.

- *Class discussion.* We might hold many class discussions, but often teachers just develop their own skills at facilitating the conversation. We can use class discussions to "push" the skills onto students, so that they function as teachers, in a sense. Instead of asking students for evidence, for example, we could say, "OK, how might you respond to Gerald's inference?" In this way, students take more responsibility for the direction of the conversation and transfer these skills into pair and group conversations.

- *Written model.* We can also write down model conversations and show them up front to more closely analyze ideas, moves, skills, grammar, and word choice used by proficient conversers in a discipline.

STRAND 1 OF FOSTERING ACADEMIC INTERACTIONS: Use Interactions to Teach Academic Communication Skills (COM)

A powerful way to develop abilities to communicate complex ideas is through many different authentic interactions with others. For example, as a student listens and prepares what she will say next, many thoughts are forming in her brain. One thought is figuring out how to clarify her idea into the best words and connected sentences. This involves mentally calling up what has been said and learned so far in the conversation, connecting to it, and using language that her partner understands. Another thought might be figuring out how to respectfully challenge her partner's ideas, which involves weighing ideas and evidence against one another. At each turn in a conversation, she is practicing different ways to communicate ideas in a discipline. She is practicing, not coincidentally, many of the text-based and output skills highlighted in Chapters 4 and 6.

One of the overarching CCSS College and Career Readiness standards emphasizes being able to listen, build on, and then clarify one's own ideas: "Likewise, students are able independently to discern a speaker's key points, request clarification, and ask relevant questions. They build on others' ideas, articulate their own ideas, and confirm they have been understood" (CCSS Introduction 2013). Yet interactions differ across disciplines. It is helpful to consider the different types of talk we might hear from professionals in different disciplines. Students need to gradually be apprenticed into talking the talk of different content areas, even in early grades. Consider the following ideas discussed by scientists, mathematicians, historians, and authors.

- Scientists discuss scientific ideas such as hypotheses, evaluations and comparisons of data, analyses of causes and effects, and descriptions of physical, biological, molecular, and geological relationships. The main goal of many conversations in science is to explain scientific phenomena or to solve science-related problems. (Refer to the Next Generation Science Standards.)

- Mathematicians and others such as engineers and scientists who use math tend to discuss multiple ways of solving problems, multiple ways of representing and modeling what is happening in a problem, justifications based on mathematical principles, ways to clarify complex theories, and novel ways to show and apply concepts.

- Historians tend to discuss historical relationships such as causes and effects; historical arguments and perspectives; interpretations and corroborations of primary-source documents; the significance of events, ideas, and people throughout history; and history's applications to the present and future.

- Authors and artists tend to discuss how works of art, media, and literature are used to show and teach what it means to be human; how to live, and how others think and live; argue for and against a text's various themes and evidence; how to best communicate profound ideas in creative ways to particular audiences; and how the language and literary styles of a wide range of works are used to communicate.

An essential element of constructive conversation work is building students' independence in these skills. Students have come to depend on teachers for most of what happens conversationally in school. Yet as soon as possible, we want students to be like teachers in a conversation; that is, we want them to be able to use teacher-like moves to sustain and deepen conversations—to not be dependent on the teacher or other adults or students to move the conversation forward. We want them to pick up the tools for sculpting and start forming ideas. For example, one important teacher-like communication skill that students must begin to use on their own is prompting partners to think. Much of the time, students are absorbed in their own thoughts, trying to express them or persuade others to agree with them. Yet the habit of prompting others to think puts the focus on and interest in the other's thinking. It also helps students to build on ideas, rather than popcorn out a random list of unformed ideas.

Another vital communication skill is genuinely validating a partner's ideas. Many students, especially English learners, do not see themselves as true students with academic ideas that are worth sharing. They tend to think of school as a factory where they do as little as possible to learn, get points, and avoid embarrassment. When a partner values a student's ideas, the student begins to develop a sense of "studentship," or academic identity that is missing in many places where students have been beaten down by talk of their low test scores.

Two important meta-skills in all conversations are storing and discarding. Our minds generate many different ideas that we want to share, but we shouldn't share them all because they don't support the focus of the discussion at the moment. For example, you can model for students how to quickly write down extra ideas and thoughts that might be useful later, even tomorrow. Remind students that good conversers store their not-relevant-right-now thoughts during a conversation. Some we write down, and others we forget. A related skill is discarding (pruning) ideas that are likely to be unhelpful. Some ideas lead conversations to dead-end places, some are focused on personal issues and events, and some are just not logical or relevant enough. Students should learn to discard their own ideas before sharing them and tactfully ask partners to discard their ideas if they aren't focused on the conversation topic.

❖ Teach Constructive Conversation Skills

Interactions in school can have many names: collaborative conversations, academic conversations, discussions, seminars, and so on. What we call constructive conversation is back-and-forth talk that builds ideas and accomplishes a useful learning purpose. Students in many settings have been trained to think about short answers (e.g., choose a, b, or c; find the antonym; use a sentence frame to answer a question). Many students have had less training and practice in building out complex ideas and concepts in a discipline with others.

In many classroom interactions, students tend to "popcorn share" a variety of fledgling ideas. For this reason, we often say, "Don't leave a building [an idea] half finished." When an idea emerges, students need to work with it as much as possible before moving on to new ideas. As new ideas are brought up, they need to connect to (1) the most recent idea and (2) the purpose of the conversation. We must teach students to do everything that they can with one idea before moving on. They can use several skills to help them do this building: creating, clarifying, fortifying, and negotiating.

- *Creating ideas.* Humans value the creation and ownership of ideas. Students need lessons and activities in which their original ideas are valued and fostered. In science and math, for example, students can converse to create ideas about their observations, patterns, problem-solving strategies, hypotheses, etc. In history, students can co-analyze primary sources to create novel perspectives on a famous historical figure. Highly effective content learning often comes from tasks that are designed to foster students' creation and synthesis of ideas. It might be easier just to tell them (as many "explicit" and "direct" teaching approaches argue to do), but just telling them tends to (1) foster "learning" that doesn't last, (2) not promote practice and pride in doing and thinking like disciplinary experts, and (3) lack the vital kinds of practice and engagement that come from working with others.

- *Clarifying ideas.* Most of the time, what we say to others is not understood exactly the way we intended. Each response in a conversation usually tells us if the partner understood what we said or not. If two partners don't clarify what is being discussed, they don't have enough shared understanding to build an idea. Clarification is a multifaceted skill. One has to know when to prompt the partner to clarify, when to clarify one's own ideas, and how to do so with a wide range of different partners. Clarification also involves both partners figuring out ways to represent the idea, such as using analogies and metaphors. This skill includes elaboration, explanation, questioning, and paraphrasing, all of which make the current ideas clearer for all involved in the discussion.

Academic English learners are very diverse in how they think and talk. They seldom say enough in the right way the first time to clearly articulate their ideas. In other words, the intended message is often way across the ravine from the perceived message. The listener must help the speaker clarify, putting the responsibility for this skill as much on the listener as it is on the speaker. The listener must show, in a respectful and interested manner, the need for clarity. The listener might need to ask a focused question, key in on a certain phrase and ask for elaboration, paraphrase, ask to define a word, ask for a drawing on a napkin, and so on in order to clarify the idea.

- *Fortifying ideas.* Another skill that is strongly emphasized in the CCSS and other standards is supporting ideas with evidence. In conversations, students should be able to identify and evaluate multiple examples of evidence that fortify ideas. In essence, this is training them to see how knowledge in a discipline is structured and valued. See the Evaluate the Evidence activity in Chapter 4 for more information on how to apprentice students in finding and deciding which evidence is best to use in their arguments. Even when students do understand how to find sufficient evidence, they sometimes lack the vital sub-skill of explaining how the evidence supports the idea. Without this explanation, also called a warrant, students cannot show that they have a solid grasp of the effectiveness of an idea and its support.

- *Negotiating ideas.* Often, ideas are put to the test and strengthened when partners negotiate their meanings. Negotiating ideas includes challenging an idea by presenting counterexamples or other ideas that oppose or compete with it. The goal should be to come to some form of agreement. This might mean making concessions to reach a compromise, agreeing to disagree, or completely embracing either idea. Students should have the academic attitude that all ideas, even if they oppose one another, should be explored and even valued by both partners throughout the conversation. This is how students come to *own* ideas and the language of them (refer to AEL Shift 1 in Chapter 1).

We must also think of these skills as "double" skills. This means that students need to (1) learn how and when to use the skill as they talk; and (2) how and when to prompt their partner to use the skill. For example, I need to know how to read a quizzical expression on my partner's face and automatically clarify what I am saying; and I need to know how to ask my partner for clarification when I don't see how his idea is related to the question asked by the teacher.

These conversation skills can be used in conversations across disciplines and grade levels. Following are several activities for further developing these skills. And for ideas on how to articulate the development of these skills vertically and horizontally in a school, see Chapter 10.

CONSTRUCTIVE CONVERSATION SKILLS POSTERS

Figure 8.4 (also in Appendix B) is a poster that you can put on the wall or give out to students to remind them of the four constructive conversation skills. In the poster are prompt-and-response sentence starters from which you can choose a few (not all) that relate best to the type of talk in the discipline. There are also icons to visually remind students, and you can teach them hand motions for a kinesthetic way to reinforce the skills: put one hand on top of the other to create; act like you are adjusting a telescope or magnifying glass to clarify; put four fingers underneath the other hand to support; hold both hands out to the side to act like a seesaw to negotiate. You can emphasize a different skill every three weeks or so, building up to using all four by the second half of the year. Some teachers put the skills on cards and paste them to an 8.5-by-11-inch card over time. There is a math version of the poster in Appendix B as well.

FIGURE 8.4

Constructive conversation skills poster

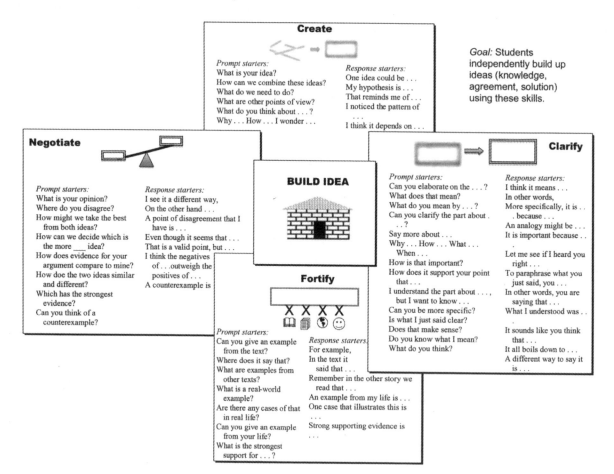

Create

Prompt starters:
What is your idea?
How can we combine these ideas?
What do we need to do?
What are other points of view?
What do you think about . . . ?
Why . . . How . . . I wonder . . .

Response starters:
One idea could be . . .
My hypothesis is . . .
That reminds me of . . .
I noticed the pattern of . . .
I think it depends on . . .

Goal: Students independently build up ideas (knowledge, agreement, solution) using these skills.

Negotiate

Prompt starters:
What is your opinion?
Where do you disagree?
How might we take the best from both ideas?
How can we decide which is the more ___ idea?
How doe the two ideas similar and different?
Which has the strongest evidence?
Can you think of a counterexample?

Response starters:
I see it a different way,
On the other hand . . .
A point of disagreement that I have is . . .
Even though it seems that . . .
That is a valid point, but . . .
I think the negatives of . . . outweigh the positives of . . .
A counterexample is

BUILD IDEA

Fortify

Prompt starters:
Can you give an example from the text?
Where does it say that?
What are examples from other texts?
What is a real-world example?
Are there any cases of that in real life?
Can you give an example from your life?
What is the strongest support for . . . ?

Response starters:
For example,
In the text it said that . . .
Remember in the other story we read that . . .
An example from my life is . . .
One case that illustrates this is . . .
Strong supporting evidence is . . .

Clarify

Prompt starters:
Can you elaborate on the . . . ?
What does that mean?
What do you mean by . . . ?
Can you clarify the part about . . . ?
Say more about . . .
Why . . . How . . . What . . . When . . .
How is that important?
How does it support your point that . . .
I understand the part about . . . , but I want to know . . .
Can you be more specific?
Is what I just said clear?
Does that make sense?
Do you know what I mean?
What do you think?

Response starters:
I think it means . . .
In other words,
More specifically, it is . . . because . . .
An analogy might be . . .
It is important because . .
Let me see if I heard you right . . .
To paraphrase what you just said, you . . .
In other words, you are saying that . . .
What I understood was . .
It sounds like you think that . . .
It all boils down to . . .
A different way to say it is . . .

CLASSROOM EXAMPLE

Mr. Allen, a sixth-grade teacher, is teaching students to interpret literature. The standard is "Determine a theme or central idea of a text and how it is conveyed through particular details" (CCSS.ELA-Literacy.RL.6.2). Mr. A. is having students look for themes and support them with details from the text. Mr. A. hands out the Clarify card that students glue onto their evolving mini-posters (like Figure 8.4). Mr. A. uses the card with a student to model ways to clarify: "Interesting. Can you explain a little more your idea that Esperanza is learning about tensions between social classes?"

The student replies, "In other words, Esperanza was learning that people respect others differently. And it depends on money or not. She saw it was bad. . . . "

After the model conversation, other students then practice the skill in their conversations about the themes they were finding. Mr. A. circulates to remind students to clarify their ideas.

CLASSROOM EXAMPLE

First-grade teacher Ms. Alvarez is having students practice turn-taking and fortifying ideas with examples in the beginning of the year. She knows that students need plenty of support early on, but also wants them to think and describe their own ideas. She decides to have them start with four sentences starters. She is teaching a unit on citizenship and rules in society. After a discussion on multiple reasons for having rules in society, Ms. A. has them form pairs and tells Partner A to begin with "Why do we have rules?" Partner B starts his or her response with "We have rules because we . . ." Partner A then asks, "Can you give an example?" And Partner B begins with, "For example, . . ." When they are done with that reason, they switch roles and Partner A must come up with a different reason that they then both support with examples, taking turns.

CLASSROOM EXAMPLE

Third-grade teacher Ms. Gerard is also teaching fortifying ideas in the beginning of the year. She wants students to see and feel the idea of supporting ideas so she has them each get five plastic cubes (usually used in math activities). She then hands out square cards made of heavy paper that say, *Many animal species form groups to help members survive* (NGSS.3-LS2-1). "These are idea cards. Ideas need to be supported with examples and evidence, which are the cubes you have. Each cube represents an example to support your idea on the card. So in your conversations, I want you to turn this idea into a well-supported three-dimensional table. See?" Ms. G. also shows students the hand motion (putting four fingers underneath the palm of the other hand to support it). "Before you have a constructive conversation, you need to find examples in the text and other places. I will let you circulate around, without writing, to get ideas from other students before you talk in pairs. *(Students read and circulate.)* OK, now in pairs, as you respond to the prompt with a good example, I want to watch you put a block underneath to support the idea card. Watch me. Also, if your partner just says, 'Zebras form herds to see more,' what can you ask to make the idea stronger? *(A student responds.)* Yes, you can ask him or her how seeing more helps them survive. Remember that you are both helping each other strengthen all your examples so that your big idea is well supported."

❖ If–When Chart for What to Say Next

Two challenges in many classrooms are the shallowness and shortness of conversations. Students often don't know what to say next. In fact, most of us adults can't clearly describe how we know what to say next in a conversation. It is often based on instinct and improvisation. It can even be humbling to reflect on the many conversations that could have been much better had we been more skilled. Oh well. Fortunately, our students can benefit from our work with them and some handy tools like the one in Figure 8.5. This chart, still a work in progress, is partly constructed from portions of the Common Core State Standards such as: engage effectively in collaborative discussions, build on others' ideas, express own ideas clearly, ask questions to check understandings, and delineate a speaker's argument and claims.

This chart was designed in our work with teachers who wanted to provide more scaffolding for conversation depth and duration. It is a draft that we all can adapt and work from. The "You" in the second column refers to the student, not the teacher, although teachers can benefit from this chart, too, for conversations with students.

FIGURE 8.5

If–when chart for what to say next

IF . . . OR WHEN . . .	YOU CAN . . .
The conversation doesn't start well or at all,	Say, "Let's understand (clarify, define) this. . . . What we need to do is . . . " Ask, "What does . . . mean in this case/context/situation?" Say, "Let's scan through the text again and look for . . ." Say, "Let's take two different sides; which one do you want?"
Your partner offers a short response,	Ask for specific clarification or elaboration Ask a question ("I wonder why/how . . . ") Ask what a word or expression means Ask for an example that supports it Give an example and ask if your partner agrees
Your partner offers a long and confusing response,	Paraphrase it and relate it to the conversation purpose Ask to clarify the most relevant part of the response Ask for additional evidence or examples
Your partner shares a piece of evidence,	Ask how the evidence supports the idea Ask how well the evidence supports the idea Ask for additional evidence and examples: "What is other evidence that might support your idea?" Compare and contrast it to similar opposing evidence: "I wonder if that is more supportive of the argument than . . ."
Your partner's idea has been sufficiently built up with multiple examples from both partners,	Ask what the partner thinks is the most/least influential evidence Share your own idea and support it Disagree or challenge with an opposing idea Play "devil's advocate" and argue against the idea just for thinking and communication practice What are different perspectives on this?
You share your idea and get little response ("Yeah, OK, Uh-huh, Hmmm"),	Ask your partner what he or she thinks about your idea Ask your partner for his or her evidence for your idea Tell your partner to disagree with you so you can make your idea stronger Ask, "Do we have enough evidence to argue this idea?"

CLASSROOM EXAMPLE

Ms. Thompson, a third-grade teacher, noticed that some students were responding to their partners' ideas about civic duties with short responses such as "I agree" and "Sounds good to me." She tells students to use some of the ideas shown in the last row of Figure 8.5, which are written on the board in the front of the room. She works with one pair of students, one of whom, Sasha, says, "I don't like all the rules, you know, of civic duties."

Her partner, Edwin, responds, "I don't like them either," and the conversation stalls. Ms. T. suggests to both of them to think about what they might say next. Edwin looks at the if–when chart and says, "I could say, 'Why don't you like civic duties?' or I could even argue with her, just to make it fun."

Sasha says, "And I could say, like, 'What is a rule you don't like? And why?'" Ms. T. encourages them to use these moves to keep building ideas in the conversation.

CLASSROOM EXAMPLE

Mr. Greene, a sixth-grade language arts and history teacher, adapts this activity and adds a short motto to help students remember key skills in a conversation. He says, "Remember our 'Respect, Connect, Build, and Support' motto. It helps us use appropriate language while working in groups. To *respect* means to acknowledge what others say without criticizing the person talking, responding instead to his or her idea. Even if an idea is wrong, silly, or way off-topic, we need to respond academically with such responses as 'I don't think it says that in the text, but let's check,' 'That might be a bit off-topic for now,' and 'That's one idea, but let's make sure to stick to the topic of . . .' To respect also means to listen actively and put one's own thoughts aside. To *connect* means to link the current idea that prompted the conversation, like the question asked by me or others in the class. To *build* means to do as much as you can with one idea before moving on. One way to build is to *support* ideas with examples from the text, other texts, the world around you, and your own life. Now I will look for these as I observe your constructive conversations about whether or not Qin Shi Huangdi was an effective emperor."

❖ Conversation Observers

An important element that is often lacking in conversation practice is feedback from an observer. In this section we describe how to observe and provide feedback to the partners during and after their conversation. The third observer has the advantage of being more "meta" and looking for the shape or direction of the conversation, rather than being forced to think on one's feet as the two partners in conversation need to do.

First, it is necessary for us teachers to hone our skills and tools for observing paired interactions. We can start observing with a formative assessment tool like the one in Figure 8.2. The observer can have the skills and features of academic interactions on a note card or in his or her head (e.g., Focus on learning; Turns build, Turns are clear and linked; and Nonverbals). And if, for example, the lesson's focal skill is fortifying, the observer will watch for students strengthening an idea with evidence in their turns.

The following sample of an interaction in a seventh-grade biology classroom was prompted by a question about how and why squids have adapted. Two focal standards for the unit were "Follow rules for collegial discussions, track progress toward specific goals and deadlines, and define individual roles as needed" (CCSS.ELA-Literacy.SL.7.1b) and "Pose questions that elicit elaboration and respond to others' questions and comments with relevant observations and ideas that bring the discussion back on topic as needed"

(CCSS.ELA-Literacy.SL.7.1c). If you were an observer of the following exchange, what might you offer as feedback?

Karina: I wonder why this squid has all this ink.

Rogelio: And I wonder why it has these suction things on its arms.

Karina: Tentacles.

Rogelio: OK, tentacles. And what about the sliminess?

Karina: I think we are supposed to say *why*.

Rogelio: OK. Why is it slimy?

Karina: Not ask why, well yes, ask why, but say why it is slimy and stuff.

Rogelio: I don't know.

You might start off with some positive feedback on the scientific questions that they raised and for Karina's reference to the prompt. You might then suggest they build on one idea, for example, on Karina's first idea about why the squid has ink. You could say to them, "Remember. We are trying to build up ideas as we talk. So, Rogelio, for example, how could you build on Katrina's first idea of wondering why a squid has ink? You could clarify by asking her, 'If ink is an adaptation, why do we think this happened?' This would relate to the prompt. Then later you could build up your idea about its sliminess."

OBSERVER CARDS FOR SUPPORTING PAIR WORK

It can be beneficial at times for the observer to help the pair during the conversation, but without getting too involved orally. To do this, you can generate observer cards that have suggested conversation moves on them. The observer (teacher or student) can put the card in front of either partner or out in the middle, when appropriate. This should happen when it is clear that they need help: they are not talking, they are off-topic, they are arguing unacademically, etc. Examples of cards an observer might use are in Figure 8.6. These are based on our observer moves in many observations of student conversations.

FIGURE 8.6

Observer card ideas

Ask for another **example** to support the idea	**Paraphrase** what the partner said or the whole conversation up until now	**Negotiate** the ideas; come to a compromise
Share an **opposing idea**	Ask what the term _____ **means in this case** (clarify)	**Show** you are **listening** (body and eyes)
Ask **why** or **how**	Refer to the conversation **prompt**	Talk less Talk more

Students can watch you model how to observe and support conversations with the cards like the ones in Figure 8.6. Observing also helps the observers, who act like conversation coaches, as much as it helps the participants. Observers get a chance to meta-analyze how conversations work so that they can do well in their own conversations. Some teachers simply have triads rotate roles (Student A, Student B, Observer) throughout a unit of study. Other teachers have pairs use the cards without coaches. Students can refer to the cards and even "play" them as they converse.

❖ Use Whole-Class Discussions to Teach Constructive Conversation Skills

Whole-class discussions can help you model and scaffold the most effective moves for building ideas in constructive conversations. When a student has an idea, you can coach students in their next responses, guiding them in ways that clarify, fortify, and negotiate ideas. For example, when a ninth-grade student said, "I don't think the United States should get involved in wars," the teacher responded with, "Interesting idea. What might we say to get Samuel to clarify or fortify his idea?" Students offered different responses such as "Why not? What evidence could support your idea?" "I agree; one example is Vietnam." "What does it mean to get involved?"

Effective teachers have crafted other ways to use whole-class discussion. One teacher has students show one finger to share a way to clarify, support, or add to a current idea; two fingers to challenge the idea; and three fingers to share a new idea. The teacher often points out how she tends to exhaust the one- and two-finger responses before moving on to the three-finger new ideas. Another teacher sits down and shows his own finger-based signals as he remains as silent as possible. He raises five fingers to prompt students to come up with a juicy prompt or question to get started. Then after a student responds, he raises one finger, which signals students to clarify or support the idea, and so on. Another teacher uses the constructive conversation skills poster during whole-class discussions. She goes over it beforehand, asks students what they think they should work on today (or she nudges them toward a skill), and they begin to discuss. They check in partway through the conversation and then self-assess afterward.

❖ Students Write Constructive Conversations

A powerful way to directly show students' conversation skills to them (and to us) is to have them work with a partner to write their conversation down on paper or on a computer. This takes more time than actual talking, but it gives them a chance to see how a conversation forms and what they can do to strengthen it. It allows you to see what everyone is thinking as you look at their written transcripts. It also helps you see the "within turn cohesion," to point out how to better connect sentences in each turn. One student said, "Wow, I didn't realize that a conversation could be good or bad. I thought we just talked." You can also use some of these conversations as models up front to point out certain skills and content understandings.

❖ What and Why Info-Gap Math Cards

In this math activity, Partner A has the general problem on a card and Partner B has the information needed to solve it on the "data card" (Figure 8.7). Data cards can also contain diagrams, tables, graphs, etc. Partner A needs to realize what is needed and ask for information that is provided on Partner B's data card. There is an information gap and students need to orally exchange information to bridge the gap. Partner B should not share information unless Partner A specifically asks for it. Neither partner should read their cards to the other or show their cards to their partners. As they work the problem, they justify their responses using clear and connected language.

FIGURE 8.7

Sample info-gap math cards

Emma wants to paint the four walls of her room. But she isn't sure if she has enough money to buy the paint. Does she have enough?	The floor of Emma's room is 12 feet by 10 feet. The walls are 8 feet tall. A gallon of paint covers 100 square feet. A gallon costs $24. Emma has $75.

PROCEDURE

1. The problem card partner (Partner A) reads his or her card silently and thinks aloud about what information is needed. Partner B reads the data card silently.

2. Partner B asks, "What specific information do you need?" Partner A needs to ask for specific information from Partner B.

3. When Partner A asks, Partner B should ask for justification: "Why do you need that information?" before telling it to Partner A.

4. Partner A then explains how he or she is using the information to solve the problem. Partner B helps and asks for explanations, even if he or she understands what Partner A is doing.

5. As a follow-up step, have both students use blank cards to write their own similar problem card and data card for other pairs to use.

CLASSROOM EXAMPLE

Ms. Gomez is using cards like the ones in Figure 8.7 with her fourth graders. She models with these cards to show students how to ask for and provide information. She begins, "I need to know a few things. First I need to know how much money she has. Ana, you can tell me the number, but you can also ask why I need to know."

Ana says, "She has $75. Why do you need to know?"

"Because ultimately I need to find out how much it will cost to paint her room and compare it with the amount of money she has. And I need to know the size of the room."

Ana replies, "10 feet by 12 feet."

"Is that a wall or the floor?" asks Ms. G.

Ana says, "The floor. The walls are 8 feet high. So, how will you use this information?"

Ms. G. emphasizes to the class that the more they talk and explain, the better they will develop their thinking and language.

❖ Supported-Then-Unsupported Conversations

This strategy can be applied to many different types of interaction activities. In essence, it is practicing a conversation with supports and then without them. This activity is a clear form of micro-scaffolding in which support is taken away during a lesson, allowing students to push themselves in a certain skill.

PROCEDURE

1. Before students start the activity, remind them of the skill(s) that you will be looking for as they interact. You might want them to focus on turn-taking,

using connected sentences, using transitions, appropriately challenging a partner's ideas, etc.

2. Give them the conversation prompt that they will use after taking notes. This helps them prepare for the conversation.

3. Have students read or listen and take notes to prepare for their conversations.

4. In the first conversation, allow students to use visuals, notes, texts, and sentence frames to help them extend and deepen their conversations.

5. Have them switch partners.

6. Have them engage in the second conversation without the aids in the first conversation. Encourage them to clarify their thoughts and incorporate ideas from the first partner into the second conversation.

CLASSROOM EXAMPLE

Mr. Lee is teaching his first-grade students about what plants need to survive. The students had been in small groups that analyzed different plants. They took notes on their plant with words and drawings. Now they will orally converse about their topic with others in pairs. With respect to skills, Mr. L. wants them to focus on taking turns and having both partners ask and answer questions. He models the process with a student named Malik. Mr. L. glances at his notes, looks at Malik, and begins the following conversation.

Mr. L.:	Plants need sunlight. Now what might you ask me?
Malik:	Why they need sun?
Mr. L.:	They use the sunlight to make food and to grow. What need do you want to tell me about?
Malik:	Water.
Mr. L.:	Wow, tell me more. Why do plants need water?"
Malik:	*(Looking at his notes)* It helps like to carry inside.
Mr. L.:	Oh, like blood in our bodies, right?
Mr. L.:	*(After moving to a second partner, he addresses the class.)* OK. Do you think Malik and I can talk to new partners without looking at our notes? Let's try.
Malik:	*(To his new partner)* Plants need water to carry things inside like blood in our bodies. And they need sunlight to grow.

❖ Artifact-Centered Conversations

Students use a set of images or a visual organizer that is situated between them during the conversation. A picture book can also be used, and students should be told to refer to the pictures as they converse. The visual supports the conversation by providing information that does not bog them down as often happens when students look for words and sentences in a text. Remember, there is a difference between referring to textual evidence and using up loads of conversation time silently looking for evidence in a text.

PROCEDURE

1. Choose artifacts such as visuals or objects that will help students to focus their conversations and pose relevant questions.

2. Choose the type of thinking and conceptual understanding that you want to observe, and create a prompt.

3. Have students use the artifact to build ideas in conversation with partners.

4. Optionally, you can have one partner in a pair or small group view the artifact to create more of an information gap, as in the example that follows.

CLASSROOM EXAMPLE

A second-grade teacher, Ms. Johnson, had students read a text on important inventions. To prepare students for conversations about the inventions, she has students get into pairs with A's facing away from her and B's facing toward her in the front of the class. She shows a picture of an invention and has B's describe the invention without saying its name. A's have to wait until B's are completely finished with their descriptions (at least three sentences) until they can guess the name of the invention. After guessing or being told the right answer, the A's need to ask the B's why the invention is important. The teacher has several B's share their descriptions and reasons for the invention's importance with the whole class. Then the teacher goes to the back of the room and shows a picture to A's to repeat the process. Then Ms. J. has students get into different pairs and puts a picture of the four inventions between each pair. Students need to be historians and discuss which inventions are most important in history and explain why.

STRAND 2 OF FOSTERING ACADEMIC INTERACTIONS: Use Interactions to Improve Students' Disciplinary Thinking Skills (TNK)

The Common Core Standards are chock-full of thinking skills that all students need to develop. Interactions provide engaging and varied opportunities for students to practice their thinking skills in a discipline in authentic ways. Think about the thinking involved when you are arguing to make a change in some system, policy, or person's actions. You are constantly thinking of the most influential reasons and evidence to make your point. Or when you are discussing possible reasons for a historical event, you are referring to how history works, seeing other people's perspectives, and analyzing causes and effects. If you are a mathematician or engineer, your conversations ignite your math modes of thinking such as problem solving, modeling the problem, analyzing extreme cases, looking for patterns, and so on. And the thinking in science conversations often includes hypothesizing, designing experiments, isolating variables, interpreting and extrapolating from data, and applying.

Conversation offers intense workouts for building the connections between language and thinking. Lev Vygotsky describes this relationship:

> The relation of thought to word is not a thing but a process, a continual movement back and forth from thought to word and from word to thought. In that process the relation of thought to word undergoes changes that themselves may be regarded as development in the functional sense. Thought is not merely expressed in words; it comes into existence through them. Every thought tends to connect something with something else, to establish a relation between things. Every thought moves, grows and develops, fulfills a function, solves a problem. (1986, 218)

Effective conversers in any discipline need to be able to zoom in and out from the big ideas and general principles of a discipline to specific examples—and back out from the specific to the general. They must be able to fluidly change their thinking from abstract ideas to concrete evidence and back again. Students must therefore learn the core ideas, truths, laws, theories, principles, themes, and essential understandings in a discipline. Then students must use these big ideas to shape conversations. For example, they might refer to balancing equations in math, entropy in physics, symbolism in literature, and bias in history.

Students should also learn to discuss patterns and relationships in their conversations. Experts tend to look for patterns and relationships that align with what they already know. For example, a biologist might see patterns in how plants adapt to certain wet and dry environments. Experts also look for new patterns and relationships. They might then formulate new theories and insights about the field. For example, a historian might look at a primary source document and find information that clashes with what was previously known about the author. In conversations, students can build habits of seeing patterns and either confirming them or creating new theories for them.

The following activities are ideas for helping teachers zoom in on developing thinking skills during interactions.

❖ Math Paired Conversation Protocol

In this activity, two students engage in CCSS mathematical practices as they negotiate meaning to solve a complex math problem. The protocol guide (Figure 8.8) helps students to structure their interactions. Notice that in the first two boxes students need to talk after reading through and thinking about the problem. They also need to justify their responses throughout the process. As you see in the protocol guide, an important feature is working through at least two different ways to go about solving the problem. One method might be visual such as using a drawing or graph, while another might be using algorithms, symbols, or algebraic expressions.

PROCEDURE

1. Tell students to read the problem and clarify it with their partners. Students should discuss what is given, what is asked, what the units are, how it relates to what they are currently learning in math class, and possible plans and methods for solving.

2. Have students individually come up with an estimate for the answer and then share it and justify it to the partner. They then compare their estimates and justifications.

3. Students take another look at the problem to think about it individually.

4. Each shares a possible method for solving it and they agree on a first method (Method A) to try to solve the problem. They can name it now or later. They might choose a visual method, putting the drawing in the box, or they might choose a method using symbols and put it in the box. If they do both, the symbols should be related to the visual, not a new method. For example, if they choose to draw a submarine that descends 300 feet and boxes that represent blocks of positive 100 and triangles for negative 100, the symbols should refer to the shapes and the picture.

5. Students should agree on a justification for the method. They should be able to verbalize the justification to one another and to the teacher when asked. They can use a frame such as "One reason we chose this method was . . ."

6. Students then solve the problem with the first method and compare the answer with their estimates.

7. Students discuss ideas for Method B, practice justifying it with one another, and solve it.

FIGURE 8.8
Math paired conversation protocol form

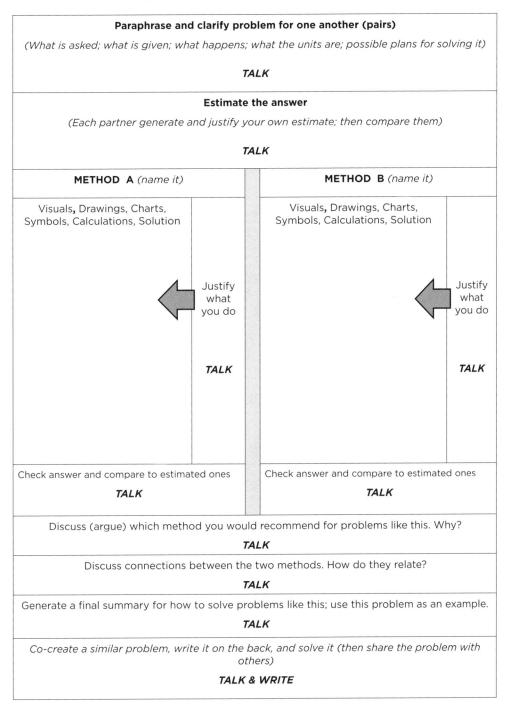

8. Students compare the two answers and the estimates and discuss any inconsistencies and possible reasons for them. They also discuss how the two methods relate.

9. Students come to an agreement on which method is "better" (e.g., clearer, more efficient, easier). The teacher can have students argue for different methods to spice up the conversation. They should end up with solid justifications for the methods they chose.

10. Students collaborate to write a similar yet slightly more challenging problem. This problem can be tackled by other students in the class.

CLASSROOM EXAMPLE

Ms. Thoresen, an eighth-grade algebra teacher, is teaching students that "solutions to a system of two linear equations in two variables correspond to points of intersection of their graphs" (CCSS.Math.Content.8.EE.C.8a). She provides the problem about cost increases of a product at two different companies over time. Students are asked to find when to switch companies to save money. Students use the protocol form to clarify what is asked and what is given; then they estimate and justify their estimates.

Julia: I think we should use a graph.

Simranjit: Why?

Julia: Because it's easier to see it and then use a ruler to see which cost is higher when.

Simranjit: But the numbers are very big. We can try it, but I think it will not be exact. Then for B we can, hmmm. What did the teacher do? Both equations equal to the other. Then solve.

Julia: That's kinda like the graph method, right? They are equal where they cross.

And the conversation continues. They eventually decide that it is more fun to draw on the graph, but setting the equations equal to each other is more precise. Finally, they write their own problem about prices of clothes in different stores.

❖ Evaluation Scorecards

Evaluation, as its name implies, means assigning value to something. We assign value when we judge a thing (object, idea, event, person, etc.) or its parts according to certain criteria.

In our communication with other people, we all must agree on the criteria that we use; then we must agree on how the information matches up with, or is described by, the criteria. For example, when I evaluate the ramifications of cutting down the rain forest, I use the criteria of short- and long-term financial gains, water runoff, loss of habitat, loss of potential medicines, impacts on people living there, and the ethics involved in each.

FIGURE 8.9
Sample evaluation scorecard

EVALUATION SCORECARD

Eleanor	Javier
Bravery 1--X---------5 Because . . .	Bravery 1----------X-5 Because . . .
Passionate 1------X-----5 Because . . .	Passionate 1----------X-5 Because . . .
Important 1--------X---5 Because . . .	Important 1----------X-5 Because . . .

The activity allows students to practice the challenging thinking skill of evaluating subjective categories. It encourages students to think about why we value certain traits, products, and ideas more than others, and it can prompt students to consider how and what we value in society. This activity can then be used with other comparisons of texts and concepts such as heroes, novels, movies, character traits, themes, choices made in a war, types of experimentation, aspects of culture, laws, human rights, and so on. The main conversation advantage is the negotiation that naturally happens as students discuss and try to agree on the "scores" across each row.

PROCEDURE

1. Tell students that they will be evaluating the worth of two things that are not easy to compare. Tell them that this is much more difficult than comparing the price or quality of two shirts. Sample prompts include, With whom would you prefer to have dinner, and why? Which is more applicable to your life? Which is more important to history? Which is more ethical? Which is worth more monetarily?

Which would be missed more if it didn't exist? Which will be best remembered in 100 years? Which character trait is most important? What is the top reason to not watch television?

2. They must first come up with solid criteria for evaluating. Have them brainstorm, in pairs, the qualities or traits they will consider.

3. Students create a list of traits that you turn into a scorecard, like the one in Figure 8.9. This step is important because it prompts students to come up with criteria.

4. Students evaluate the two things with the scorecards. They can do this individually or in pairs.

5. Students share with a partner or other pair. They discuss discrepancies and come to a final agreement. They should refer to evidence or background experience and then evaluate how solid or credible this evidence is. For example, they can refer to a quotation where the person yelled at the skies to show his passion.

6. Students write a final summary paragraph that answers a final question you pose about the two things.

7. Variations: You can make the chart larger with three or more categories or characters at the top. You can also adapt this activity to support the comparing that students do during the Argument Balance Scale activity in Chapter 6.

❖ Disciplinary Thinking Lenses

A thinking lens is a visual organizer that helps students to think more like experts as they discuss content. The lens provides a visual reminder of key thinking processes that should happen as they discuss content in the discipline. Sections of a science lens might include hypothesizing, observing, connecting to basic properties and laws, causes and effects, applying, and experimenting. A language arts lens might include cause and effect, interpreting, evaluating, arguing, empathizing, and applying. A math lens might include defining problems, interpreting, modeling, using multiple representations, looking for patterns, and justifying methods and solutions.

PROCEDURE

1. Choose which types of disciplinary thinking that students will need to use as they read and talk about the text. The six sections of the history lens in Figure 8.10 are identifying and inferring causes, identifying and inferring effects, recognizing bias in primary and secondary sources (i.e., sourcing and corroborating), empathizing

FIGURE 8.10

Disciplinary lens for history

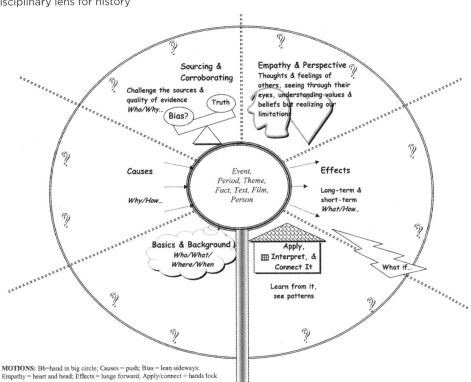

MOTIONS: Bb=hand in big circle; Causes = push; Bias = lean sideways;
Empathy = heart and head; Effects = lunge forward; Apply/connect = hands lock

and seeing different perspectives, applying and interpreting, and understanding the key events and people involved (i.e., contextualizing).

2. Choose the topic that will go in the middle of the lens, which is up on a poster. For history, the topic could be a significant event, person, or issue worthy of discussion.

3. Ask students to generate questions based on the lens sections. You can attach them to the poster in the section where they best belong. You can also add your questions to the lens that focus on the lesson's objectives and have potential for sparking rich conversations.

4. Students then read the text and generate additional questions.

5. Students use the questions in each section of the lens to prompt and guide their conversations.

CLASSROOM EXAMPLE

Fifth-grade teacher Mr. Katz is teaching from a textbook passage on the Louisiana Purchase. As students read the text, they put their questions in the six sections of the lens. They then share the questions with the whole class. For causes and effects, they put "Why did Napoleon sell the land? How did it benefit the United States? What role did the slave rebellion in Haiti play?" For the perspective section, students ask, "What was Napoleon thinking? Why were some Americans against the purchase?" For the sourcing and corroborating section, students ask, "How do we know all this? How was this letter biased?" For the application-interpretation section, they ask, "Was the sale constitutional? Should we give it back to France? Have purchases like this happened recently?" Students add these questions to their lenses. Students then reread the text. Finally, they pair up to discuss the possible answers to the questions.

❖ Conversation Cards

Conversation cards can be used with any content area, but in this description we focus on how they can be used in science. The Next Generation Science Standards (NGSS), like the CCSS, focus on higher levels of thinking and language use. The NGSS, for example, highlight the importance of constructing explanations and developing designs; arguing and evaluating evidence; and obtaining, evaluating, and communicating information.

Each student has a card with differing information that he or she uses in a conversation to achieve a particular scientific purpose. Using different cards leverages the power of having gaps in information between people that they need to fill in by talking. Another dimension of this activity is giving students authentic practice in connecting sentences to describe their thinking processes. Before they engage in conversation, they practice using the cards to create two or more connected sentences. For example, if on a card it says, "High amounts of energy are found in ocean waves," a student might come up with, "High amounts of energy are found in ocean waves. Because of this, we should invent ways to harness the energy."

PROCEDURE

1. Model for students how to take notes on the most important parts of a text (article, textbook chapter, research report, etc.) and have students do so with different texts or parts of the text. Student A might read an article while Student B reads a part of the textbook chapter. You can also prepare the cards if you want more control over the content and language that they will discuss.

2. Tell students the possible purposes for their conversations. Four possible purposes of science conversations are outlined here: *argue, answer, design and test, and model.*

    - *Argue* for or against issues such as nuclear power, spending more money on deep space exploration, or reviving extinct species

    - *Answer a question*: How do we stop global warming? How do brain cells store information? Why do plants produce fruit?

    - *Design and test*: Design an experiment to measure the speed of sound; design a way to use magnets to generate power; gather data from a local pond

    - *Model*: Show how your cells get nutrients; communicate to younger students how gravity works; create a model of a chemical reaction

    Students might pursue more than one purpose in their conversations. For example, after arguing and coming to an agreement on an issue, they might discuss how to gather data or explain the issue to others with a model.

3. Create the cards. Students can create the cards using separate texts or parts of texts. Remind students that they need to include information that they will share to help both achieve the purpose. You can also create the cards. Figure 8.11 includes sample cards for the following purpose: discuss whether or not scientists should continue to create "man-made" cells.

FIGURE 8.11

Sample conversation cards

CARD A	CARD B
We don't know the potential effects on ecology or on the health of humans.	The man-made cells might be used to convert algae into fuel, create vaccines, and clean up large oil spills.
Man-made cells might allow bioterrorists to create deadly new viruses.	Humans throughout history have gained control of nature, such as the domestication of animals and the creation of antibiotics.

4. Have students look at their cards, read them orally to one another, and then negotiate the information to come up with a final decision.

5. They can then prepare what they will say to a larger group or the whole class (with three or more connected sentences).

CLASSROOM EXAMPLE

Ms. Vance, a seventh-grade science teacher, has students look at articles to create notes in preparation for conversations with partners about scientists creating artificial life. Two students generate the cards in Figure 8.11 and give them to Ms.V., who checks them and gives them to a different pair of students. The pair reads them and begins to synthesize and negotiate the ideas.

Nelida: We shouldn't be creating life, because if it gets out, it
will kill everyone.

David: That's in movies. Like we need new cells and life to
help us fight off disease and even oil spills.

Nelida: How do they do that?

David: I don't know. I read that they make bacteria that eat oil.

Nelida: That sounds like the movies to me.

Their conversation continues. Ms.V. listens in and reminds them to refer to the articles for evidence to support their ideas.

STRAND 3 OF FOSTERING ACADEMIC INTERACTIONS: Use Interactions to Develop Students' Content Understandings (UND)

Interaction is a powerful way for students to clarify and remember key understandings in a discipline. As students interact, they share ideas. Often these ideas are unclear or differ in their meanings from student to student. For example, if a student says that she believes that freedom is sacred, her partner should help her clarify the ideas of freedom and sacred.

Everything we know is on sliding scales of understanding. We all understand gravity, cell division, algebra, character development, theme, plate tectonics, and democracy in many different ways. Understanding typically entails being able to explain processes and relationships, apply conceptual knowledge to new situations, and interpret ideas in intended ways. Understanding is very different in different disciplines. Thus, in order to help students understand, we must keep seeking to understand what it means to understand—without getting too dizzy in the cycle. Interacting with others can help.

The activities in Strands 1 and 2 also develop content understandings, but the activities in Strand 3 are extra focused on clarifying, solidifying, remembering, and applying understandings across disciplines.

❖ Role-Based Improv Conversations

This activity develops complex language and content understanding at the same time. Rather than filling in blanks, memorizing dialogs, or answering questions, students get to be in conversations that approximate the twists and turns of real-world interactions. As students take on different roles and respond to one another in real time, they learn to adapt and clarify what they say to build and challenge ideas. You can also introduce additional ideas by guiding and even taking a role in the conversation.

PROCEDURE

1. Start off with some fun and easy improvisation practice. Put students in pairs and give them a situation, such as talking about an actor, planning a party, complaining about food, discussing a movie, or arguing about use of texting. Once the idea of an improv conversation is understood, you can move on to the academic versions of it.

2. Pick a concept from the essential standards of a unit or text. For example, you might choose magnetism, a novel's theme, an important historical controversy, a famous historical figure, an environmental problem, and so on. Try to find a concept that can have two to three participants in conversation.

3. Figure out the roles. Students can also submit their own ideas on separate slips of paper.

4. Have students help you to write rough notes on what will be discussed in the improv conversation. Visualize where you want students to go, what they will do, and what they will say. Most will be improvised.

5. Describe the scenario and give students a few minutes to discuss what they might say. They should not have time to memorize, just to create some ideas.

6. Pick several students to model and guide them in the role play, similar to a rehearsal.

7. You can insert an additional character (often you in a new role) to make it even more interesting. See Figure 8.12 for ideas.

8. Other students can respond to questions that you give them when you stop the conversation at times, similar to when you stop during a read-aloud. They can coach students who are modeling, if appropriate.

9. Have student pairs or groups draft, practice, and hold their own improv conversations.

FIGURE 8.12

Situations and optional additions

SITUATIONS	OPTIONAL ADDITIONS
Two brothers on opposing sides of the Civil War, arguing their side	Their mother enters and says that they must choose one side.
Romeo and Juliet in the afterlife, discussing what happened	Shakespeare enters and asks them how he should have changed the story.
Howard Carter discussing King Tut's treasure with Cairo authorities	King Tut enters and tells them what they should do.
An environmental engineer discussing acid rain with a senator to draft a bill that limits air pollution	A representative from the main factory producing the pollution enters and explains the costs and loss of jobs.
Harriet Tubman and Harriet Beecher Stowe discussing the joint creation of a poem about freedom	Diego Rivera enters and says he would like to paint a mural that goes with the poem.
Ponyboy talking about the future with his brother at home	A social worker comes to ask about recent events to decide if Ponyboy should be in a foster home.
Galileo discussing his theories with a judge who is about to put him in jail	Einstein shows up to set the record straight.

❖ Prepare to Be an Author

This activity develops interactions that focus on becoming better authors while they also develop students' creative juices. Furthermore, it gives an additional reason to analyze literature. For many students, figuring out themes in a story just to write about it for points or to become a better person is not enough motivation. Becoming an author and creating stories like those being read can be more motivating. And, because much of the writing that we ask students to do is not engaging or creative (e.g., reports, literature analysis essays, summaries), students can lose interest in writing. This activity helps students think as authors as they bounce and build ideas that they might put together to write powerful pieces of literature. Even if they don't write the eventual products (e.g., a novel), the conversations help them to build core thinking and communication skills. Finally, while this description focuses on talking about narrative literature, you can adapt the activity to any type of text. Students could converse as authors of textbook chapters, articles, biographies, and so on.

PROCEDURE

1.   Remind students that someday they might want to write literature, poetry, stories, screenplays, or other creative works.

2. Have pairs reflect on stories, novels, films, and television shows that have taught them positive themes about life. Emphasize that they should support their theme ideas with specific examples.

3. Have students, throughout the year, analyze literature as examples of what they would like to write or not write. They consider the features of each work that they want to emulate or incorporate into their own writing.

4. Have students generate an initial list of themes that they want to write about: themes that they think their classmates or school or world need to know in order to understand what it means to live a fulfilled life, understand how others live and think, or to be a good citizen of the world.

5. Have students engage in constructive conversations on a theme and what kind of story might teach it. Students should start with one partner's theme and build up idea(s) on how a character would change or learn, related to the theme. Then do this with the other partner's top theme. Themes and their stories can change throughout the conversation.

6. Pairs can fill in a story map or outline when they have a more solid idea of their story. They then share their maps or outlines and receive feedback. The partner can ask questions such as

   • What is the main conflict and how will it be solved?

   • How will the main character change on the inside to show the theme? How will the character's dialog or actions show this change?

   • Remember that I will be looking for evidence in your story of the theme. What kinds of evidence will there be?

   • That sounds a lot like the book we read (or the movie we have seen); how can your story be different and new?

7. Students take notes based on their author conversations and then begin to write their stories.

8. After the first draft, they meet with the original partner and two others to get additional feedback. Remind students that you will be listening for great author conversations; the written stories are secondary for the moment. Talking about their own and peer stories can be more engaging and academic than conversations about works by famous authors (but don't tell them this).

CLASSROOM EXAMPLE

Eighth-grade language arts teacher Mr. Olvera is finishing up a unit focused on the standard, "Determine a theme or central idea of a text and analyze its development over the course of the text, including its relationship to the characters, setting, and plot" (CCSS. ELA-literacy.RL.8.2). Mr. O. wants students to converse about their ideas for themes of short stories that they might write in order to expand their creativity. Students are to talk with three different partners and build up their ideas each time. At the end of each conversation, they need to tell one another one new idea about the theme or character development related to the theme that they might incorporate into their stories. Mr. O. is writing his own story, to model his thinking processes. He finds a partner, Keisha, to model a conversation.

Mr. O.:   I want to write about the theme of how important it is to read literature. *(Waits)* What can you ask me or add?

Keisha: So you want a character to learn that it is good to read books, right? Like in that story we read, "No More Ink," where things are different cuz of no books?

Mr. O.:   I like that idea. Maybe the character loses her favorite stories and things get worse for her. Yet I would like to have a different plot from other stories I have read. Hmmm.

After the modeling, the rest of the class pairs up to have their own conversations.

❖ Co-create an Assessment Trio

There are very few essays and multiple-choice tests in the daily "real world," but there are endless ways in which people are assessed by what they produce. Such production takes many forms, yet in most cases people must be creative in how they apply their knowledge and skills in order to create a high-quality product. They know they must draw upon the focal concepts and skills they gained while learning, and now they must synthesize and adapt that learning to craft assessments. When students participate in and wrestle with ideas, they tend to learn them better. Sometimes, students will generate surprisingly insightful and challenging ways of applying and assessing their own learning.

This activity asks students to collaborate in pairs to come up with three types of assessment: (1) a performance task that shows, as well as possible, their learning of the most important concepts of the unit (the task may or may not be feasible to do in school); (2) an expository writing prompt with a complete sample response and rubric; and (3) a short-answer test with an answer key. Whether or not the Assessment Trio is completed, the conversations about each part of the task are very beneficial for developing content understandings.

PROCEDURE

1. Student pairs arrive at a clear understanding of what the target standards mean and how they relate to the central questions, problems, challenges, and themes in a unit.

2. Students come up with the problem to solve, product to create, or performance needed, any of which become the performance task. It should show understanding of being able to apply the concepts and standards that support the central ideas of the unit. Students are encouraged to argue for different tasks and how they will show learning of the key concepts in the unit or not. Sample tasks might include the following:

    *   A doctor needs to isolate a bacterial infection by comparing symptoms and the effects of treatments.

    *   A museum curator needs to design the next exhibit by interpreting an artist's works, synthesizing background documents, and communicating to patrons.

    *   An author needs to research the topic about which he or she will write by analyzing primary documents, classifying the information, synthesizing it, and empathizing with the people in the research to create characters.

    *   A marine biologist analyzes plankton levels to predict whale migrations and then use a cause-and-effect argument to persuade other scientists to change their minds about whale behaviors.

    *   An attorney analyzes student's rights to free speech at school, interpreting current laws and evaluating the extent to which the school rules conflict with them.

    *   A reporter during the Civil War needs to empathize with people on both sides, interpret their words and actions, and synthesize it into an article.

3. Students collaborate to create the expository writing prompt that takes a more academic and removed (not as creative) stance to directly state what they have learned. They create the rubric and then cowrite a model (or at least an outline) that responds to the prompt, shows their understandings of the content, and scores well on their rubric.

4. Finally, students cowrite several key short answer questions that were not covered in the longer writing prompt in number 3.

5.   You synthesize their ideas, pick the most effective ones, and have students actually do them to show their learning.

CLASSROOM EXAMPLE

Mr. Holt, a fourth-grade teacher, has been teaching a unit on the influence of the missions in California. He wants to both improve and assess his students' conceptual understandings by having them converse to create Assessment Trios for the unit. He guides them in a whole-class discussion first to help them see what a performance task would entail. They write a list of ideas on the board: Write a letter to the president to give back the lands, write a documentary about the relationships built by the missions, write a historical fiction story that shows the feelings of the Native Americans, and write an article as a historian claiming that the missions were necessary for California. Students converse to choose the most important prompt and to write the background for it.

Juan: I think it should be the letter to the president.

Daisy: I don't think he'll read it; I think we need to know how the Native Americans felt, like we should have students write stories.

Juan: You mean like the book about the girl and her brother? But we need to show what we learned about missions.

Daisy: A story can do all that, plus it shows how they felt about everything.

This interesting argument continues and Mr. H. gets insight into what they understood in the unit and what they want to emphasize in their assessments.

Strengthening Common Activities for Fostering Academic Interactions

Many practices and activities have gained popularity with educators who teach academic English learners. Most of the practices and activities, such as those in the first column of Figure 8.13, can be effective, but they often (1) need some tweaking to maximize high-quality interaction, and (2) need to be strategically combined with other activities to develop deep and enduring complex language and interaction skills (see Chapter 1). For example, many interaction activities give the impression of authentic two-way interaction, but can actually end up being inauthentic, being one-sided, or allowing too many students to not participate.

FIGURE 8.13

Strengthening common practices and activities for more effective interaction

COMMON PRACTICE OR ACTIVITY	COMMON LIMITATIONS	HOW TO BUILD INTERACTION SKILLS INTO AND FROM THE ACTIVITY
Whole-class discussion	- Most responses are by the teacher and a handful of very verbal students. - Teacher often controls the conversation.	- Train students to respond to one another and to use teacher-like moves and constructive conversation skills. - Show and analyze model classroom discussions.
Socratic Seminars	One person talks at a time. It is intimidating to talk in front of others. It is easy to pass or let others dominate.	- Have inner circle discuss topic and outer-circle partners coach each inner-circle participant. Take time-outs and have coach and coachee discuss next things to say; have circles turn and talk in pairs at times.
Sentence starters and frames	- Looking at sentence frames during conversation can stall the conversation.	- Focus on a thinking skill and a few of its frames. - Have students memorize the frames. - Students find different partners and try to use the frames without looking (e.g., cover up the posters).
Visuals and hands-on activities	Students can overrely on commonly experienced visuals or the objects to communicate. Students might just point to them rather than using complex language.	- Create information gaps in which students use different visuals and need to describe them. - Take away the visuals and objects and provide prompts that ask students to talk about the ideas face-to-face with a purpose.
Pair-shares and turn-and-talks	Pair-shares often offer quick quantity but lack quality in terms of complex language and ideas. Often partners share similar information one turn each.	- Structure the turn-taking (Partner A starts first) and the responses: "After A shares an idea, clarify and build on that idea as much as you can. Then B can share, connecting somehow to the idea just built up." - Have different partners respond to different prompts.
Wait time and prep time	- We often don't give enough time for students to prepare their thoughts before talking. - We can wait all day and still many students won't want to share.	- Give students time to take notes, draw, organize, find evidence, etc., before having constructive conversations. - Have students think up mental paragraphs (see Chapter 6) to help them start off with strong ideas. - Have them draw or diagram ideas to share.
Commonly used assessment practices (written; multiple choice)	- For many students, writing and multiple-choice tests frustrate them, which can turn them off to learning. - Multiple-choice tests tend to assess facts, vocabulary, grammar, and abilities to choose answers.	- Assess conversations that precede or follow writing assignments and tests. - Have students generate ideas for interaction assessment tasks. - Have student pairs write down an ideal conversation about the topic of the unit or the essential question.

As mentioned in other chapters, a core purpose of this book is to build habits of using and modifying existing activities, lessons, and assessments to maximize student learning of complex language and literacy. Figure 8.13 outlines only a few of the common practices and activities that can be strengthened for and by developing students' interaction skills. The purpose of the chart is to seed ideas for building our habits of being critical users and adapters of all practices and lesson activities that we see in professional development sessions and resources.

Summary

Many academic English learners don't see themselves as being good at conversing about school topics, as creators of ideas, or as academics. A powerful feature of conversations is the choice that students have for how they choose to shape and build ideas in a discipline. Such choices provide ownership (not just access) and agency, which help them develop their academic identities. Usually, students come to think and communicate in far greater ways than they ever expected. They use language and explore ideas that go well beyond the prompts and the sentence frames. They become so engaged in an idea that they forget that they are learning.

For the majority of academic English learners, schools are the main avenues for learning academic interaction skills across disciplines. We therefore have a duty to (1) teach students how to interact productively in each subject area and (2) teach content and language through the use of interactions. It is a major shift to do both, but it is one of the most important sets of skills that we can offer our students.

The next chapter describes sample lessons that emphasize the use and development of complex language in interaction-based activities.

CHAPTER 9

Lessons That Focus on Fostering Academic Interactions

Learning often lingers longer after loud lessons.

This final chapter of model lessons builds on the lessons introduced in Chapters 5 and 7, which emphasized the practices of using complex texts and fortifying complex output. This chapter includes the third lessons in each sequence of lessons. It emphasizes how teachers can foster complex language growth through academic interactions and vice versa. As in the other chapters, look for ways in which teachers support interaction work with the crosscutting and foundational practices of clarifying, modeling, guiding, and designing. Also, look for things that teachers might have changed in order to better foster students' interactions.

Second-Grade Math: Lesson 3

OBJECTIVES

In Ms. Stevens's Lesson 2 (Chapter 7), students learned how to understand and solve two-step word problems and use language to describe how they solved them. Ms. S. continues with the focal content standard "Use addition and subtraction within 100 to solve one- and two-step word problems involving situations of adding to, taking from, putting together, taking apart, and comparing, with unknowns in all positions, e.g., by using drawings and equations with a symbol for the unknown number to represent the problem" (CCSS.2.OA.A.1). Today's content objective is to solve two-step problems with unknowns at the beginning and middle positions, and to argue for a best way to solve a problem. Ms. S. also highlights two mathematical practice objectives of the day: CCSS.Math.Practice.MP3, Construct viable arguments; and CCSS.Math.Practice.MP4, Model with mathematics.

Ms. S. continues to develop her English learners' mastery of the 2012 WIDA ELD Grade 2 Standard 3 (p. 60): "Students at all levels of English language proficiency will ANALYZE text of word problems." Ms. S. uses the descriptions of the five different proficiency levels to help her differentiate the challenges that she gives to students as they converse about the problems, solutions, and concepts. The leveled functions of matching, finding, sequencing, locating clues, and categorizing are woven into the lesson's prompts and tasks.

Ms. S. identified the following language objectives for the day: being able to describe math understandings of a problem and logically argue for methods and representations used to solve problems.

INTRODUCTION

After briefly explaining the objectives, Ms. S. begins the lesson by connecting to the key ideas and skills learned the day before. She reminds students that they used different ways to solve problems with multiple steps and described their reasons and methods orally and in writing.

Ms. S.: OK, window partner, share what we did yesterday in math to solve problems. You can look at the problem up here. Wall partner, you need to build on and add to what you hear.[1] *(Pairs talk.)* OK, what did you come up with?

> [1] Ms. S. has pairs build clear explanations for what they did yesterday to solve problems in math.

Asha: Yesterday we solved word problems with two changes. Like more is add and less is minus. We made 'quations to solve for the boxes at the end.

Ms. S.: Thank you. And today we will solve problems with unknown answers at the beginning, middle, and end of the equations.[2] We will also have some great math conversations.

> [2] Ms. S. introduces students to new learning by connecting to yesterday's lesson.

LAUNCH

Ms. S. introduces a new type of two-step problem with the unknown at the beginning. She uses a variation of the Math Conversation Protocol (Chapter 8) that she adapted for her students. This launch problem allows students to ponder the new problem and experiment with different possible ways to approach its solution(s). The problem is this: *Leopold found some marbles in an old shoe. He gave 7 marbles to his sister and 5 to his brother. He had 11 left for himself. How many marbles did he find in the shoe?*

Ms. S.:	OK, today I want to hear good conversation about our problems. Not just one person do the work and the other talk. Ask each other why you are doing or thinking or drawing a certain thing. So now, after I read the problem aloud, I want you to look at it and silently think about it. The first thing I want you to talk about, even before you write anything, is what the problem is about and what it is asking for. *(Wait time)* Now I want you to estimate, or guess the answer, without writing. Look for words and clues. Tell your partner and tell him or her why. Start with "I think the answer will be . . . because . . ."[3] And if your partner doesn't give a reason, ask why.

[3] Ms. S. builds the habit of estimating and gives a language frame for claim and support that students can use in pairs.

(Pairs work.)

Alex:	*(To Lara)* I think the answer will be 20 cuz it's more than 11. And he gave some away.
Lara:	I think it'll be 30.
Alex:	Why?
Lara:	Cuz he needs to give them all away and that is enough.

EXPLORATION

In this stage of the lesson, the teacher provides time for students to work on the problem and verbalize their understandings and ideas to others. She refers to their version of the constructive conversation skills poster for math (Appendix B) on the wall, emphasizing that she wants students to explore and experiment with ways to solve the problem and then give reasons. Ms. S. reminds students to give good reasons for what they think they should do. As students talk, Ms. S. listens in for misconceptions and strong responses. She supports students in putting sentences together to create logical ideas.

(Whole class)

Ms. S.:	OK, now talk about how to solve this. And if you look at the page, there are two sides.[4] That means there are

[4] Ms. S. uses the visual organizer to emphasize that there is more than one way to solve the problem.

two ways, at least, to solve this problem. Remember to give reasons for what you do. And ask for reasons if your partner doesn't give them right away.[5]

(In pairs)

Kevin: I think we should draw them. Here is a shoe with marbles.

Ana: But we don't know how many marbles, right?

Kevin: So we draw lots of them. I wonder if they smell cuz they were in a shoe. Ha–ha. Then we take away 7 for the sister and 5 for brother. And he has 11...

Ana: So we draw 11 out here. Or we can keep 11 in the shoe. So now what?

Kevin: He gave the marbles away, so that would be subtract. But we don't know what to subtract from. We can add the 7 and the 5.

Ana: Why?[6]

Kevin: I don't know. Hmmm. They are both numbers that he gave away. It's not he found 7 and lost 5.

Ana: So that is ... 12. Then we subtract 11 minus 12? No, that's too small.

Kevin: We can add them! 11 plus 12 is 23. That's the answer.

Ana: Why?

Kevin: I don't know, but it looks like it works.[7]

(Whole class)

Ms. S.: I saw some great math thinking and heard some great conversations! Let's hear one method for solving it.

Kevin: We used ... *(Describes the drawing method that they used).*

Vicki: We made a equation like yesterday. We didn't know the beginning number so we put an empty box there. Then he gave away 7 so we put minus 7, then minus 5 cuz he

[5] Ms. S. reinforces the need for students to justify and ask for justification during math conversations.

[6] Ana asks a *why* question at the right time to clarify Kevin's idea.

[7] Students get the answer but don't really know how. The lesson will then help them focus on explaining the *how*, which is just as important as getting the right answer.

	gave away 5. Then equals 11 cuz that's what he had at the end.
Ms. S.:	Hmmm. Interesting. Let's work with this. Think about what you might do if the first thing isn't a number. We don't know what to do to it, do we? Tell a partner what you might do.

(Wait time)

Ana:	We drawed pictures but we added those numbers. The sister had 7, the brother had 5, and Leo had 11. So he started with 23.

Ms. S.:	Nice work! See how you connected the drawing you did to the equation that Vicki and her partner used?[8] So we see two methods here. Now I wonder, which is better? Argue respectfully with your partner.[9] Wall partner, argue for the drawing method; window partner for the equation method. I will listen for good reasons on either side of the argument.

[8] Ms. S. uses and shows the relationships between two different methods from student launch problem conversations.

[9] Ms. S. has students practice arguing for one method against the other.

(In pairs)

Carina:	I like the picture method better. Because it is easier to see what happened. And I like to draw. And that last one was weird. There was minus signs and we had to add.
Rafael:	I think the equation is good. Drawing too much time. The equation is math. Is what we are learning. Not drawing. I don't know. They both work. But I don't want to draw so much every time.

DISCUSSION

In this stage, the teacher focuses on helping students to engage in mathematical conversations for understanding and solving the word problems.

(Whole class)

Ms. S.:	Nice job, everyone. I heard some good reasons to support your arguments. Here it is on our math conversation skills poster. So now before you practice this on your own, I want to first model this with a

partner on a new problem.[10] How about you, Ana?
First, we make sense of the problem and estimate. What
do you think it asks?

[10] Ms. S. fishbowl models
with a student the type of
conversations she wants
to see.

Ana: It asks how many roses bloomed the second week.

Ms. S.:   And we know several things. In the beginning there
were 38 roses; at the end there were 52. In the first
week Ted cut down 16 to sell. What do you estimate as
the answer? Try saying, "I estimate that the answer will
be around . . . because . . ."[11]

[11] Ms. S. steps into the
teacher role to provide
language she wants
students to use to justify
their solution methods.

Ana: I estimate that the answer will be around 20 because 20
plus 16 is 36.

Ms. S.:   And I estimate it to be around 30 because Ted has
around 40 roses and loses around 20, then needs around
30 to get back up to around 50. So how should we
solve it?

Ana: An equation?

Ms. S.:   *(To the whole class)* What would I ask Ana next? OK.
Why should we use an equation? You can answer with,
"A big advantage of using an equation is . . ."

Ana: A big advantage of using an equation is you don't have
to draw lots of flowers. And equations *are* math, not art.
And it gives the right answer.

(Conversation modeling continues.)

PRACTICE

Now students practice their developing skills at solving the problem and discussing their
reasons. Ms. S. offers a new problem and tells them to use the math paired conversation
organizer (Figure 8.8) to clarify, estimate, generate multiple methods, and argue for one
at the end. She refers to this problem on the board: *Lisa went to the bookstore and bought
28 books. She also bought 5 books at the book fair. On her way home, she left some books on the
bus. She got home and counted her books. She had 22 books. How many did she lose?*

Ms. S.:   OK. Start this problem on your own. Read it three
times.[12] When I give the word, clarify and estimate
with your partner. Then continue to solve it with two
methods, if you can.

[12] Ms. S. removes her support
as she has students read
the problem more than
once and think about it on
their own before clarifying
it with a partner.

(In pairs)

Alex: Let's draw. We can show the books. Bookstore 28. Book fair 5. Bus, we put a question mark. We look for it. End, 22.

Nayra: It takes too long to draw them. . . . OK, so we draw 5 more and add to 28, right? Then we minus how many?

Alex: We don't know. But it gets to 22.

Nayra: So we cross out books to get to 22. We count the crossed ones. 33, 32, 31 . . . We get 11. OK, now I think we should try the equation way. It's math, and we don't use time drawing.[13]

[13] Nayra argues for the need to use an equation method, justifying it by saying it's more time-efficient.

Alex: OK, so 28 then plus 5 cuz she buys more. That's 33 and it equals 22 cuz that's final number.

Nayra: I don't know. Where's the box? And 33 is not 22. I think it goes here, plus box. After the 5.

Alex: Why is it plus the box? She loses books and we don't know how many.[14]

[14] Alex challenges the use of addition and provides a reason to help Nayra correct her equation. He provides a clue from the text.

Nayra: Oh yeah. OK. She starts with 28 and here is the 28. She buys 5, here is plus 5. She loses we don't know, so minus box. Got 22 at home, so equals 22.

(Whole class)

Ms. S.: Now discuss which method of the two that you used is better. Explain your reasons. You can start with *(writes on the board),* "For problems like this one, I think the ＿＿＿ method is better. First of all, it . . ."[15] *(Pairs talk.)* What did you decide?

[15] Ms. S. provides language to help students' reasoning for their "arguments" about which method is better.

Pablo: We liked the drawing but we thought the equation was easier because of the box. But we didn't like it when the box was the first thing.

Ms. S: Yes. When the numbers get really big, we can't draw everything. That's why they invented math! Now for extra learning, take a minute to describe to one another how the two methods connect to each other![16] You can draw arrows if you want.

[16] Ms. S. has students look for patterns and relationships in the two methods (CCSS MP1).

(Pairs work.)

CONCLUSION

Ms. S. concludes the lesson by describing how the learning met the objectives. She emphasizes the conversation skills and thinking she observed, and she highlights the need for some students to say more to explain their reasons in future math conversations. She highlights some of the dialog she heard as she circulated and supported student pairs.

Ms. S.: I noticed that Ana was listening to her partner, Vicki, and that they asked each other to support their ideas and say why they were doing something. I noticed how Nayra and others were sharing their thoughts and reasons as they solved problems, and when they disagreed, they disagreed respectfully. That is what mathematicians do! Now I want you to self-assess how well you talked and learned today. Use the checklist up here: *Did you take turns? Did you explain your reasons? Were you respectful to your partner? Did you understand the math?*[17]

[17] Ms. S. validates specific learning that she saw and then has students self-assess for both language and content.

Fifth-Grade Language Arts: Lesson 3

OBJECTIVES

Ms. Flores continues to teach her students how to identify and explain themes in a short story. The focal standard is "Determine a theme of a story, drama, or poem from details in the text, including how characters in a story or drama respond to challenges or how the speaker in a poem reflects upon a topic; summarize the text" (CCSS ELA-Literacy. RL.5.2). The content objective is the same as in Lesson 1: Determine the theme(s) of a short story based on character actions and words, and support ideas from the text.

Ms. F. continues to use the California ELD Standards (2012) focused on supporting ideas by using the text, CA-ELD.5.2.I.11: "Support opinions or persuade others by expressing appropriate and accurate reasons using textual evidence."

With today's emphasis on interaction, Ms. F. reflects on the thinking and language that is needed for the interaction related to this objective. She realizes that students need to practice using some of the language of explaining the value of the evidence that students gathered yesterday. They will also work on skills of building on an idea in conversations. The language objective includes message-organizing strategies such as explaining warrants with relevant and logically linked sentences, and using terms such as *evidence, support, claim,* and *outweigh*.

INTRODUCTION AND CONNECTIONS

After presenting the day's objectives, Ms. F. connects to previous learning by having students take out their written responses from yesterday, many of which were finished as homework. Ms. F. uses this introduction activity to listen in on ideas and as a way to get students thinking about themes that they will talk about during the lesson.

Ms. F.: First, let's connect to what we did yesterday. Take out your three-part written summaries of your current ideas for the text's theme. What's the motion for claim? (*She puts her fist out and down.*) For support? (*She puts her other hand under the fist.*) And your explanations? (*She moves her hands up near her eyes.*) Read your sentences to your partner and have your partner do the motions as you read. (*Ms. F. circulates and observes.*)[1]

[1] Ms. F. has listeners engage in activity (the motions) as they listen to partners reading their written ideas that contain claim, support, and explanations.

(In pairs)

Carlos: I claim that the theme for this story is don't judge a book by its cover (*puts his fist out*). Evidence is kids thought Francisco was dumb, but he wasn't (*puts hand under fist*). This showed that kids judged him from the outside (*moves hand and fist up to face*).

Ixchel: I think the theme is that you gotta work hard to get ahead. He worked hard and stayed in school and even became an author! His hard work made him get ahead in life, so we should work hard, too.

NEW LEARNING

Ms. F. models and provides input for the new skills and language of the lesson, such as conversing about themes. She models how to deepen and build on ideas in a conversation, rather than just popcorn out ideas. She observes in order to formatively assess and make adjustments as needed.

Ms. F.: I heard some great ideas out there. Today we are going to work on being better at constructive conversations. This means that we work together to build ideas. Even if we disagree, we need to build up both ideas. Let's take out our constructive conversation posters to look at how we can build on ideas.[2] So, Kiera, can you come up and model with me? Kiera, what is your theme? Without reading it, please.

[2] Ms. F. uses the constructive conversation poster organizer to reinforce ways to build ideas.

Kiera:	I think the biggest theme in the story was being who you are.
Ms. F.:	What do you mean?
Kiera:	It means that every person should be who you are inside, to not be like others, to be proud of your life and family.
Ms. F.:	*(To whole class)* Class, what should I ask next?[3]
Juan:	Ask for evidence?
Ms. F.:	OK, Kiera, and is there some evidence in the story?
Kiera:	For example, Francisco spoke Spanish to his friend. That showed he wasn't afraid to speak up in his language, like who he is.
Ms. F.:	Hmmm. OK, class, what can I do now?
Sara:	You can say your idea.
Carlos:	You can ask her for more evidence or you can help her if you know evidence.
Ms. F.:	I could do either, but I will help her build her idea with my own evidence.[4] Ready? *(To Kiera)* I also thought that his drawings were examples of who he was. He expressed his ideas by drawing because he couldn't write well in English. . . . OK, thank you, Kiera. *(To whole class)* So, conversation observers, what did we do first? Did I immediately disagree and say my idea?
Samuel:	No. You helped Kiera build up her idea first.
Ms. F.:	Yes. In fact, helping her with her idea also made my idea stronger. So I want you all to practice this with your partner.[5]
(Pairs)	
Jasmin:	I thought the theme of the story was being patient and waiting to do good. And the symbol was the caterpillar.
Isabel:	Can you explain that?

[3] Ms. F. uses fishbowl modeling to show how to respond and build on partner ideas. She engages all students to listen and think about what to do or say next.

[4] Emphasizes the conversation choice of helping a partner build ideas rather than pushing for more evidence or bringing up a different idea.

[5] Uses the modeling to focus students on building on partner ideas in their next conversation.

Jasmin: The caterpillar just crawls around and is ugly. And he is trapped in the jar. Francisco was kinda trapped. He had to wait to learn English and be happy.

Isabel: So you think Francisco was like the caterpillar cuz he waited. Like he didn't quit school or yell at the teacher. Like when she took his drawing away. Maybe he thought she didn't like it. But it won a ribbon.[6]

Jasmin: Yeah, and when he got the ribbon and that guy liked the drawing, that made him happy, like a butterfly. (*Pause*) What's your theme?

Isabel: Mine is different. I think the theme is to try hard. Francisco was scared like when he looked at the jar, when other kids looked at him. But he stayed and tried hard to learn English.

Jasmin: And another part for try hard was he looked at the books to learn. He tried to learn . . . *a pesar de* [in spite of] not able to read English.[7]

Isabel: And he made art to show his interests. He tried to make beautiful pictures and he did and won the prize. But the caterpillar part? Maybe the caterpillar tries hard to make his cocoon thing.

Jasmin: And that helps him to turn into a butterfly.[8]

[6] This is a nice example of student paraphrasing a partner's idea to clarify the idea and add to it.

[7] Jasmin helps to build up Isabel's idea for a theme with additional evidence. This also gave time and sparked more building on Isabel's part in her next response.

[8] The students use the conversation as a chance to pose questions and hypotheses about the symbol.

PRACTICE

In this stage, students practice their skill of building on ideas in a conversation by using a new story from the same author. The teacher provides a varying amount of support and feedback to students.

Ms. F.: OK, you just practiced building on each other's ideas. I heard some great additional examples that helped your partners build their ideas. After we read this new story from the same author called "Learning the Game," we will converse about its themes. First of all, we start to read a story, what do we do? What do we look for?[9] Share with a partner what to do. (*Waits*) Let's hear some ideas.

[9] Ms. F. reminds students of the skills of wide-angle reading when starting to read a new text.

Samuel: We look at characters and for a problem.

Julia: And for themes and symbols, like the caterpillar.

Ms. F.: OK. So be looking for these things as I read the first part of the story aloud. I will stop so you can take notes on possible themes and evidence, as we did with the story before. (*Ms. F. reads first half of story and stops.*) OK, I think I have a theme forming in my mind. Do you? (*Wait time*) I think it might be about sticking up for others who are smaller. My evidence is Francisco begging Carlos to let Manuelito play. And for the title, I am not sure if it is literal or figurative, like a real game or a game in life.[10] Now, I will let you read the rest. (*Students read.*) Now, before you have your constructive conversations, let's generate some ideas for possible themes. Think about the title and the new characters. Quickly share ideas with your partner. (*Waits*) What did we come up with?[11]

James: We think don't cheat in games.

Alicia: You shouldn't make up rules of the game, like Carlos making up his own rules. And not letting Manuelito play.

Jasmin: And then Gabriel gets mad. It's not a game but Diaz, the boss, he isn't fair.

Ms. F.: Aah, so do you see any comparisons in this story? Remember the last story with the caterpillar and how Francisco changed. In your conversations I want you to think about themes that are based on comparisons. And the title. Remember that authors include things for a reason and they love to put symbols and metaphors to teach us themes and lessons. (*Wait time*) Now I will go around and assess your conversations with my checklist. If I don't get to you, you will have time to self-assess afterward. Our focal skill for today is building on partner ideas by fortifying them with evidence (*hand under fist*). But we also want to use skills from the last two days, such as making a claim (*fist out and down*), and explaining them (*hands up to face*).[12] Begin.

(*In pairs*)

[10] Ms. F. models how to form ideas for a theme while reading and how to form rough ideas about the title and its meaning. She purposely shares a less obvious theme in the chapter.

[11] Whole-class generation of ideas prompts students to think and generate ideas for conversations for all to consider.

[12] Ms. F. uses formative assessment and reminds students of lesson objectives.

Ixchel: I think we need to talk about the game and how Carlos makes up rules. And about Gabriel and the fight and Francisco and the game.

Ismael: They're like each other.

Ixchel: What do you mean?

Ismael: Carlos makes his rules. That isn't fair. Diaz makes Gabriel pull a plow. That not fair. And he fired him. Also not fair.

Ixchel: Oh. OK. Diaz makes his own rules, like Carlos for the game. So it's like rules of life, but they are wrong. And Francisco stands up to Carlos, like Gabriel did to Diaz. So the theme?

Ismael: The theme maybe is not follow rules if the rules not fair. OK, I got mine. What's your theme?

Ixchel: That's my theme![13]

Ismael: But it's mine too, now. (*Laughing*)

Ms. F.:   If you both built the theme, you both can own it. But remember that you need to make it clear and strong. You need to use evidence and explain it.[14]

Ixchel: (*To Ismael*) So we have to do that fist thing, claim (*fist out and down*), support (*hand under fist*), and explain it (*hands to face*).

Ismael: OK. Evidence. Francisco doesn't play the game cuz he hates a rule that Manuelito . . . *no puede jugar* [can't play].

Ixchel: And Gabriel stands up to Diaz and breaks his rule. I think he was right. So Francisco learns to break unfair rules. And it's like that word (*looks at vocabulary chart on wall*) *boycott*. All his brothers stop playing and Carlos can't play.[15]

Ismael: But what about Gabriel? He gets fired. Maybe he comes back and wins, like a movie.

Ixchel: It's not a movie.

[13] After gathering up ideas from the text, students organize them into a possible theme.

[14] Ms. F. reminds them that the purpose of the conversation is to clarify, support, and explain the claim; it's not a competition.

[15] Ixchel explains the connection between the two parts of the story. Students arrived at understandings like this by conversing and building on ideas by creating, clarifying, supporting, and negotiating.

CONCLUSION

To conclude the lesson, the teacher refers to the objectives of the day and wraps up the lesson, connecting to the learning that will happen in the future.

Ms. F.: I heard some excellent conversations! You worked hard to build up an idea that your partner shared. I even heard some academic disagreements. Respectful disagreements can help us learn because they make us fortify our ideas with evidence and compare them![16] We will practice disagreeing tomorrow. Now, in your notebooks, I want a quick self-assessment of your conversation. From 1 to 4, did you build on ideas? Write down a quick explanation. Did you take turns talking? Did you support your ideas with evidence from the text? . . . Did you use academic language? Now tell your partner one thing you think you both could work on for next time. (*Wait time*) Would anyone like to share?[17]

[16] Ms. F. emphasizes the building of ideas that can come from disagreeing and negotiating ideas.

Elisa: We thought we could do better at explaining evidence. We just said the theme and then pointed to pages in the story.

[17] Ms. F. uses a quick self-assessment to have students reflect on the quality of their talk and set goals for next time.

Ms. F: Great goal. I think others could borrow your goal, too. Now, before you forget, write down a three- or four-sentence "proof of learning" ticket based on your conversation.[18] Extra credit for using gerunds, you know, the –ing verbs that were subjects in sentences yesterday. (*Wait time*) Tomorrow we will do some respectful arguing. You will argue with a partner about which theme is the strongest. And we will talk about what it means to compare "apples and oranges" as we look at evidence. We will also start a longer writing assignment on themes. At the end, we will also start to talk about you all as authors.[19] You will choose an important theme for students at our school and write a story that shows that theme. I can't wait to read them.

[18] Ms. F. reinforces language and ideas by having students organize them into final written products.

[19] Ms. F. foreshadows the future learning of how to author stories—not just read them and look for themes.

Eighth-Grade Science: Lesson 3

OBJECTIVES

Mr. Escobar continues to build on the previous two lessons in which students learned about kinetic and potential energy as well as energy transfer. This lesson further reinforces, through conversation activities, focal Next Generation Science Standards: "Construct, use, and present oral and written arguments supported by empirical evidence and scientific reasoning to support or refute an explanation or a model for a phenomenon" (MS-PS3-5) and "When two objects interact, each one exerts a force on the other that can cause energy to be transferred to or from the object" (MS-PS3-2).

Mr. E. continues to use the 2012 WIDA ELD Standard 4 for Grade 8 (p. 97): "Students at all levels of English language proficiency will ANALYZE energy transfer." Mr. E. uses the five leveled performance indicators to help him differentiate the challenges he gives to students as they build and explain their models.

Focal science practices include asking questions and defining problems, developing and using models, planning and carrying out investigations, analyzing and interpreting data, constructing explanations and designing solutions, and engaging in argument from evidence. To support the development of communication skills content, Mr. E. emphasizes two Common Core speaking standards: "Present claims and findings, emphasizing salient points in a focused, coherent manner with relevant evidence, sound valid reasoning, and well-chosen details; use appropriate eye contact, adequate volume, and clear pronunciation" and "Integrate multimedia and visual displays into presentations to clarify information, strengthen claims and evidence, and add interest" (CCSS.ELA-Literacy.SL.8.4-5). The main language objective is to use argumentation language to engage in conversations and appropriately support one's ideas related to energy use in a machine.

INTRODUCTION AND CONNECTIONS

Mr. E. goes over the objectives, emphasizing that students will use what they learned in the previous two lessons to engage in complex conversations about their designs. He has them engage in discussions about the limitations of the models, outside forces that will skew their numbers, the challenges that exist, and what modifications might be needed to overcome each challenge.

Mr. E.:	Conversations are a vital part of science, engineering, and design. They help you to clarify and support your ideas; they help you see things you might miss—things that might save lives, in this case.[1] So to get your conversation muscles warmed up, I want you to talk

[1] Mr. E. explains the reasons for improving conversation skills in science. This helps to make the interaction time more relevant.

about the advantages of the features of your ride design. Remember, *feature* means a part of your design, like a parachute system, and *advantage* is something positive about it.[2] Now find a partner from another design team.

[2] Mr. E. realizes that students might benefit from a quick reminder explanation of two important academic terms.

(In pairs)

Tesfaye: Our ride has soft platform. It catches cage. It has gears and changes the kinetic energy to electricity.

Yesenia: Good. Our feature is a giant rubber ball under it. It bounces the cage back up.

Tesfaye: What if it pops?

Yesenia: I don't know. Maybe another ball inside of it?

NEW LEARNING

Mr. E. introduces and models the constructive conversation skills that students will practice later in the lesson.

Mr. E.: Take out your constructive conversation skills mini-posters we have been using. Today we will focus on fortifying ideas, with some negotiating, especially if you disagree or challenge someone's idea.[3] So, Sara, will you help me model? First of all, we need a reason to talk. In this case we will talk about which features are the most important for conserving energy in the design of the ride. What do you think is the most important?

[3] Mr. E. uses the visual organizer to focus students on the target skills for their conversations. They will work on fortifying science ideas as they talk.

Sara: Rollers for electricity.

Mr. E.: Can you clarify that idea for me?

Sara: Rollers touch the frame on the way down and make electricity. It goes into a battery.

Mr. E.: How can you support that idea?

Sara: We have the numbers from our model. It slows the cage down, but it changed the motion energy into electricity.

Mr. E.: Hmmm. And you could have it adjust so it slows the cage all the way to a stop. That way you get as much energy as you can and you stop the car so it doesn't crash. Do you think you can capture all the energy?

Sara: Not all the energy. A lot probably changes into heat and sound and wind resistance, too.

Mr. E.: Interesting! *(To whole class)* Did you notice how well Sara explained her idea? And did you notice how I built on and strengthened Sara's idea? I had a different idea but I waited and helped her build up her idea first.[4]

[4] Mr. E. models building on Sara's idea in a "fishbowl" format, and highlights how he helped to strengthen her idea, not just his.

PRACTICE

In this stage, Mr. E. supports students as they engage in paired constructive conversations about their designs. They can use their own design features but are also encouraged to use the best ideas from the class.

Mr. E.: All right. You just saw a sample conversation that focused on building ideas. And even when you challenge an idea, this can help to build it up. Now you will form new teams of two vice-presidents of the amusement park company. You are deciding which features should go into the new ride.[5] You have the list we made up here to work with, along with the models around the class. I will be looking for how well you build on ideas and how well you explain the energy transfers happening during the ride.

[5] Mr. E. has students take on real-world-like roles to explain, evaluate, negotiate, and choose the features created by the teams.

(In pairs)

Liam: I think we should use a huge rubber ball under it.

Nissa: Why?

Liam: Cuz it will look cool and it is a good way to get it back up the tower. Watch. *(He uses the model to show the cage falling and bouncing back up.)*

Nissa: I think we should put a big fan on the bottom to catch the air.

Mr. E.: Nissa, before you share your idea, remember what our focus is.[6]

Nissa: Building up ideas.

Mr. E.: And describing the energy transformations.

Nissa: OK. So, do you have any numbers?

Liam: It will save like 200,000 joules.

Nissa: I like it. It is like a trampoline or using bungee cords, I guess. So it transfers kinetic energy at the end of the fall to elastic energy in the ball, right?[7]

Liam: Yes. Then it goes back into kinetic. What about yours?[8]

Nissa: I think we put a big propeller on the bottom that winds up a rubber band, like on those little wooden planes.

Liam: Why?

Nissa: Well, it is safer than a lot of ideas. It slows the cage down. It is clean energy from the wind.

Liam: Then what?

Nissa: Then we lock the propeller at the bottom and let people on. We let it go and it lifts the cage back up.

Liam: So you change kinetic energy of the cage to kinetic air resistance energy. That turns into elastic energy when you stop it.

Nissa: Then we let it go and it is kinetic again. Not sure how much energy it will save. So, can we put both ideas into the ride?[9]

Liam: I don't know. The propeller would slow it down so there is less bouncing back up from the big rubber ball.

(Whole class)

Mr. E.: Three, two, one. Wow. Lots of great conversations. I heard several students describing the energy transfers between kinetic and potential energy. And

[6] Mr. E. intervenes to guide Nissa in building on Liam's idea before moving on to sharing hers.

[7] Nissa validates Liam's idea and keeps building on it by adding extra information about the energy transfers.

[8] Liam asks to hear Nissa's idea, rather than Nissa sharing it unsolicited.

[9] Nissa asks a powerful design question about combining features, but they run out of time.

a few academic arguments came up. Now I want to ask Maribel and Tesfaye to share a part of their conversation.[10]

Maribel: I like your idea about the solar panels, but they don't use the motion energy.

Tesfaye: They change sun energy to electricity.

Maribel: So light waves change to electric energy, and this energy changes into a battery.

Tesfaye: Battery is chemical energy. It's potential, like a phone battery gets charged.

Maribel: I think you need to figure out how much energy you get from the sun. Might not be a lot. I will think about it if you show me good numbers.

Mr. E.: *(To whole class)* Notice how they built on each other's responses and described the science going on? Maribel challenged the solar panel idea in a respectful and scientific way.[11] Well done. Now I would like you all to self-assess your conversations using the observation tool I am handing out.[12]

[10] Mr. E. has two students model part of their conversation (that he identified while he observed) to show students effectively building on ideas.

[11] Mr. E. highlights how Maribel respectfully and scientifically challenged the idea.

[12] Mr. E. has students self-assess and set goals using a self-assessment tool (adapted from Figure 8.2).

CONCLUSION

In this stage, Mr. E. has students share how the conversations helped them understand the concepts of kinetic and potential energy and the transformations between them.

Mr. E.: All right. Now in the last few minutes let's reflect on how our conversations helped us learn.[13]

Adrian: I think I was more interested and listened better when I talked with one person.

Calvin: I got to practice talking like a scientist, like using *potential* and *gravitational* words.

Darla: I liked talking about the models that we made. Jon explained where energy was lost.

Griselda: I like talking and not listening all the time. It helps me to remember. And I like talking to one other person, not in front of everyone.

[13] Mr. E. uses the last few minutes to reinforce the content ideas and the rationale for working on conversation skills in science class.

Mr. E.: Great job, everyone. We will use the ideas and language we used today as we look at other types of energy transfer tomorrow. But for homework, I want you to have a conversation with someone about energy transfer. Energy is a big challenge these days and you can talk about possible ways to make clean energy. You can use the ride as an example. You can talk about cars, lights in the house, etc. Just see what happens. It can be a friend or family member. And bring back this card signed by the person.[14]

[14] Mr. E. has students practice their conversation skills with an atypical homework assignment that involves conversing with another person.

Eleventh-Grade History: Lesson 3

OBJECTIVES

Mr. Rodríguez continues to teach his students about World War II. They will be learning from a primary source document about the military participation of Navajo soldiers in the war. Focal standards include "Analyze how a complex primary source is structured, including how key sentences, paragraphs and larger portions of the text contribute to the whole" (CCSS.ELA-Literacy.RH.11-12.5); and "Determine the central ideas or information of a primary or secondary source; provide an accurate summary that makes clear the relationships among the key details and ideas" (CCSS.ELA-Literacy.RH.11-12.2).

Mr. R. continues to focus on NY-ESL Standards 3.9-12, "Students will listen, speak, read, and write in English for critical analysis and evaluation," and 3.9-12.1, "Develop and present clear interpretations, analyses, and evaluations of issues, ideas, texts, and experiences; justify and explain the rationale for positions, using persuasive language, tone, evidence, and well-developed arguments."

With today's emphasis on interaction, Mr. R.'s language objective is being able to better interpret the language of primary sources for historical purposes, cite evidence, and negotiate differing interpretations with peers.

INTRODUCTION AND CONNECTIONS

Mr. R. begins by asking the class what they know about the Navajo people. Mr. R. then tells the class that this particular group of Native Americans played a key role in the war, which will be the focus of the lesson. He also explains that part of their job of working with primary source documents is to have extended conversations with their partners as historians might have.

Mr. R.: So, what are some of the things we need to do as listeners and as speakers when we are having a constructive conversation about history?[1]

Randy: If I am the speaker, I say what I believe or think is true. But I should ask my partner if they agree or disagree or have a different opinion.

Trini: Yeah, and if I am the listener, I really need to listen.

Mr. R.: What do you mean by that?

Irma: I shouldn't be thinking about what I am going to say next. I just need to listen to what my partner is saying.

Mr. R.: So, what do you do in your head when you listen?

Irma: I listen for the idea and how the speaker supports it. Like if he thinks what happened didn't happen like that, I ask to explain.

Mr. R.: Great! And you might add ideas to it, or you might pick a part and ask for clarification or fortification. For example, if you are my partner and I tell you that I think a primary source letter is biased.

Randy: Can you support your idea about why the letter is biased?

Lupe: Is there evidence in the letter or somewhere else?

Mr. R.: Good. Remember that we are conversing with partners as historians, and we are building up and comparing ideas, and making historical claims based on evidence. Today we will focus on citing evidence and negotiating ideas when we disagree.[2]

[1] Mr. R. starts the lesson with a recap of how to engage in constructive conversations.

[2] Mr. R. emphasizes the focal historical thinking and conversation skills to work on during the lesson.

NEW LEARNING

Mr. R hands out a graphic organizer called the primary source conversation guide (see Appendix B). He explains that the class will be looking at a primary source document about the military participation of Navajo soldiers and that they will be using the guide to help them analyze and talk about the primary source.

Mr. R.: First of all, historians always have a purpose for looking at a primary source. In this case, we are historians who are deciding if the story of the Code Talkers should be included in the history textbook.[3] This conversation guide is going to help us analyze a primary source and converse about it. The left side helps us analyze the text. In order to model this, we will use a short excerpt from Philip Johnson's *Proposed Plan for Recruiting Indian Signal Personnel* (http://archive.library.nau.edu/cdm/compoundobject/collection/cpa/id/44712/rec/1).

Now work with a partner to jot down notes for the prompts on the left side. You can talk about these, too. *(Pairs work for a few minutes.)* Now on the right side of the guide are interaction prompts. These are reminders for how to have a solid history conversation. Laura, can you help me model?[4] What do you think was the author's purpose?

Laura: I think to persuade the army to get Native Americans to join and help them with messages.

Mr. R.: I agree, because of the title, especially. But I wonder if it was all true. For instance, when he wrote "could not, under any circumstances, be interpreted by the enemy." How did he know? It seems like opinion.[5]

Laura: He didn't know yet. But now we know that he was right. So, should this be in the textbook?

Mr. R.: Perhaps a paragraph or two. There is a lot of other history to cover.[6]

Laura: I think it deserves a whole section or chapter! This is important to show the forgiveness and, like, the dedication of the Navajo and others who participated.[7] They were put on reservations by the American Army and now they were being asked to give their lives to help the army.

Mr. R.: Hmmm. Perhaps you are right. This is a good example of doing the right thing even though they didn't have to, after their treatment. It was a little like someone taking over your home, moving you to one room in it, and then asking you a few years later to help them protect the rest of the home that they took from you.[8]

[3] Mr. R. gives his student historians a real-ish purpose for analyzing primary sources and to guide their conversations.

[4] Mr. R. fishbowl-models conversation moves using a text that connects to, but is different from, the text that students will use.

[5] Mr. R. models questioning strong statements in the text.

[6] Mr. R. intentionally sets up a disagreement here.

[7] Laura brings up perspectives and themes beyond typical events and causes in history.

[8] Mr. R. builds on Laura's ideas and models how to use an analogy to clarify historical events and concepts.

Laura: So, more than two paragraphs, right?

Mr. R.:   Yes. You convinced me. *(To class)* Did you notice the negotiation?[9]

> [9] Mr. R. models negotiation and points it out to the class.

PRACTICE

Mr. R. distributes another primary source, *Enlistment of Navaho Indians* (http://www. archives.gov/education/lessons/code-talkers/images/letter-01.jpg) to his students. He has students work in pairs to answer the left-hand side of the guide before and during reading. Then they use the interaction prompts as needed to work on skills of citing evidence and negotiating ideas. Mr. R. circulates to support students' interactions.

Nelly: I think this source is fact because the commanding general is saying why it would be good to enlist the Navajo. What do you think?

Amit: Yes, but in the last sentence he says, "It is therefore recommended," so I think it might be persuasive.[10]

> [10] Amit uses some evidence to propose a different interpretation of the purpose of the text.

Nelly: To make something persuasive, you gotta take a stand. It's about being for or against something. I don't see where he makes a stand. I think he is just stating facts. Do you see anywhere that he takes a stand?

Amit: I don't know. So he is not taking a stand, exactly. But the purpose is to recommend, like persuade. Here, "It is therefore recommended that an effort be made to enlist 200 Navaho Indians for this force." So he is persuading, I think.

Nelly: I guess.

Mr. R.:   You both did a nice job negotiating right there. Now you might want to focus on additional evidence and the language used in the text to decide if and how much of this to put in a textbook.[11]

> [11] Mr. R. provides some positive feedback for the negotiation and guidance for sticking on topic.

Nelly: In point 3 I think it's evidence. He says the Navajo is the only tribe that has not been infested with German students. The word *infested* showed his attitude for the Germans, like they were rats or something.

> [12] Students analyze how language is used in the memo and compare it to the speech from the lesson before.

Amit: Yeah, they were the enemy. Remember the bad words in that Pearl Harbor speech? So do you think he used *infested* on purpose?[12]

Nelly: Yeah. Look at the next sentence. He says the Germans studied other dialects under the "guise" of art students. Like they were disguised or spies or something.

Amit: Hmmm. But why Germans? I thought the Navajo were used against the Japanese.[13]

Nelly: Maybe as an example of what all enemies do?

Amit: And he says other tribes can't understand the language and only 28 Americans know it, so it is like a secret code.

Nelly: But is he saying that Navajo people and Americans are different? Like the Navajo isn't an American? They were the first Americans! Shouldn't he have said something like 28 Euro-Americans? I think it is racist.[14]

Amit: That was the past, though. Remember yesterday when we discussed the posters that women hardly worked and African Americans could only work in kitchens? So maybe this isn't being racist in his time.

Nelly: I don't know. I think racism is racism. If people disrespected others or thought they were less valuable cuz of their race, it's wrong, whenever in history. That make sense?[15]

Amit: I guess so. What about the main question of should it be in a history book?[16]

Nelly: Definitely. It shows the commitment of the Navajo to protect this country even though they were not valued. This memo showed that even people asking for help were racist because he thinks Navajos aren't Americans.

Amit: And they forgave enough to help the army. And they sacrificed their lives. And they helped win the war.[17]

Nelly: I think history is messy, like Mr. R. said once.

[13] Amit asks a historian-like question based on the text.

[14] Nelly builds from Amit's quoting of the text to bring up an unexpected conversation topic, racism.

[15] Nelly and Amit negotiate the idea of racism in the past vs. present and Nelly clarifies the concept.

[16] Amit gets the conversation back to the opening purpose.

[17] Amit builds on and builds up Nelly's idea that this aspect of history, of helping former enemies despite mistreatment, should be learned by all.

CONCLUSION

To conclude the lesson, Mr. R. refers to the objectives of the day and wraps up the lesson, connecting to the learning that will happen tomorrow.

Mr. R.:   I heard a lot of great conversations. You were all actively engaged. You were using your primary source guides to keep your deep conversations going. Now, let's self-assess with fist-to-five. Remember to hold up five fingers if you did it consistently and on down to a fist, which means you didn't at all.[18] Ready? How well did you do taking turns talking? How well did you support your ideas with examples from the text? How well did you build on your partner's ideas? How well did you clarify ideas? How well did you negotiate your ideas? I am impressed that most of you were between a three and a five most of the time. I did notice lower numbers on clarifying, so we can work on that. Can someone share what they want to work on for next time?

[18] Mr. R. gets formative feedback for what they need to work on in future conversations.

Irma: I want to get better at building on my partner's ideas. I have lots of thoughts and want to share them and sometimes I don't listen. So I can't build if I don't know what she said, you know.

Mr. R.:   I know. Good example. And others I think might have similar goals. Right? OK, so to wrap up our learning for today, we are going to do a 3-2-1. Write down three reasons to include or not include this part of history in a textbook, two things about the Navajo dialect that made it a perfect secret code, and one historian question you now have and would like answered tomorrow.[19]

[19] Mr. R. has students write down the key content ideas that they learned to use as formative assessment.

CHAPTER 10

Coaching, Collaboration, and Capacity

Only by locking arms and thinking together will we turn this enormous ship into the wind.

Now that we have looked at the essential teaching practices for developing complex language and disciplinary literacy, we can look at another set of vital practices for directly supporting teachers, working together, and strengthening the system as a whole to meet the needs of academic English learners. Effective coaching, for example, provides teachers with focused feedback and reflective conversations. Collaboration among teachers and others generates and strengthens new ideas for meeting the needs of diverse students. And the third *C*, capacity, creates strategic school systems along with policies that sustain the growth of teacher effectiveness and student learning over time.

We realize that each *C* merits a separate chapter, book, or series of books. Here we simply present the core elements that (1) don't seem to get enough attention in professional development efforts, (2) relate most to working with academic English learners, and (3) are essential for supporting the teaching and assessment of complex language and literacy of the Common Core and similar new standards.

Coaching Practices for Complex Academic Language and Literacy

Instructional coaching is a highly effective way to help teachers develop teaching practices for several reasons. It provides individualized support and feedback. It is ongoing. It is grounded in a relationship. It offers modeling, observation, and reflection on specific lessons and students. All of these apply to coaching for complex language and literacy development, the focus of this section.

First of all, there are several challenges to address when it comes to coaching teachers in the practices found in this book. These challenges include the following:

- Coaches have received extensive training for teaching, but very little training on how to work with adults, some of whom have taught for many years.

- Most instructional coaches have not been trained to coach teachers for language and literacy development across disciplines.

- Most coaches, especially in the upper grades, tend to work with teachers of varying disciplines. A coach might be a former math teacher who is coaching several language arts teachers. For basic classroom management and lesson design, this can work, but delving into the language and literacy of the discipline often requires more content expertise.

- A coach cannot be in each teacher's classroom every lesson, and there is seldom enough time to engage in extended planning or post-observation conversations.

- It is difficult to assess the effectiveness of one's coaching for complex language and literacy development.

The rest of this section helps coaches (and others who support teacher development) to meet these challenges and improve their knowledge and skills for coaching teachers of AELs.

EFFECTIVE COACHING PRACTICES FOR DEVELOPING LANGUAGE AND LITERACY

Research has yielded a set of practices for effective professional development and support offered by coaches. Two general practices are (1) providing opportunities for teachers to reflect on their learning and instructional practice, and (2) developing classroom curriculum in collaboration with coaches (Lawless and Pellegrino 2007). Coaching that is specific to developing language and literacy includes the following:

- *Zoom in on student language use.* Coaching activities should focus on students' growth in using language, given its huge role in learning. Teachers need to know how various practices and instructional moves can facilitate complex language development and disciplinary literacy development among their students.

- *Model instructional strategies.* Coaches should model instructional strategies that integrate language development into teaching and learning, providing teachers with the opportunity first to experience these practices and strategies as learners, and second, to reflect on the effectiveness of such strategies from the perspective of teachers.

- *Engage in cycles of inquiry.* Inquiry cycles are particularly effective because they allow teachers to dig more deeply into the complexity of an important educational challenge. They look at ongoing sets of data and make changes as needed. Coaches can help teachers formulate inquiries that focus on complex language and literacy.

LEARNING WHAT COACHES NEED TO KNOW

The best coaches are zealous learners who continually develop their knowledge of teaching, learning, and assessment. There are three critical areas of knowledge for effective coaching that focus on language and literacy across disciplines: content, language, and learners.

Content knowledge includes the concepts, facts, skills, and standards of the discipline that students need to learn. It also includes knowing how students learn this type of content, also known as "pedagogical content knowledge" (Shulman 1986). During observations and conversations, a coach must know how to "formatively assess" the teacher's content and pedagogical content knowledge. Finally, a coach must also know how to use artifacts such as video clips and student work as well as conversations to help teachers reflect on their practice (Luft et al. 2010).

Coaches must have a solid knowledge of the language demands of each lesson and how language is used to communicate important concepts, facts, skills, and standards of a discipline. This is also called "pedagogical language knowledge" (Bunch 2013; Galguera 2011; Zwiers 2008). Coaches should know what complex language is and what it looks like in classroom tasks and texts, and they should be able to argue for its importance. They should know a variety of effective strategies and practices for building complex language, some of which are described in previous chapters. Finally, they need to know the language and literacy demands of the Common Core, Next Generation Science, ELD, and other standards. You can also refer to the charts at the beginning of Chapters 4, 6, and 8 for more detailed looks at the language demands of selected standards.

Coaches also need to know how academic English learners learn. They need to know how to build on students' cultural and linguistic backgrounds and how to motivate them to learn in spite of the many challenges they face. They need to know how students view and respond to the pressures on them to use language for academic purposes in school.

And finally, coaches need to know how to use lesson observations and conversations to help teachers know and look for these previously mentioned things over time.

CO-PLANNING PRACTICES

In addition to developing and applying their knowledge, coaches need to be effective at helping teachers plan for language and literacy development. This is challenging because it is often tempting for the teacher and even the coach to focus solely on content while planning a lesson. While few standards specifically outline the language that students need in order to learn and to show their learning, many content standards describe concrete concepts and skills. This concreteness makes it easier for coaches and teachers to focus on them than on the language needed for them. One of the purposes of this book, in fact, has been to clarify the complex language and literacy skills that undergird learning in school and to highlight their importance.

Lesson planning is a challenging art because a teacher needs to come up with multiple masterpieces each day. It is also a science because of all the "data" that teachers must use before, during, and after lessons to make them as effective as possible for many different students. The following paragraphs provide several ideas for coaching teachers in the art and science of lesson planning for complex language development.

In co-planning a lesson for complex language and literacy, begin by engaging in the three strands of designing lessons: identify complex language to be learned (OBJ), design activities that allow and push for authentic uses of language (AUT), and build on students' backgrounds and previous learning (BLD). For example, in working with a teacher who is planning a science lesson on continental drift, the coach asks the teacher to consider (1) what the tasks are and the language students will need to use for them (e.g., to share and compare their own theories), (2) how to have students use new language to share information that their partners might not know, and (3) how to connect to previous learning about volcanoes and earthquakes. Throughout the conversation, the coach and the teacher discuss how the lesson activities (video clip, text, group work) will best be organized in order to spirally develop (i.e., return to and reinforce) key concepts and language.

A coach helps teachers analyze all teaching activities for ways to strengthen the high-impact practices of using complex text, fortifying output, and fostering interaction skills. Most of the activities in a lesson involve one or more of these practices. When using text in any form, a coach can co-plan with a teacher ways to preread texts (e.g., wide-angle reading described in Chapter 4), highlight text structure, and use sentence connectors. In history, for example, a coach might point out how the history textbook uses boxed vignettes to add personal views and engagement to a chapter. The teacher can have students decide how valuable these evidence vignettes are for supporting ideas in the chapter and for describing history accurately. When coaching a math teacher, for example, a coach might notice an activity with output such as displaying answers on mini-whiteboards and answering questions orally. The coach asks the teacher to consider having students write reasons on their boards, not just numbers, and having students come up with two or more sentences for answering orally after practicing their responses first with a partner. A coach might help a science teacher craft an engaging prompt for having students converse about how to reduce earthquake damage.

For all activities being planned, a coach should also ask how the teacher plans to incorporate the crosscutting practices of clarifying, modeling, and guiding complex language learning. For example, a fourth-grade teacher wanted to have her students decide which theme in a short story was most applicable to all fourth graders in their school. They needed to interpret to find the theme and then evaluate to decide which was most applicable. The coach encouraged the teacher to clarify and model the language needed for interpretation and evaluation by using a model paragraph about a different story. The teacher planned to have students notice the strong topic sentence, transitions, and terms such as *interpret, theme, evidence, outweigh,* and *pertinent,* which she would explain by gestures and additional examples. After talking with the coach, the teacher also planned to have students engage in extended conversations during which she would observe, prompt for and provide language when needed, and give specific feedback on how effectively students were using the new language.

Coaches and teachers can use the lesson planning toolbox at the end of Chapter 2 to foster their collective thinking about how to design lessons.

OBSERVATION PRACTICES

A whole lot happens in an effective lesson. Coaches need to be highly skilled at observing with multiple eyes that simultaneously look at behavior, engagement, classroom culture, transitions, content, literacy, and complex language development practices. Before a lesson, it helps to ask the teacher what he or she would like you to observe with respect to language or literacy. Likewise, it helps to tell the teacher what you would like to focus on, based on previous conversations and lesson observations.

Here are several observation practices that can strengthen coaching.

- Carefully notice (1) if and how the language objectives support the content objectives, (2) if and how the language development in the lesson matches the language objective(s), and (3) if and how the lesson activities and interactions help students to understand, practice, and learn the language of the language objective(s) in meaningful ways.

- Focus on one or two students. If you can, ask the teacher which students you should observe closely. They can be students who are "average" in order to get a sampling of the class, who have shown lots of recent growth, or who spark the curiosity or concern of the teacher. Position yourself near the student(s) and watch and listen for engagement, original ideas, complex language, and reading, writing, oral, and interaction behaviors that result from the teaching and the prompts. You can use the student observation tools like the ones at the beginning of Chapters 4, 6, and 8 as a start.

- Audio- and video-record. Place the camera on the side of the room, with window light behind, if possible, and capture teacher and students in whole-class, group, pair, and individual work.

- Transcribe portions of interactions between students and between the teacher and students. Choose portions of interactions that show the building on and up of ideas. Capture expert moves that help the conversation to keep going in "discipline-valued" ways and in support of the learning objectives.

- Use practice frames to take notes on the teacher's practices. In Appendix C there is a one-page form with the three high-impact frames on one page to use during a lesson. You won't fill in every box but should note down areas of strength and growth needed in the practices and their strands.

COACHING CONVERSATION PRACTICES

The most powerful component of coaching is conversation. Conversation does many things: helps to clarify the links between content and language, facilitates teacher reflection on teaching practices, provides teachers with new ideas, values teachers' current practices while slightly pushing them to higher levels, and even models the interactions that they should have with their students.

Conversations can take a variety of paths that range from ineffective to highly effective. Even one word can send the conversation either way. For this reason, any person who supports teachers must be highly strategic in and reflective of his or her conversations with teachers. Coaches, mentors, supervisors, lead teachers, and fellow teachers who talk to one another all can and need to improve conversation skills each year. For example, in many settings coaches are audio-recording their coaching conversations and analyzing them to see how they can improve their coaching.

For most coaches and teachers, the goal of the conversation is to get the most out of the limited time they have to talk. Teachers don't have much time to talk and they want their talk time to be as useful as possible. We have created a simple tool to use for strengthening and streamlining our conversations with teachers. (There is always room for one more "tool," right?) We analyzed a wide range of conversations, including our own, and several categories emerged in the most effective and efficient interactions. For lack of a better acronym, it is called the WEOPT, shown in Figure 10.1. Each letter corresponds to a different column. You can take notes in the columns during and after a conversation with a teacher, or you can simply have "mental columns" that you use to take notes during the conversation.

In the column on the far left, you put specific or general information on what is to be learned, for example: complex language, disciplinary literacy, and/or content understandings. In the WHAT column, you put the specific objective and/or standard. You might already know this from the pre-lesson conference or from the beginning of the lesson. If not, ask what it was. During the lesson, in the EVIDENCE column, write down the observed evidence of students' learning of the specifics in the WHAT column. In the OBSERVED column, write down the practices and strands that you observe or wanted to observe during the lesson. Select several effective ones that you saw and one important one that you didn't see or wanted to improve. Near the end of the lesson and before the conversation, in the TARGET column, jot down what the practice (to improve upon) would ideally look like for that lesson. Then add a note about possible next steps in the PUSH column.

FIGURE 10.1

WEOPT observation, conversation, and note-taking tool

FOCUS OR INQUIRY QUESTION					
	WHAT is/was to be learned by students	**EVIDENCE** of student learning (formative assessment)	**OBSERVED** practices (TXT, OUT, INT, CLA, MOD, PRO, etc.)	**PUSH** (what is needed to get to next level)	**TARGET** level of core practice
Complex language					
Disciplinary literacy					
Content understanding					

During the conversation, before sharing your notes for each column, ask the teacher to describe what was intended and what he or she saw and heard during the lesson. Prompt the teacher to come up with initial information and then build off it or add your own information. Before ending the conversation, ask how the teacher might envision or improve the practice in a future lesson, and add anything that you jotted down. Then discuss what the next steps could be to reach that target practice. Remember that the most powerful conversations are those that support ongoing inquiries and action research. This process is described in more detail later in this chapter.

Coaching Chart for Developing Complex Language

By building a chart like the one in Figure 10.2, coaches can build and organize their ideas for sharing how to strengthen activities in each lesson. For example, you might observe a teacher using sentence frames for pair-shares in which students have only one turn apiece and share the same idea with just one sentence. The teacher counts the activity as interaction, but you know that there are additional ways to foster students' interaction skills and language. You refer to the chart and see pair-shares in the output category. You emphasize that to turn pair-shares into interactions, and to get students to use complex language such as connected sentences, the teacher can tweak a few things using principles in the second column next to the interactions box. The principles provide ideas and rationale that you both can discuss.

FIGURE 10.2

Chart for strengthening complex language in every lesson

HIGH-IMPACT PRACTICE	WHEN I WANT TO TO EMPHASIZE THE FOLLOWING PRINCIPLES . . .	. . . I CAN SUGGEST THE FOLLOWING STRATEGIES AND ACTIVITIES
Use complex texts to build language, literacy, and thinking	Encourage students to reread and engage with text in manageable chunks; focus students on complex language in a text	• Close reading • Multiple reads
	Build habit of looking at the whole message of a text and how it is structured; create visual scaffold on which students can organize ideas from the text	• Wide-angle reading • Book "walkthroughs"
	Many AELs don't thoroughly understand the terms that teachers use for supporting ideas: *evidence, weak, strong, position, example, support, outweigh, claim, warrant,* etc.	• Evaluate the evidence • Increase activities that require the use of these terms
	Can get much more language development out of reading texts aloud	• Read-aloud protocol for complex language • Borrow and build

Fortify oral, written, and multimedia output	Increased time practicing original and academic oral output	• Pro-con and variations • Pair-shares that give an amount of time for each partner to talk
	Using connected sentences in a turn or utterance; fortifying writing with oral practice; using new vocabulary in talk	• Linked sentence stems in pair-shares • Provide silent time to put sentences together in mind before talking
	Practicing: complex output with different partners; building up language and ideas using texts, ideas, and language of successive partners; face-to-face communication behaviors	• Interview grids • Opinion formation cards • Continuums • Talk lines and circles
	Talking about key ideas in complex texts more than once; using the language of the text; practicing summarizing and paraphrasing	• Jigsaw without copying or reading answers aloud
Foster interactions that use complex language	Co-building meaning during a conversation: create, clarify, fortify, and negotiate ideas (i.e., not just share ideas as output in pair-shares)	• Constructive conversation poster • Extensive modeling of building ideas in conversation
	Students extend conversations on their own	• Supported-then-unsupported Talk activity • Third observer cards
	Students use language from the text to converse, create, and modify ideas	• Borrow and build activity
	Students should have different information (partner doesn't know what other will say) to negotiate meanings	• Conversation cards
	Practice comparing, arguing, and supporting abstract and complex ideas	• Argument balance scale
	Choosing and evaluating evidence and arguments	• Evaluation scorecards
	Peer observation and evaluation to foster accountability for building ideas and staying on topic	• Conversation observer with feedback tool

Charts like this one and those at the end of Chapters 4, 6, and 8 can help coaches to see how certain activities that teachers already do can be strengthened to improve the development of complex language, literacy, and thinking across disciplines.

MODELS OF PRACTICE

In order to learn a new practice, teachers need opportunities to see clear examples of the practice and develop ways to distinguish stronger and weaker versions of a practice (Goodwin 1994; Little 2003; Stevens and Hall 1998). Coaches should model various practices for teachers and use artifacts that show instructional practices such as video. It is best for teachers to see coaches model the practices in the teachers' own classrooms. At other times, video examples of practice can be an effective resource for learning because video provides opportunities to examine the elements of these practices as they unfold over time. The coach and teacher can stop the video (unlike a lesson) or view it again (unlike a lesson) to reflect on the practices and see themselves, coaches, or other teachers in action. Modeling, coupled with repeated and reflective practice, is essential for the development of expertise (Ericsson 2002).

Modeling the Practices

It takes loads of skill to go into a classroom and practice what we preach, especially the teaching of complex language and content concepts. When coaches walk their talk, even when not perfectly executed, they allow teachers to watch lessons unfold and reflect on their own practices. Coaches can show them that it is both possible and powerful to integrate complex language development into lessons.

If a teacher has multiple prep periods for the same or similar course, you (coach/support person) can model a lesson the first class period and then observe the teacher in a later period. Having some time to converse in the interim is even more powerful. Having time to converse afterward is necessary in order to go over notes and next steps. You both can even use the tools in this book's chapters and Appendix C when you observe.

Using Video and Audio Artifacts

Since we can't stop a lesson to analyze its nitty-gritty moments, we use video and audio. Oral language, in particular, is highly fleeting: we seldom remember what was said or how it was said during a lesson. Video can help us see both in order to improve communication. As a coach or teacher colleague, you can video-record a lesson and co-analyze it for the practices. Discuss with the teacher how you will choose clips to talk about in the post-observation conversation. Suggestions for criteria are (1) the clip shows intentional teaching of complex language, (2) the clip shows expert levels in a practice and its strands, (3) the clip shows a lack of or low level of practice to improve, (4) the clip shows students who are engaged in learning, (5) the clip shows a strength in or need of formative assessment, (6) the clip shows how language supported the learning of content understandings.

For example, a middle school math coach video-recorded a lesson that focused on the Common Core standard "Use variables to represent quantities in a real-world or mathematical problem, and construct simple equations and inequalities to solve problems by reasoning about the quantities" (CCSS.Math.Content.7.EE.B.4). During the lesson, the teacher had the students generate equations for the word problems and argue the rationale for their equations. After the lesson, the teacher asked the coach to find clips that focused on clarifying the language of mathematical argument. The coach also said that she would look for a clip showing guiding because it was part of their ongoing inquiry process. The coach found a clip of the teacher that showed effective clarifying of argument and justification language. In the clip, the teacher said, "I can't just tell my partner, 'Because I say so!' I need to justify it. I say, 'Because the problem tells us that the water level is going down at a certain rate, this rate, r, should be negative.' See how it helps to refer to math rules and refer to what is given in the problem?" The coach and teacher then discussed ways to use this kind of language in the future. Then as they watched the rest of the clip, the teacher pointed out places where she could have prompted two other students to justify their equations. The teacher said, "I noticed that when Marissa said that the answer would get bigger if the denominator increased, I could have asked her to justify this to her partner using simpler forms to see if her idea was true." The coach and teacher further discussed ways to push students' thinking and the language of thinking as they watched the clip.

Collaboration

In addition to the more formal practices of coaching, all teachers should be collaborating to improve their planning, instruction, and assessment. Collaboration is vital because of the highly complex nature of teaching. There is too much information and there are too many things to do for one person each day, especially when surrounded by thirty children or adolescents for six hours of it. Collaboration requires teams that share burdens and generate creative solutions for the many diverse language and literacy challenges of each school year. Collaboration is particularly vital these days, as schools "implement" the Common Core and similar standards, making wide and deep changes in curriculum, instruction, and assessment.

Collaboration revolves around a common focus (e.g., complex language development), which can take the form of a design-based research question. According to Penuel et al. (2011), a design-based implementation approach focuses on developing and "testing" innovations for improving teaching and learning in classrooms. This approach includes four key elements:

1. A focus on persistent problems of practice

2. A commitment to iterative, collaborative design

3. A concern with developing new knowledge related to both classroom learning and implementation through systematic inquiry

4. A concern with developing capacity for sustaining change in systems

Unlike coaching conversations, where the coach or support provider has a differing role from that of the teacher, design-based collaborations leverage the collective wisdom, experience, perspectives, and creativity of colleagues in similar roles. Effective collaboration happens between grade-level and content-area learning teams that meet on a regular basis throughout the year. Teachers work together, communicate, and share strategies for facing the challenges of educating all students. As one middle school teacher said, "We share strategies, but not randomly like before. Now we share teaching ideas that come from looking at student work and research that focuses on our question." This type of sharing promotes enduring habits of reflective and selective teaching focused on current students, rather than simply following a pacing guide or filling up lesson plan templates with disjointed activities. This is a shift from isolation to collaboration at the teacher level.

For example, a group of fifth-grade teachers gathers periodically to analyze student work and share how well certain practices are working. The core practice of their own collaboration is conversation. The teachers need to effectively and efficiently converse to get the most out of the time. They often clarify goals and conversation norms to help manage the wide range of ideas, perspectives, biases, and interpretations that each person brings to the table.

BACKWARD DESIGNED INQUIRY QUESTIONS

At the beginning of the year, the group of fifth-grade teachers mentioned in the previous paragraph looks at evidence of learning to identify the largest gaps between where students are and where they should be. They discuss current and anticipated student needs as they look at data from the previous year, pre-assessments, reports from former teachers, and student observation data.

The group identifies a persistent problem of practice and agrees on a not-too-broad but not-too-narrow inquiry focus. They decide to focus on building on and fortifying partner ideas in conversations about literature and history texts. The group then crafts the draft inquiry question that will guide them and focus their conversations in a particular area of teaching: "How can we improve students' skills at building on partner ideas in conversations, evidenced by conversation observations, using graphic organizers and modeling?" The inquiry question's parts are somewhat based on "backward planning" approaches (Wiggins and McTighe 1998), in which we (1) start with what we want students to learn (outcome), (2) figure out how students will show their new knowledge and skills (evidence/assessment), then (3) design instructional experiences or tasks (strategies) to help students do well on the assessments. Daily and weekly formative assessments are used to make sure students are on the path to doing well on summative assessments such as tests, projects, and conversations. A wide variety of evidence can and should be used: audio recordings, observation notes, writing samples, quizzes, journals, test scores, reading inventories, video, etc.

Here are additional examples of inquiry questions from different grade levels and subject areas. Notice the three parts of each one.

- How can we increase students' abilities to justify their solution ideas for word problems involving negative numbers, as assessed by written explanations of problem-solving quizzes, by modeling how to use multiple representations?

- How can we improve students' use of supporting evidence in writing literature analysis essays, evidenced by daily quickwrites and weekly writing responses, by using visual organizers and conversing about them?

- How can we develop students' oral output skills of connecting sentences (and even using oral paragraphs) to explain lab results in science, assessed with audio recordings and conversation observation checklists, using language frames and oral augmenting language activities?

- How can we help students develop helpful—rather than distract-ful—strategies and thoughts for comprehension of complex text, as shown by reading quizzes and visual organizers, using wide-angle and close reading activities?

- How can we strengthen the historical thinking skills and language of noticing patterns in history, forming theories, and applying them to present day and future, as evidenced by one-paragraph essays and conversation observations, using the strategies of the thinking lens visual and paired conversations during/after reading?

Once the draft of the inquiry question is crafted, the teachers place it into the inquiry cycle diagram, described in the next section. Note that the inquiry question is often refined over time as teachers gather data and try different strategies.

INQUIRY CYCLE PROCESS DIAGRAM

A helpful visual tool for collaborative inquiry is an inquiry cycle process diagram (Figure 10.3). The cycle usually proceeds clockwise, but not always. For example, while planning, a team might go back to the evidence to help inform the development of a new variation of a strategy. The inquiry question remains in the center, serving to remind the group of the focus of the conversation.

FIGURE 10.3
Inquiry cycle process diagram

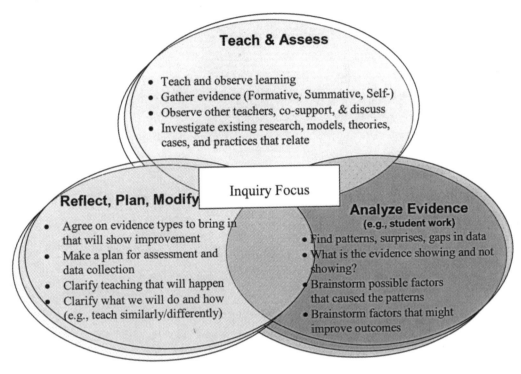

At each meeting, teachers should answer several questions so that the data that they bring back for the next meeting will be comparable and useful for answering the inquiry.

- What are we going to teach?

- How are we going to teach it?

- How are we going to assess? What evidence will we bring in to the next meeting?

- Should we teach the same and assess the same, use different teaching practices and bring in the same assessment, or bring different types of assessment for the same teaching practice?

- What else should we do before the next meeting to improve in this area and help answer our question (e.g., peer observations, read books and resources, attend trainings, have someone model a practice)?

At each meeting, teachers bring in evidence and focus on how it answers the inquiry question. After collaboratively analyzing and reflecting on the data, teachers often realize that more data is needed and/or a change in instruction or assessment should be used. Often one or more teachers will bring in very positive data and share a new strategy that helped produce the learning. This new strategy can then be part of the planning stage. In the planning stage, the team plans what and how to teach, along with what and how to assess, in order to bring in more data for the next meeting. They go out and teach and return with more data to analyze.

Teachers use these collegial conversations to dig into the highly complex "rocket science" involved in teaching language and literacy in each discipline. For many, these conversations become the most effective professional development of all because teachers get to draw on the strengths of colleagues, look closely at students' work, share their ideas and insights, and discuss their own students' learning. As they help each other and share resources, they also build professional relationships, another challenging necessity in the busy and isolated world of teaching.

CO-ANALYZE STUDENT WORK

One of the biggest areas of need for teachers and teacher leaders is improving their skills in analyzing evidence of learning. Many are already adept at "analyzing" test scores and noticing general areas of need and growth (e.g., vocabulary, comprehension), but teachers need to see more strategically into the minds of students to know what they are learning and not learning. We need to be ultra-observant and ultra-creative to climb into student heads (if we dare). This analysis opens up our "assessment eyes" to new possibilities for seeing students' development of the complex language and literacy needed to learn key content concepts and skills.

An inquiry cycle group can use a tool like the one in Figure 10.4 to support their analyses of student work. Several teacher conversation stems are provided in italics. Teachers must be mindful to analyze the evidence through the lens of their inquiry question. Teachers might look at the same artifact or different ones from a class set. First, the teacher who shared the artifacts clarifies the expectations for how the work showed or should have showed the desired learning. Second, teachers share patterns and trends that they noticed within and across artifacts. Third, they share interpretations of the evidence: what they believe students were thinking and what they learned. They do this with several different artifacts or sets of data. Finally, they synthesize ideas to inform their planning for the next period of time.

FIGURE 10.4

Tool for conversing about student work

INQUIRY QUESTION		
Expectations for student work: How should the work show learning? Starters: *I assume . . . ; I expect to see . . . ; I wonder . . . ; Some possibilities for learning that this data may present include . . .*	**Observations** of trends: What are the general patterns observed? Starters: Just the facts—"*I observe that . . . ; Some patterns/trends that I notice . . . ; I counted . . . ; The percentage of . . . ; I'm surprised that I see . . .*"	**Interpretations:** What can we interpret and infer about student learning from the data? "*I believe the data suggests __ because . . . ; Perhaps __ is causing the pattern of . . . ; I think the students need . . .*"
Questions that arise:	Questions that arise:	Questions that arise:
Plan/Design What are the implications for instruction and assessment? *We could try . . . because . . . This strategy/assessment would be most effective for this group because . . .*		

The fifth-grade inquiry team, for example, was focused on improving students' abilities to build up ideas in paired conversations. They analyzed video- and audio clips and noticed that students were not listening well enough to build on what their partners were saying. So they decided to teach listening strategies and had students write down what their responses would be to build ideas in the conversation. This became evidence. Teachers brought the samples back in, along with some audio samples to see that students had improved significantly, but many still needed to improve in how well they listened "with the prompt and purpose" in mind in order to better craft their responses to partners. This pattern fostered a rich discussion about what to do next across different subject areas.

These types of collaborative conversations between teachers, in addition to effective coaching practices covered earlier, don't grow without yet another set of practices. This is the set of practices that builds the broader system's capacity to focus on the right things for the right reasons at the right times.

Building Schoolwide Capacity for Teaching Complex Language and Literacy

It is vital to strengthen the organizational structures and conditions to grow, sustain, and spread the use of practices that support the language and literacy development of academic English learners. One reason for strengthening the system is the lack of evidence showing that commonly used professional development (PD) programs have a sustained effect on teaching after the PD program ends (Cobb, Gibbons, and Garrison 2010; Hill 2007). Professional development programs are often aimed at teams of teachers in a school without engaging the organization and its leaders in developing a system of supports to sustain and strengthen the targeted practices. For instance, rarely does a professional development program identify a meaningful role for the school principal or district leaders to assume in overseeing or guiding the implementation.

Enduring and effective development of students' language and literacy requires system-wide coordination. This means that students need all teachers to be on similar pages with respect to what and how they are teaching complex language and disciplinary literacy. This also means that the system needs to be clear, well-oiled, well-organized, and have components that reinforce each other. Here are three central principles of such a system:

1. Instructional leadership is most effective when leadership is shared among a team of people who have different roles and expertise.

2. Shared understanding of the purpose for and value of language and literacy in content-area teaching is essential for the development of new practices.

3. Generating site-based capacity to reflect on evidence creates the conditions for ongoing learning and sustained use of the practices that develop language and literacy.

The next two sections outline ways to apply these three principles in your setting.

STRENGTHENING SYSTEMS AND THEIR STRUCTURES

Each ongoing event or process forms the system. The main types of systems are meetings, teacher support, assessment procedures, and professional development efforts. The chart in Figure 10.5 can help us to strengthen the various structures and features that make up a particular system. Notice that the second column requires us to clarify how the structure can or should be used to support complex language growth, the focus of this book. This column alone can generate some lively discussion and brainstorming. The third column asks for resources and tools, while the fourth column helps us clarify the evidence for the effectiveness of the structure in the row. For example, one school team realized that there was little evidence of staff meetings being effective for language development in the school. They changed the format of their meetings to include a book study discussion on language that supports content understandings and skills. In the final column you put how the structures are connected and how communication is achieved between them. Figure 10.5 is just a sample of the more detailed version you might generate in your settings.

FIGURE 10.5

Sample chart for clarifying how structures in a system can align to foster complex language growth

NAME OF STRUCTURE	HOW IT IS, CAN, SHOULD BE USED TO SUPPORT COMPLEX LANGUAGE DEVELOPMENT IN AELS	HELPFUL RESOURCES AND TOOLS	EVIDENCE OF EFFECTIVENESS	COMMUNICATION AND CONNECTIONS
Staff meetings	Disseminate latest research articles; share teacher practices and student work; build up knowledge; model strategies	Share video clips from own and other schools	Feedback forms; observations of lessons	Organizers meet with department chairs to decide what and how to share
Weekly PLC	Inquiry focused on interactions	Inquiry cycle diagram	Student work, video clip, PLC notes	PLC team presents at staff meeting; feedback from others
Department-/ grade-level meetings	Compare common assessments and strategies; build up knowledge; model strategies	Meeting agenda template	Feedback forms; peer observations of lessons; minutes	Discuss ways to implement ideas from staff meeting
Coaching observation and conversation	Feedback and reflection strategies; take notes on language issues	WEOPT; charts for strengthening common practices	Observed changes in practices; quality of student work and talk	Coaches gather data for PLCs and PDs; facilitate PD days; join walkthroughs
School PD days	Choose to focus PDs on complex language; show data on needs; time to weave into own lessons	PD implementation form and reflection time; video clips	Observations of lessons; student work	Follow up on topics in other meetings
Instructional rounds and walkthroughs	Look for teaching and formative assessment of complex language	Essential practices frames	Data gathered during walkthroughs; how it is used for PD and inquiry cycles	Teachers are informed of walkthroughs and their focus; walkers provide feedback after
Assessment and data analysis	Analyze assessments for language demands; look for relationships between content learning with language strengths and needs	Dimensions and features chart; reflection tools	Quality of student work, talk, and test scores; lesson observations	Disseminate and explain findings at meetings

BUILDING THE CAPACITY OF PEOPLE

By building the capacity of each person in a system, we build the system's overall capacity. Thus, it is important to develop people's knowledge and skills that relate to the language and literacy demands of the Standards. These include knowledge of the language and literacy skills to be taught to students, the skills for teaching them, the resources and tools they can use, and ways to monitor and measure students' growth. The last column includes notes on relationships between people that can help to strengthen the other categories in the row. Figure 10.6 is a highly abridged version of what you might generate in your setting.

FIGURE 10.6

Sample chart for building capacity of people in a system focused on the development of complex language and disciplinary literacy

PEOPLE	KNOWLEDGE	PRACTICES AND ACTIONS	RESOURCES AND TOOLS	EVIDENCE OF EFFECTIVENESS	RELATIONSHIPS
Teacher	Role of language in thinking; disciplinary literacy activities	Uses high-impact practices for complex language and literacy	Reflection tools for practices; constructive conversation skills poster	Classroom observations, student self-assessments, and video/audio clips showing language growth	Shares ideas and burdens with coach and other teachers
ELD teacher	Language development ideas	Models for content teachers; provides PD at meetings	Student language data; language teaching lessons	Practices and strategies observed in own and others' classrooms	Shares ideas and data with content teachers
Coach	Complex language and literacy; high-impact practices	Co-plans, observes, converses, provides feedback	Reflection tools; charts for strengthening practices	Observations; student work; teacher reflections and lessons	Weekly observations and meetings with teachers
Principal	Role of language in learning across grades and disciplines	Walkthroughs; facilitates PD and meetings focused on language development	Reflection tools; charts for strengthening practices	Feedback forms; walkthroughs; student work; lesson plans; test scores	Observes and meets with teachers and coaches
District curriculum director	Role of language in learning across grades and disciplines	Walkthroughs; facilitates PD and meetings focused on complex academic language	Reflection tools; charts for strengthening practices	Student work; lesson plans; performance assessment results; teacher feedback	Meets with lead teachers and school administrators

ALIGNING EFFORTS AND EVIDENCE

Many organizations, including schools, waste energy on misaligned efforts. Just like a shopping cart with misaligned wheels, schools can be pushing a lot harder than they need to for mediocre results. Keep in mind that when we use terms like *evi-*

dence, data, and *results*, we are not talking about test scores. When you consider the high-impact practices and what they build in students (using language from texts; producing complex oral, written, and multimedia output; and engaging in academic interactions), a once-a-year machine-scored test shows just a fraction of such learning. As grade-level teams, content-area departments, schools, and districts, we must continue to improve the ways in which we gather and use evidence of students' growth in these essential language and literacy abilities during each year. And as we gather evidence, we must engage in research and inquiry cycles to strengthen instruction that is focused on the evidence.

As part of the Common Core implementation process, one middle school decided to focus on organizing information in ways that were most useful and as clear as possible. The seventh-grade teaching team, in order to align with the school focus, agreed that all seventh graders would improve their abilities to communicate their learning using slide shows, videos, and web page designs that were logically organized. They shared the work of creating detailed assignments that outlined complex language requirements and co-designed rubrics for products and presentations based on Common Core standards. They then compared their assessment evidence during the year to refine their assignments and teaching activities. One teacher commented, "This implementation process is a lot less daunting when we work together. It's even fun at times."

Vertical Alignment: Student Yearly Progressions of Complex Language and Literacy
An example of aligning efforts and evidence is clarifying where students should be at the end of each year with respect to complex language and literacy. It is important to delineate levels or points that students should reach at the end of each year in their uses of complex texts; their uses of complex language in written, oral, and multimedia products; and their abilities to engage in constructive conversations. Common Core State Standards offer some basic building blocks for what to expect, but it requires extra work to clarify the levels that students need to reach and the tasks that will display their learning. An excellent project focused on progressions, Dynamic Language Learning Progressions (www.dllp.org), is directed by Alison Bailey and Margaret Heritage, who also have written extensively on formative assessment of language and literacy.

To offer an idea of what can be done, we share a very basic example of what one district's teachers produced through collaborative meetings. They generated a chart like the one in Figure 10.7 to help outline where students should be at the end of each year with respect to complex language development. Each year roughly includes the descriptions from the previous years. They continued to edit and refine this chart over time.

FIGURE 10.7

Simplified sample chart for vertical alignment of complex language growth over time

SKILLS	END OF 1ST	END OF 2ND	END OF 3RD	END OF 4TH	END OF 5TH	END OF 6TH
Using language of complex texts	Use new words from texts in oral communication	Incorporate texts' words and phrases into oral answers and written work	Use complex and compound sentences based on those in texts in oral and written work	Organize written paragraphs in ways that are similar to texts' paragraphs	Organize multi-paragraph written work using organization ideas from nonfiction texts	Craft multimedia messages using organization ideas from nonfiction texts and web pages
Complex output	Use more than one sentence or fragment in an utterance	Use logically connected sentences and fragments	Use transitions to connect sentences and organize messages	Speak or write a general (topic/idea) sentence and then support it with two or more examples	Speak or write a point of view, support it with examples, and explain how they support the idea (warrant)	Speak or write a point of view, support it with examples, and explain how they support the idea (warrant)
Academic interaction	Partners engage in at least two turns each and focus on one idea	Partners engage in at least three turns each, focus on an idea, and clarify it	Partners engage in at least four turns each, focus on an idea, and fortify it	Partners engage in at least five turns each; they argue grade-level ideas and concepts	Partners engage in at least five turns each; they negotiate grade-level ideas	Partners engage in at least six turns each; they carefully weigh and evaluate the arguments and evidence to reach a conclusion

Horizontal Alignment Across Disciplines

It is also vital to reinforce complex language development across subject areas. This is a bit "easier" to do in elementary grades because one teacher often teaches multiple subjects and can connect to the language learning in previous lessons. For content-specific teachers in upper grades, teachers from different disciplines should agree on language and literacy skills to work on over a period of time. They can design similar tasks and activities so students can see how language and thinking can overlap across disciplines. This reinforcement is vital for getting complex language to stick over the long haul.

One high school, for example, chose to develop the cross-disciplinary CCSS skill of supporting ideas with evidence. The English teachers had students find evidence for themes in literature, the science teacher had students use evidence from lab observations, the history teacher had students find evidence in primary source documents and the textbook, and math students needed to use evidence based on math principles and reasoning processes in their written work. The teachers agreed to use similar assessments and rubrics, as much as possible, for related written, oral, and interaction tasks.

USING ASSESSMENTS

Throughout this book we have provided ideas for formatively assessing students' growth in complex language and literacy. In this section we briefly outline ways to use more formal assessment practices to improve teaching and learning.

Assessing Students' Acquisition of Complex Text Language

It is highly challenging to see how well students have learned language from texts. Usually, one exposure to a text is not enough, making it difficult to know when or how a student learned some aspect of language. Much of language develops underneath the surface of awareness, from countless exposures to it and many uses of it over time. Indeed, most of the sentences that students say and write have never been said or written before. Their brains, from processing countless words, sentences, and whole messages, figure out how to use language to convey ideas. Nevertheless, we can look for ways in which students use vocabulary, syntax, and message-organization strategies of the texts that they have been reading, especially language that we have focused on during close reading activities. We can look for this language in their written and multimedia products, as well as in oral presentations and conversations. The data we gather from such assessments can then be shared with teachers in other disciplines and grade levels.

Assessing the Clarity and Complexity of Students' Oral, Written, and Multimedia Output

Many schools already look at periodic writing assessments. These assessments can be analyzed for clarity and complexity using rubrics based on the dimensions of language in Chapter 1. For example, one school put the topmost features of the Message dimension in Figure 1.1 (clarity, appropriate register, density of ideas, organization of ideas) in the rows of a rubric for writing and oral presentations. They were not as focused on correct grammar as they were on organization and students' attempts to push themselves to use more sophisticated language. It wasn't easy, but the school used the data to shift their focus forward to designing lessons that focused more on thinking about and communicating complex messages, and less on word meanings and grammar rules.

Assessing the Quality of Interactions

Interaction, though vital, is one of the most under-assessed areas in our schools. It is a huge challenge to assess conversations, especially paired ones. As technology improves, we will be better able to record and transcribe conversations. Most smartphones have applications that can record conversations. Students might then e-mail them to the teacher or to a central location. Yet in the meantime and despite the challenges, we strongly encourage teachers to assess conversations several times a year. Using a tool like the one in Figure 8.2, a teacher can assess for language and skills while listening to live or recorded conversations. Teachers can synthesize their data on students' conversations to inform them of the types of skills that students need to work on until the end of the year.

ADDRESSING THE AEL SHIFTS

A tool (Figure 10.8) that we have found to be useful is based on the academic English Learner Shifts described in Chapter 1. Educators can use this tool or a variation of it to reflect on changes over time. You might, for example, use this tool this week, putting "scores" and/or explanations in the pre-rating column. You then notice the need to focus lessons more on authentic communication and students' abilities to communicate whole messages (Shifts 1 and 2). One of these shifts, or a combination of them, might then become an inquiry focus for which you gather evidence over time.

FIGURE 10.8

Tool for observing and roughly measuring AEL shifts

AEL SHIFTS	PRE-RATING (1–4) AND EXPLANATION	POST-RATING (1–4) AND EXPLANATION
1. *From Access to Ownership:* Do students, after using a complex text, have stronger abilities to think and authentically use its language?		
2. *From "Piece" Skills to "Whole-Message" Skills:* Do students spend less time on word meanings, memorizing, and grammar rules and more time on interpreting and communicating complete messages of value in a discipline?		
3. *From focusing on content to focusing on language-literacy-content.* Do students engage in more activities that strategically develop their disciplinary literacy, language, and thinking skills?		
4. *From Individual to Collaborative.* Is there less lecturing (filling students' heads) and individual seat work and more student collaboration to create, practice, and use new language and ideas?		
5. *From Playing School to Learning.* Is there less activity focused on points and grades and more activity focused on the development of student thinking and communication of engaging ideas?		
6. *From Checklists of Strategies to Frames of Practice.* Is there more strategic integration and use of high-impact practices for developing complex language and disciplinary literacy?		

7. *From Tests to Assessment and Beyond.* Is there less focus on having students score well on tests and more focus on designing assessments of vital knowledge, language, and skills for college and career?		
8. *From Silos to Capacity.* Is there more focus on collaboration, supporting teachers, communicating effective practices, analyzing useful data, and creating policies that strengthen the development of complex language and literacy across the system?		

CULTURE

A vital element of capacity building is another *C*, culture. Culture is how people work together and get things done in a particular setting. Granted, culture usually has deep roots that are hard to change, but its cultivation must always be part of the efforts to improve a system. In the very limited space that we have here, we emphasize several ideas for fostering a culture that develops complex academic language and disciplinary literacy.

First, strive to build a classroom "worldview" that values creativity, curiosity, risk taking, respect, and collaboration. When students experience these during learning, they are free to develop sophisticated levels of thinking, content, and language. Yes, we know that these things can clash with "explicit, test-focused, and teacher-centered tactics of instruction," but we need to make some choices about what our diverse students deserve (i.e., cut bait or fish). For example, a third-grade teacher has students create screenplays of their "sequels" to stories that they have been reading. Students do extra research in teams and take risks as they perform pieces in front of peers. Along the way, the teacher emphasizes being clear and academic in their writing and discussions.

Second, we must develop our own "professional-level" culture of creativity, curiosity, risk taking, respect, and collaboration. Teachers, administrators, staff, and parents need to work together to meet the challenges of teaching academic English learners. Such a culture values the role of every person in the system and uses the ideas of each person as part of meeting challenges. For example, in one school the principal would use part of staff meetings for sharing creative solutions to ongoing challenges. A fifth-grade teacher shared how she taught students how to give feedback on language use when peer editing persuasive letters. Others then met with her to benefit from her experiences and ideas.

Third, we must be constantly pushing ourselves to improve the clarity of our and our students' communication. This requires ongoing attention to how ideas are developed and communicated during a lesson, between teachers, and throughout an organization. It includes encouraging all students to push themselves to learn and use new language each day, unit, and year. Right answers are not enough. We and our students must shoot for clarity in all communication. For example, in one school all the teachers have agreed to refer to posters on the wall that include ways to express ideas in academic ways as scientists, authors, mathematicians, engineers, and historians do. Before the final sharing out of group tasks, teachers ask students to make the messages as clear and academic as possible.

Fourth, we must cultivate a culture of implementation. One of the purposes of this book has been to help educators "implement the Common Core State Standards" well in settings with academic English learners. *Implementation,* in a nutshell, is the process of putting a program, idea, or activity into place in a given setting. Yet the process of implementation never really ends in dynamic and diverse educational settings. In such settings, we must cultivate beliefs, attitudes, and behaviors that view implementation as a positive and ongoing way to be and do.

Summary

This chapter focused on several core components of supporting teachers to effectively use and improve the essential practices described in previous chapters. These "practices" include coaching, collaborating, capacity building, and culture building. Several key threads holding these *C*'s together are the ongoing alignment of goals and activities, inquiry-based cycles of reflection, continual building of knowledge, and pushing for improved communication and conversations throughout the system. These practices and their threads, for the purposes of this book, all work toward increasing students' complex academic language and literacy across grade levels and disciplines.

Conclusion

Neither the Common Core State Standards nor any other standards are the answer to the many challenges facing the education of academic English learners. Yet the new standards have sparked a wide range of important discussions on the role that language plays in learning for success in college, career, and life. It's a powerful role.

In our zeal for using data and the many data tools around us, we have hyper-focused on looking for the things that were easiest to see—especially in schools that weren't producing good numbers. We, like in the analogy, looked for our watch under the lamp, where the light was best, and not down the dark alley where we know we lost it. We focused on increasing the quantity of more testable things, rather than striving to increase the quality of less testable things. As a result, in too many settings, teaching veered into ruts of disconnected facts, drills, points, and passivity. Now, as the Common Core and other standards describe the need for learning increasingly complex knowledge and skills, we are realizing the exciting challenges in teaching and assessing them.

The practices in this book are not new. Yet how we use them to teach is. We must use them to teach more complex ways of using language to read, write, listen, speak, and interact, as outlined in the new standards. For example, we should advance our practices of modeling from that of modeling the use of an academic sentence stem (e.g., In my opinion, . . .) to modeling how to communicate an opinion with evidence and explanation. And this opinion activity should be authentic, not just a display for points. We must shift, as much as we can in each lesson, from enabling students to "play school" to preparing students to think and communicate in the future.

Without the skills to interpret, create, communicate, and negotiate complex ideas, many students are destined to become mere consumers of pieces of knowledge that come their way. We sincerely hope that you join us in helping to accelerate the growth of students' language and literacy such that they become users, critiquers, creators, and owners of knowledge. This means setting aside the mile-wide and inch-deep lesson plans, test-score-raising quick fixes, and assembly-line approaches so that we can effectively teach students what they need in order to reach their potentials in and out of school.

We hope that our descriptions of the essential practices and how they fit together have somewhat helped to clarify the rocket science of teaching complex language and literacy in every discipline. We hope you have seen ways to use the practices in your settings to make some of the shifts mentioned in Chapter 1. And we hope that we can continue to partner with you in the development of resources beyond this book in order to meet the needs of all academic English learners.

Appendix A: Research

I n the initial stage of the research that led to the creation of the practice frames, we conducted a literature review on the teaching of academic language and literacy to English learners (ELs). We reviewed dozens of research studies, approaches, checklists, and protocols such as SIOP (Echeverria, Vogt, and Short 2007), CLASS (Pianta, La Paro, and Hamre 2008), PLATO (Grossman 2011), QTEL (Alvarez et al. 2012), and others. We used this review to identify a subset of initial instructional practices that best represented the intersection of teaching content, thinking, academic language, and literacy to academic English learners. In the second stage, we viewed videos of teaching in a variety of diverse classrooms and edited the practices to incorporate descriptions that specifically addressed the complex language development of AELs in content-area classrooms. Using this list, we conducted a Delphi study in which we surveyed twenty-two experts in the areas of language learning and English learner education. In the first round, participants analyzed the initial list, edited the language of each practice, and added practices. We synthesized the results and generated a refined list for the second round of analysis. A smaller group of experts then gathered and commented on this set of practices. We synthesized the results into a list of seven essential practices with three observable components, or strands, in each.

Alvarez, L., N. Catechis, H. Chu, H., L. Hamburger, S. Herpin, and A. Walqui. 2012. Quality Teaching for English Learners (QTEL) Impact Study. San Francisco: WestEd.

Echevarria, J., M. E. Vogt, and D. Short. 2007. *Making Content Comprehensible for English Learners: The SIOP Model.* 3rd ed. Boston: Pearson Allyn & Bacon.

Grossman, P. 2011. Protocol for Language Arts Teaching Observations. Presentation accessed on August 30, 2013, from http://www.gse.harvard.edu/ncte/news/NCTE_Conference_PLATO_Grossman.pdf.

Pianta, R. C., K. La Paro, and B. K. Hamre. 2008. *Classroom Assessment Scoring System.* Baltimore: Brookes.

Appendix B: Lesson Resources from Chapters 5, 7, and 9

Chapter 7: Eleventh-Grade History

WWII Poster Rubric

CRITERIA	5	3	1
Purpose	The purpose of the poster is clear. There is no ambiguity. It is historically accurate.	The purpose of the poster is a bit murky. It isn't as clear as you would like, but you have some idea of the purpose. It might be historically accurate or not.	Can't tell what the purpose is. It appears that the author is still searching for the purpose. It might be historically accurate or not.
Visual theme	All the elements of the poster (color choice, written slogan, image, etc.) support the visual theme and purpose. They work together and don't cause any dissonance with the viewer.	Some of the elements of the poster (color choice, written slogan, image, etc.) support the visual theme and purpose. There is something that seems out of place or that doesn't fit.	Most of the elements of the poster (color choice, written slogan, image, etc.) don't support the visual theme and purpose. It appears that the elements were thrown together without any thought for purpose or what the viewer might think.
Persuasive technique	It is clear which persuasive technique(s) is illustrated on the poster. It could be used as an example for next year's class.	The persuasive technique is identifiable but you feel like you are guessing to find it.	Unclear which persuasive technique is being used. Seems like the author didn't know either.
Audience	It is clear who the target audience is. The visual theme as well as the visual images are appropriate for the audience.	It is unclear who the target audience is. The visual theme isn't appropriate for the audience; neither are the visual images.	It appears the author wasn't sure who the audience was. There is no hint of the targeted audience. The visual theme and the visual images are inappropriate for the audience.
Attractiveness	The use of color, visual images, and fonts clearly communicates and works with the intended message. It is neat and has no convention errors.	The use of color, visual images, and fonts works with the intended message. They don't distract from the message yet they don't add to the message either. It could be neater and there are a few convention errors.	The poster uses very little color or visual images. They seem random and don't communicate the intended message. It isn't very neat and there are convention errors that distract from the message.

Chapter 9: Fifth-Grade Language Arts and Eighth-Grade Science

Constructive Conversation Skills Poster

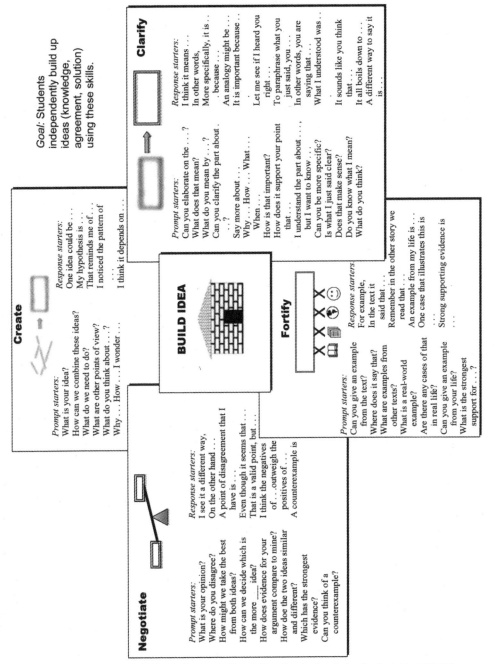

Chapter 9: Second-Grade Math
Math Constructive Conversation Skills Poster

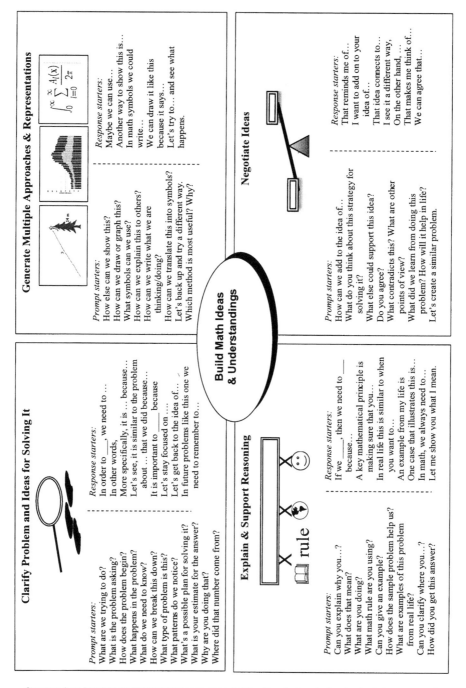

Generate Multiple Approaches & Representations

$$\int_0^\infty \sum_{i=0}^x \frac{A|(x)}{2\pi}$$

Prompt starters:
How else can we show this?
How can we draw or graph this?
What symbols can we use?
How can we explain this to others?
How can we write what we are
  thinking/doing?
How can we translate this into symbols?
Let's back up and try a different way.
Which method is most useful? Why?

Response starters:
Maybe we can use...
Another way to show this is...
In math symbols we could
  write...
We can draw it like this
  because it says...
Let's try to... and see what
happens.

Negotiate Ideas

Prompt starters:
How can we add to the idea of...
What do you think about this strategy for
  solving it?
What else could support this idea?
Do you agree?
What contradicts this? What are other
  points of view?
What did we learn from doing this
  problem? How will it help in life?
Let's create a similar problem.

Response starters:
That reminds me of...
I want to add on to your
  idea of...
That idea connects to...
I see it a different way,
On the other hand, ...
That makes me think of...
We can agree that...

**Build Math Ideas
& Understandings**

Clarify Problem and Ideas for Solving It

Prompt starters:
What are we trying to do?
What is the problem asking?
How does the problem begin?
What happens in the problem?
What do we need to know?
How can we break this down?
What type of problem is this?
What patterns do we notice?
What's a possible plan for solving it?
What is your estimate for the answer?
Why are you doing that?
Where did that number come from?

Response starters:
In order to ___, we need to ...
In other words,
More specifically, it is ... because...
Let's see, it is similar to the problem
  about ... that we did because...
It is important to ___ because
Let's stay focused on ...
Let's get back to the idea of... ̸
In future problems like this one we
  need to remember to...

Explain & Support Reasoning

rule

Prompt starters:
Can you explain why you...?
What does that mean?
What are you doing?
What math rule are you using?
Can you give an example?
How does the sample problem help us?
What are examples of this problem
  from real life?
Can you clarify where you...?
How did you get this answer?

Response starters:
If we ___, then we need to ___
  because...
A key mathematical principle is
  making sure that you...
In real life this is similar to when
  you want to...
An example from my life is
One case that illustrates this is...
In math, we always need to...
Let me show you what I mean.

Chapter 9: Eleventh-Grade History
Primary Source Conversation Guide

Read and Prepare to Talk

1. Why am I reading this document? How might a historian use it?

2. What kind of document is it? What might it tell us? Is it believable?

   o Correspondence (letter, memo, telegram, etc.)
   o Official documents (speech, congressional record, press release, judicial review, treaties, etc.)
   o Personal (diary, personal notes, journal, eyewitness account, etc.)
   o Oral (news footage, interview)
   o Visual (poster, cartoon, map, photo, etc.)
   o Article (newspaper, journal, magazine, etc.)
   o Other_____

3. What was going on at the time it was written?

4. What was the purpose of the document?

5. What do I know about the author?

6. Who was the intended audience?

7. How was the text structured? What was included and excluded to convey the message?

8. Does this text corroborate what we commonly believe happened at that time? Does it match up with other sources?

History Interaction Prompts

☐ What do you think was the author's purpose?
Where in the text does it support your conjecture?

☐ Is this fact, opinion, propaganda, or a combination of all three? Can you cite evidence from the text?

☐ What do you think?
Do you agree?
Do you have another point of view?
Can you add anything?

☐ How does this fit into what we have been learning?

☐ Why is this important history to learn?

☐ How can we summarize our conversation?

Appendix C: Practice Frames Observation Tool

USING COMPLEX TEXTS (CON, LIT, BLT)		
Clarifying Complex Language (CLR, DIF, CHK)	Modeling Complex Language (MLZ, FOC, DEC)	Guiding Language Learning (PRO, FAS, FBK)
Designing Activities and Lessons (OBJ, AUT, BKG)		

FORTIFYING COMPLEX OUTPUT (ORL, WRT, MMM)		
Clarifying Complex Language (CLR, DIF, CHK)	Modeling Complex Language (MLZ, FOC, DEC)	Guiding Language Learning (PRO, FAS, FBK)
Designing Activities and Lessons (OBJ, AUT, BKG)		

FOSTERING ACADEMIC INTERACTIONS (COM, TNK, UND)		
Clarifying Complex Language (CLR, DIF, CHK)	Modeling Complex Language (MLZ, FOC, DEC)	Guiding Language Learning (PRO, FAS, FBK)
Designing Activities and Lessons (OBJ, AUT, BKG)		

Common Core Standards in Diverse Classrooms: Essential Practices for Developing Academic Language and Disciplinary Literacy by Jeff Zwiers, Susan O'Hara, and Robert Pritchard. Copyright © 2014. Stenhouse Publishers.

References

August, D., L. Artzi, and J. Mazrum. 2010. *Improving Science and Vocabulary Learning of English Language Learners.* Austin, TX: CREATE.

Anstrom, K., P. DiCerbo, F. Butler, A. Katz, J. Millet, and C. Rivera. 2010. *A Review of the Literature on Academic Language: Implications for K–12 English Language Learners.* Arlington, VA: George Washington University Center for Equity and Excellence in Education.

Bailey, A. L., ed. 2007. *The Language Demands of School: Putting Academic English to the Test.* New Haven, CT: Yale University Press.

Belland, B. R., K. D. Glazewski, and J. C. Richardson. 2008. "A Scaffolding Framework to Support the Construction of Evidence-Based Arguments among Middle School Students." *Educational Technology Research and Development* 56:401–422.

Belton, S. 1998. *From Miss Ida's Porch.* New York: Aladdin Paperbacks.

Bunch, G. 2013. "Pedagogical Language Knowledge: Preparing Mainstream Teachers for English Learners in the New Standards Era." *Review of Research in Education* 37:298–341.

California ELD Standards. 2012. English Language Development Standards. Accessed on September 2, 2013, from http://www.cde.ca.gov/sp/el/er/documents/sbeeldstdg5c.pdf.

Carr, J., U. Sexton, and R. Lagunoff. 2006. *Making Science Accessible to English Learners: A Guidebook for Teachers.* San Francisco: Wested.

Cazden, C. 2001. *Classroom Discourse: The Language of Teaching and Learning.* Portsmouth, NH: Heinemann.

CCSS. 2012. Common Core State Standards for Math, English Language Arts, and Literacy. Accessed on September 2, 2013, from http://www.corestandards.org.

CCSS Introduction. 2013. English Language Arts Standards >> Introduction >> Students Who Are College and Career Ready in Reading, Writing, Speaking, Listening, and Language. Accessed on September 2, 2013, from http://www.corestandards.org/ELA-Literacy/introduction/students-who-are-college-and-career-ready-in-reading-writing-speaking-listening-language.

CCSS Math Appendix A. 2013. Designing High School Mathematics Courses Based on the Common Core State Standards. Accessed on September 2, 2013, from http://www.corestandards.org/assets/CCSSI_Mathematics_Appendix_A.pdf.

CCSSO (Council of Chief State School Officers). 2012. *Framework for English Language Proficiency Development: Standards Corresponding to the Common Core State Standards and the Next Generation Science Standards.* Washington, DC: CCSSO.

Chafe, W. L. 1982. "Integration and Involvement in Speaking, Writing and Oral Literature." In *Spoken and Written Language: Exploring Orality and Literacy,* ed. D. Tannen, 35–53. Norwood, NJ: Ablex.

Clancy, M., and B. Hruska. 2005. "Developing Language Objectives for English Language Learners in Physical Education Lessons." *Journal of Physical Education Recreation and Dance* 76 (4): 30–35.

Cobb, P., with L. K. Gibbons, and A. L. Garrison. 2010. *Teacher Networks and the Role of the Mathematics Coach: How Institutional Factors Influence Coach Centrality.* Paper presented at the annual conference of the North American Chapter of the International Group for the Psychology of Mathematics Education, Columbus, OH.

Cortes, C. E. 1994. "Multiculturation: An Education Model for a Culturally and Linguistically Diverse Society." In *Kids Come in All Languages: Reading Instruction for ESL Students,* ed. K. Spangenberg-Urbschat and R. Pritchard, 22–35. Newark, DE: International Reading Association.

Delpit, L. 2006. *Other People's Children: Cultural Conflict in the Classroom.* New York: New Press.

Dennis, J., S. Griffin, and R. Wills. 1981. *English Through Drama: An Introduction to Language-Learning Activities Developed by Mark Rittenberg and Penelope Kreitzer.* San Francisco: The Alemany Press.

Dickinson, D., and S. Neuman. 2006. *Handbook of Early Literacy Research: Volume II.* New York: Guilford Press.

Duke, N., and D. Pearson. 2002. "Effective Practices for Developing Reading Comprehension." In *What Research Has To Say About Reading Instruction,* 3rd ed., ed. A. E. Farstrup and S. J. Samuels, 205–242. Newark, DE: International Reading Association.

Dutro, S., and C. Moran. 2003. "Rethinking English Language Instruction: An Architectural Approach." In *English Learners: Reaching the Highest Level of English Literacy,* ed. G. García, 227–258. Newark, NJ: International Reading Association.

Echevarria, J., M. Vogt, and D. Short. 2008. *Making Content Comprehensible for English Language Learners: The SIOP Model.* 3rd ed. Boston: Allyn & Bacon.

Ericsson, K. A. 2002. "Attaining Excellence Through Deliberate Practice: Insights from the Study of Expert Performance." In *The Pursuit of Excellence in Education,* ed. M. Ferrari, 21–55. Hillsdale, NJ: Erlbaum.

Fairbairn, S., and S. Jones-Vo. 2010. *Differentiating Instruction and Assessment for English Language Learners: A Guide for K–12 Teachers.* Philadelphia: Caslon.

Fang, Z., and M. Schleppegrell. 2010. "Disciplinary Literacies Across Content Areas: Supporting Secondary Reading Through Functional Language Analysis." *Journal of Adolescent and Adult Literacy* 53 (7):587–597.

Forman, M. 2011. *Fortunately, Unfortunately.* London: Andersen Press.

Fox, M. 2013. "What Next in the Read Aloud Battle? Win or Lose?" *The Reading Teacher* 67 (1):4–8.

Galguera, T. 2011. "Participant Structures as Professional Learning Tasks and the Development of Pedagogical Language Knowledge Among Preservice Teachers." *Teacher Education Quarterly* 38 (1): 85–106.

Gibbons, P. 2002. *Scaffolding Language, Scaffolding Learning.* Portsmouth, NH: Heinemann.

Goodwin, C. 1994. "Professional Vision." *American Anthropologist* 96: 606–633.

Halliday, M. A. K. 1989. *Spoken and Written Language.* Oxford: Oxford University Press.

Harklau, L. 2002. "The Role of Writing in Classroom Second Language Acquisition." *Journal of Second Language Writing* 11:329–350.

Hattie, J. 2009. *Visible Learning: A Synthesis of Over 800 Meta-Analyses Relating to Achievement.* London: Routledge.

Heath, S. 1983. *Ways with Words: Language, Life and Work in Communities and Classrooms.* Cambridge: Cambridge University Press.

Hill, H. 2007. "Teachers' Ongoing Learning: Evidence from Research and Practice." *The Future of Children* 17:111–128.

Hilton, J. 1933/1993. *Lost Horizon.* Mattituck, NY: Amereon.

Hobbs, R., and R. Frost. 2003. "Illuminating Constructivism: Structure, Discourse, and Subjectivity in a Middle School Classroom." *Reading Research Quarterly* 37:278–308.

Hurston, Z. N. 1937/1998. *Their Eyes Were Watching God.* New York: Harper Perennial Modern Classics.

Irujo, S. 2004. "Differentiated Instruction: We Can No Longer Just Aim Down the Middle." *ELL Outlook.* Retrieved from http://coursecrafters.com/ELL-Outlook/index.html.

Jewitt, C. 2008. "Multimodality and Literacy in School Classrooms." *Review of Research in Education* 32:241–267.

Jimenez, F. 1997. *The Circuit: Stories from the Life of a Migrant Child.* Albuquerque: University of New Mexico Press.

Keene, E., and S. Zimmerman. 2007. *Mosaic of Thought, Second Edition: The Power of Comprehension Strategy Instruction.* Portsmouth, NH: Heinemann.

Krashen, S., and C. Brown. 2007. "What Is Academic Language Proficiency?" Singapore Tertiary English Teachers Society. Accessed on September 2, 2013, from http://www.sdkrashen.com/articles/Krashen_Brown_ALP.pdf.

Lambert, J. 2002. *Digital Storytelling: Capturing Lives, Creating Community.* Berkeley, CA: Digital Diner.

Lawless, K., and J. Pellegrino. 2007. "Professional Development in Integrating Technology into Teaching and Learning: Knowns, Unknowns, and Ways to Pursue Better Questions and Answers." *Review of Educational Research* 77:575–614.

Lemke, J. 1990. *Talking Science: Language, Learning, and Values.* New York: Ablex.

Little, J. W. 2003. "Inside Teacher Community: Representations of Classroom Practice." *Teachers College Record* 105 (6): 913–945.

Long, M. 1981. "Input, Interaction and Second Language Acquisition." In *Native Language and Foreign Language Acquisition,* ed. H. Winitz, 259–278. New York: Annals of the New York Academy of Science.

Lowry, L. 2002. *The Giver.* New York: Laurel Leaf.

Luft, J. A., J. Neakrase, K. Adams, J. Firestone, and E. J. Bang. 2010. "Bringing Content into Induction Programs: Examples from Science." In *Past, Present, and Future Research on Teacher Induction: An Anthology for Researchers, Policy Makers, and Practitioners,* ed. J. Wang, S. Odell, and R. Cliff, 205–220. Lanham, MD: Rowman and Littlefield.

Mercer, N. 2000. *The Guided Construction of Knowledge: Talk Amongst Teachers and Learners.* Clevedon, UK: Multilingual Matters.

Mercer, N., and K. Littleton. 2007. *Dialogue and the Development of Children's Thinking: A Sociocultural Approach.* London: Routledge.

Mohan, B. 2006. *The Role of Lexical Cohesion in Explanations in Science Classrooms.* Paper presented at the annual meeting of the American Association of Applied Linguistics, Montreal, Canada.

O'Hara, S., and R. Pritchard 2009. "Hypermedia Authoring as a Vehicle for Vocabulary Development in Middle School English as a Second Language Classrooms." *Clearing House: A Journal of Educational Strategies, Issues, and Ideas* 82 (2): 60–65.

O'Hara, S., J. Zwiers, and R. Pritchard. 2013. Research Brief: Framing the Development of Complex Academic Language and Literacy. Accessed on August 26, 2013, from http://aldnetwork.org/sites/default/files/pictures/aldn_brief_2013.pdf.

Pearson, P. D., and M. Gallagher. 1983. "The Instruction of Reading Comprehension." *Contemporary Educational Psychology* 8:317–344.

Penuel, W., B. Fishman, B. Cheng, and N. Sabelli. 2011. "Organizing Research and Development at the Intersection of Learning, Implementation, and Design." *Educational Researcher* 40 (7): 331–337.

Richardson, W. 2010. *Blogs, Wikis, Podcasts, and Other Powerful Web Tools for Classrooms.* Thousand Oaks, CA: Corwin Press.

Rutledge, P. 2011. "Social Networks: What Maslow Misses." *Psychology Today.* Accessed on September 5, 2013, from http://www.psychologytoday.com/blog/positively-media/201111/social-networks-what-maslow-misses-0.

Scarcella, R. 2003. *Academic English: A Conceptual Framework* (The University of California Linguistic Minority Research Institute, Technical Report 2003-1). Berkeley: University of California Linguistic Minority Research Institute.

Schleppegrell, M. J. 2004. *The Language of Schooling: A Functional Linguistics Approach.* Mahwah, NJ: Erlbaum.

Schleppegrell, M. 2005. *Helping Content Area Teachers Work with Academic Language: Promoting English Language Learners' Literacy in History* (Final Report: Individual Research Grant Award #03-03CY-061G-D). Santa Barbara: University of California Linguistic Minority Research Institute.

Schleppegrell, M., and C. O'Hallaron. 2011. "Teaching Academic Language in L2 Secondary Settings." *Annual Review of Applied Linguistics* 31:3–18.

Shulman, L. 1986. "Those Who Understand: Knowledge Growth in Teaching." *Educational Researcher* 15 (2): 4–31.

Skinner, E. N. 2007. "'Teenage Addiction': Writing Workshop Meets Critical Media Literacy." *Voices from the Middle* 15:30–39.

Smith, D. J. 2002. *If the World Were a Village: A Book About the World's People.* Toronto: Kids Can Press.

Stevens, R., and R. Hall. 1998. "Disciplined Perception: Learning to See in Technoscience." In *Talking Mathematics in School: Studies of Teaching and Learning,* ed. M. Lampert and M. Blunk, 107–149. New York: Cambridge University Press.

Swain, M. 1985. "Communicative Competence: Some Roles of Comprehensible Input and Comprehensible Output in Its Development." In *Input in Second Language Acquisition,* ed. S. Gass and C. Madden, 235–253. Rowley, MA: Newbury House.

Swartz, R. 2001. "Infusing Critical and Creative Thinking into Content Instruction." In *Developing Minds: A Resource Book for Teaching Thinking,* ed. A. L. Costa, 201–223.

Alexandria, VA: Association for Supervision and Curriculum Development.

Taylor, M. 1976. *Roll of Thunder, Hear My Cry.* New York: Puffin.

Toulmin, S. 2003. *The Uses of Argument.* Cambridge, UK: Cambridge University Press.

Urquhart, A. H., and C. J. Weir. 1998. *Reading in a Second Language: Process, Product, and Practice.* New York: Longman.

Van den Branden, K. 2000. "Does Negotiation of Meaning Promote Reading Comprehension? A Study of Primary School Classes." *Reading Research Quarterly* 35:426–443.

Vygotsky, L. 1986. *Thought and Language,* trans. A. Kozulin. Cambridge, MA: MIT Press.

Walqui, A. 2006. "Scaffolding Instruction for English Language Learners: A Conceptual Framework." *International Journal of Bilingual Education and Bilingualism* 9 (2): 159–180.

WIDA. 2012. *2012 Amplification of the English Language Development Standards.* Madison: Board of Regents of the University of Wisconsin.

Williams, J. 2008. "The Speaking–Writing Connection in Second Language and Academic Literacy Development." In *The Oral/Literate Connection: Perspectives on L2 Speaking, Writing, and Other Media Interactions,* ed. D. Belcher and A. Hirvela, 10–25. Ann Arbor: University of Michigan Press.

Wiggins, G., and J. McTighe. 1998. *Understanding by Design.* Alexandria, VA: Association for Supervision and Curriculum Development.

Wong Fillmore, L. 2012. "The Common Core State Standards, ELs and Language Minority Students: What Instructional Support Is Needed?" Accessed on December 19, 2012, from http://assets.pearsonpd.com/asset_mgr/current/201211/CCSS%20EL%20&%20Language%20Minority%20Students%20Maui.pdf.

Wong Fillmore, L., and C. Fillmore. 2011. *What Does Text Complexity Mean for English Learners and Language Minority Students?* Paper presented at Understanding Language Conference, Stanford University, Stanford, CA.

Wood, D., J. Bruner, and G. Ross. 1976. "The Role of Tutoring in Problem Solving." *Journal of Child Psychology and Psychiatry* 17:89–100.

Zhao, Y. 2003. "Recent Developments in Technology and Language Learning: A Literature Review and Meta-Analysis." *CALICO Journal* 21:7–27.

Zwiers, J. 2008. *Building Academic Language: Essential Practices for Content Classrooms.* San Francisco: Jossey-Bass.

———. 2010. *Building Reading Comprehension Habits in Grades 6–12: A Toolkit of Classroom Activities.* 2nd ed. *Newark, NJ: International Reading Association.*

Index